1986

DARWIN WAS WRONG —
A STUDY IN PROBABILITIES

I.L. COHEN

New Research Publications, Inc.
Greenvale, New York

Inquiries should be addressed to:

New Research Publications, Inc.
P.O. Box 231
Greenvale, N.Y. 11548

Printed in the United States of America, 1985

Library of Congress Cataloging in Publication Data

Cohen, I.L., 1922—
    Darwin was wrong.

    Bibliography: p.
    1. Evolution.   2. Evolution--Statistical methods.
3. Probabilities.   I. Title.
QH371.C75   1984   575   84-22613
ISBN 0-910891-02-8

Dedication

This book is dedicated to those trained to think scientifically and who are not afraid to reach conclusions dictated by their objective logic—no matter how unpopular the results may temporarily be.

Table of Contents

List of Illustrations

Introduction

A spirited debate has been raging for decades between evolutionists and creationists. The latter had a simple base on which they relied: the Old Testament. The God of the Hebrews had stated that God created mankind. That particular statement was sufficient evidence for the creationists to accept it at face value, on "faith," and erect all subsequent arguments.

The evolutionists, however, could not accept a mere statement as the basis for one's conclusions and beliefs. There had to be a scientific explanation, hypothesis that would fit the facts, theory that could be tested, law that would successfully predict occurrences, before any such belief was warranted.

During the middle of the nineteenth century, Charles Darwin developed his theory of gradual evolution. In essence, the original premise was based on certain specific concepts:

a) At the beginning, there was only heaven and Earth.

b) Life started spontaneously from inanimate inorganic matter.

c) A simple single cell first formed from interactions of pressures, water (perhaps mud), chemicals, temperatures, etc. These first forms of life were to be found in water.

d) That simple cell multiplied and split, forming newer forms of life: 2-cell organisms, 10-cell species, 100-cell species, etc.

e) With the passing of untold millions of years, these organisms developed into fish with gills; additional millions of years later, some fish moved onto dry land.

f) By a process involving "mutations," "survival of the fittest," and "natural selection" the first few fish on hand managed to develop lungs instead of gills — over a period of millions of years.

g) Eventually, various forms of land animals developed.

h) Within further millions of years, a branch of these land animals evolved wings and the ability to fly, while another branch continued to develop and eventually blossomed into fully formed men and women.

i) Still another branching from the original simple single cell underwent a different development leading to the establishment of additional millions of species of plants.

j) The development of organs took place again by a process of "natural selection." For example, the eye was supposed to have started as a light-sensitive cell on the surface of the skin, and after millions of years of progress became a complex instrument of sight.

k) Change from one stage to the next was achieved by certain methods:

> 1) Evolution took place in gradual, but imperceptibly small improvements, from stage to stage.

> 2) Species improved through survival of the fittest individuals.

> 3) More advanced species were created through the genetic transmission of acquired physical characteristics.

> 4) Haphazard mutations created a variety of species and organs.

> 5) This process was steady and continuous over untold millions of years.

2

These were, in general, the original, basic precepts of the theory of evolution. With time, many changes were introduced. As aspects of the theory were found to be unworkable, or wrong, newer concepts were added and molded to fit the particular shortcomings — a process that is normal and to be expected with any scientific theory. Eventually the Lamarckist concept of the transmission of acquired characteristics was completely discarded as it proved to be scientifically untenable. Likewise, the idea that life sprang spontaneously from dead inorganic matter was quietly set aside, underemphasized, and virtually forgotten even though a number of modern scientists still believe in it.

During the years that followed, fossils and skeletal remnants were anxiously sought since they were the crucial evidence that would demonstrate all the postulated intermediate stages of development. Unfortunately, the many fossils dug apparently indicated the contrary: half-way stages were the preponderant exception, not the rule. Geological strata, going back hundreds of millions of years, almost invariably gave us faunas and floras of fully developed orders, families, genera and species. Once such an assemblage was located in its strata, individual species persisted unchanged during the hundreds of millions of years of their known existence. This hard fact was contrary to the concept of gradual incremental changes that took place over millions of years.

To remedy this unexpected contradiction of a cornerstone of evolutionary theory, a new concept was introduced, *punctuated equilibria*. In effect this substitutes for gradualism the notion that evolution took place in leaps — jumping from one plateau to the next, from one completely formed species to another. It suggests that the rate of transformation from one form to the ensuing form was enormously more rapid than indicated by Darwins's slow incremental concept.

All of these theoretical considerations continued to be hotly debated; unfortunately no convincing evidence was forthcoming, except for what scientists wanted to see *in* it. Arguments deteriorated into little more than sophism relying on mental gymnastics and extraordinary imagination.

With time, and as newer findings frustrated the awaited proof, we reached a stage of polarization between evolutionists and creationists. Positions became frozen and degenerated into a blind, stubborn repetition of old arguments ana name calling. On the one hand the creationists were clinging to their one sentence in the Bible and insisting that creation was a fact, *because* God had said so. On the other hand, evolutionists were continually patching up the original theory and calling on convoluted logic, couched in elegant, educated terminology, to create an aura of science.

Indeed, the bitter debate became more and more sterile, leading nowhere. The one lacked conclusive evidence, the other lacked conclusive proof. The one relied on a statement pronounced about 3,250 years ago — the other on a statement made 125 years ago; in both cases, the clinching arguments were statements lacking convincing proof. The one stood fast on an immutable text, no one could change — the other changed volumes of text so as to stand fast with an immutable theory. Ultimately, while one group remained frozen in a long-standing "faith," the other degenerated into a like class of "faith" — both simply because they *wanted* their theory to survive, no matter what the evidence indicated.

In the 1950s, while this indecisive tug-of-war was still being waged, a momentous event occurred — the discovery of the DNA and RNA within the cell. For the first time, we had a general understanding of the blueprint of life. Even though a great many details were sketchy or missing, the DNA/RNA was shown to be an extraordinarily complex and supersophisticated system within the cell, programming and directing every aspect of growth. It was the same blueprint for animals, humans or vegetation. All living forms consisted of the same building blocks and relied on the same controls to direct their growth.

At that moment, when the DNA/RNA system became understood, the debate between evolutionists and creationists should have come to a screeching halt. We now had a precise mechanistic tool with which to measure and evaluate our concepts of evolution. It was no longer a matter of stretching the imagination to consider the possibility of an event that might or might not have taken place millions or billions of years ago. It was no longer necessary to postulate amorphous concepts of mutations and "survival of the fittest" to explain the appearance of new species. Instead, every single aspect of life was translatable into a precise mechanistic and mathematical language. The debate should have ended — the implications of the DNA/RNA were obvious and clear.

The present book evaluates the highlights of past concepts of evolution, and tries to translate them into the new, practical, mechanistical meaning of the DNA/RNA.

In the final analysis the whole argument of this book will boil down to answer a very basic question:

> Are the millions of species on Earth the end result of accidental, haphazard arrangements and rearrangements (mutations) of DNA molecules that took place without infusion of outside intelligence — or are they attributable to purposeful, predetermining intelligence?

The answer to this question will indicate to us whether evolution could have taken place on this planet as described by Darwin. And, if it would have, what was the probability of occurrence?

The subject on hand is exceedingly broad; dozens of books could, and probably will be written to cover a multitude of additional details and arguments. Within the confines of this one, enough highlights have been incorporated so as to give the reader the basic facts that support the conclusions submitted in this book.

In the process of depicting other points of view, I chose to quote mainly from the writings of three scientists: Loren Eiseley, the late anthropologist; Stephen Jay Gould, the biologist and geologist at Harvard University; and Niles Eldredge, curator at the American Museum of Natural History, New York City. These scientists have an eloquent capacity to express their thoughts. They possess a gift of literary articulation rarely found among scientists. All three are identified with and support Darwinian evolution, in one form or another. Still, a certain skepticism pervades their writings. They seem to sense that a number of aspects of evolution agree neither with the available physical evidence nor with scientific logic — nevertheless they continue to espouse the principles they absorbed during their formative years as scientists.

I selected the writings of these three brilliant men, out of dozens of others, as being representative of the thinking scientists who believe they "know," admit the flaws, yet cannot detach themselves from the dogma of their discipline. My arguments will not be directed against them as persons, but against the concepts they articulate.

Forcibly a number of repetitions had to be introduced in the text. Since this book submits one main thesis, said thought had to be constantly compared to existing concepts of evolution, thus creating, unfortunately, a repetitious effect.

For the purpose of the arguments submitted in this book, the concept of evolution has been taken as a single school of thought — which, in fact, it is not. The theory, first enunciated by Charles Darwin and Alfred Wallace, now comprises many subdivisions, such as Lamarckism, Neo-Lamarckism, Darwinism, and Neo-Darwinism. In this book, the words "Darwin" and "evolution" are used in their broadest sense as representing all the schools of thought that subscribe to the general concept that the origin and subsequent development of life on Earth was based on haphazard occurrences and events.

The book invites the reader to continually ask a very simple question each time an evolutionary argument is being evaluated:

If we translate the specific occurrence into DNA nucleotides and apply mathematical probability principles to the argument at hand, what magnitude of figure do we obtain?

The answer to this question is the fundamental crux to the entire confrontation between those who accept Darwinian evolution as scientific law from those who do not. From that point of view Table 1 and/or Table 2 should be frequently referred to as they contain the key to the arguments.

The conclusions submitted in this book have not been reached on the basis on any religious beliefs — they are the end products of logic, based on established scientific principles called for in the study and application of DNA, fossils, and mathematics.

I have no doubt but that flaws will be found in certain details of this book — as can be done on almost any scientific book dealing with evolution. Nitpicking on details, or quarreling with semantics, although interesting *per se*, should not divert attention from my basic mathematical argument: the improbability of random occurrence of millions of nucleotides in very specific sequences as found in the DNA of the cells.

I wrote this book also because I am troubled — troubled with the rigid dogmatic position taken by a number of evolutionists. They imply that they — and they alone — know the "truth." As such any further questioning is considered to be superfluous. There is little difference between the certainty expressed by such modern powers-that-be, and those who imprisoned Galileo and threatened him with torture for writing that the Earth was circling around the sun. Then, too, the authorities *knew* exactly what the "truth" was — or so they thought.

We become frightened and scandalized by limitations imposed on our freedom of expression of thoughts, when groups of powerful people suppress and ridicule ideas that do not coincide with theirs. We have fought wars to preserve our freedom of expression. In the scientific field, that fright is now more pronounced because we have been trained to call the shots objectively, no matter how uncomfortable the results might be. Any suppression which undermines and destroys that very foundation on which scientific methodology and research was erected, evolutionist or otherwise, cannot and must not be allowed to flourish.

In a certain sense, the debate transcends the confrontation between evolutionists and creationists. We now have a debate within the scientific community itself; it is a confrontation between scientific objectivity and ingrained prejudice — between logic and emotion — between fact and fiction.

Over the years we adopted certain cliches in our criticism of creationism and defense of evolution. These cliches became so well entrenched in the mental process of the debaters, that any differing concepts became the scientific equivalent of anathema. The net result was a constant rehashing of old ideas defended with standard replies.

For example, one of the favorite arguments of evolutionists takes the following form:

Even if the theory of evolution is not the answer to our enormous enigma, are we not just as well off to support it pending an acceptable and proven one?

This type of argument begs the question and is not a procedure normally applied in scientific matters. Even if we had no other explanation (which is not the case here), we still should not push a defective theory just for the sake of having an explanation on the books. Normally, theories that do not stand up to scrutiny, are thrown out and no further time wasted on them. In the case of evolution, it is true that we had a variety of arguments, which *seemingly* satisfied our requirements — before we understood the intricacies of the cell. We should be devoting our time and attention to exploring new avenues, not defending something stripped of scientific evidence and logic.

The present book submits the theme and argument that evolution could not have taken place along the lines depicted by evolutionists. Mathematically speaking, based on probability concepts, there is no possibility that evolution was the mechanism that created the approximately 6,000,000 species of plants and animals we recognize today.

The conclusions submitted in this book will not be pleasing to a segment of the scientific community. I beg of them to rethink the subject with an objective, scientific logic so as to evaluate *facts* and not imaginary events that might or might not have taken place hundreds of millions of years ago. The cell is real, DNA/RNA strands exist and can be tested today. Mathematics and probability concepts are based on solid scientific foundations. Let us apply them to understand the probable occurrence of events that are supposed to have taken place haphazardly. Let us be guided by the answers we obtain — mathematics is the most "scientific" of all sciences; it is not an inconsequential evaluator of facts.

In the final analysis, objective scientific logic has to prevail — no matter what the final result is — no matter how many time-honored idols have to be discarded in the process.

To paraphrase Gertrude Stein: a fact is a fact is a fact!

1
Gemmules-Eozoon-
Bathybius

In the mid-nineteenth century the new scientific era was consolidating a growing hold on society's thought processes. Darwin contributed significantly to the impetus by rationalizing his evolutionary theory on some of the most logical and scientific bases yet seen. During the next few decades most scientists jumped on the bandwagon and in attempting to convince each other that Darwin was correct, many put forward quite specious and flawed reasons why it had to be so. Within a relatively short time few scientists had the courage to question what was becoming an entrenched theory.

Some went further and described exactly what evolutionary links were going to be discovered and even where they would be found, so certain were they about this new theory of evolution.

One well-known scientist, Louis Agassiz, wrote that in deep waters of the ocean "we should expect to find representatives of earlier geological periods." According to such scientists, the deep waters would contain the same conditions under which life had originally emerged millions of years ago. The deep ocean beds were assumed to harbor the "Urschleim" — the original slime that evolutionists believed constituted the mud pond, from which all living matter originated.

The reputation of these men among the scientific community in and of itself gave credence to such hypothesis which was then repeated as though it were scientific law. Among other rationalizations, some postulated that in the depths of the ocean *alone* was the same type of pressure being exerted as when the world was created — millions of years before. Hence any fish found there would be the most primitive. These were powerful and sweeping statements, but such was the fame of these leaders of science that few others would question their speculations. Naturally, most scientists simply nodded their heads in complete agreement.

Thomas Huxley, a well known scientist of the time, made the following statement of the creatures to be found in the ocean depths: "The things brought up will ... be zoological antiquities which in the tranquil and little–changed depths of the ocean have escaped the causes of destruction at work in the shallows, and represent the predominant population of a past age."

The same view was presented by zoologist Charles Thompson, who also forcefully predicted that "missing links" in the evolution of life would be found in the ocean depths in the form of "living fossils."

A scientific expedition was arranged and in 1872 the ship *Challenger* set sail to collect specimens from dredgings of the deep beds of the ocean. After four years and 69,000 miles of cruising, having collected hundreds of specimen, the *Challenger* returned to port. The results were quite disappointing. Instead of proving the advanced theories of the evolutionists, the expedition pointed to the contrary: there was no Urschleim; there were no representative elements from early geological periods; there were no new links for the evolutionary ladder, nor were the fish encountered of primitive form, i.e. "living fossils." In short, the fanciful postulates built up by the scientific community crumbled to their dismay and disappointment.

But the attraction of Darwin's theory was too strong to be stopped by such failure. Shortly, scientists overlooked the lack of primitive ocean-dwellers, or of geological and biological proof, and went on to elaborate Darwin's theory of evolution as though the results of the *Challenger* expedition never existed or were of no consequence.

Some scientists' enthusiasm for the new theory went overboard. During Darwin's time, noted scientists competed for the honor of being the first or the most vociferous to predict the exact forms of primitive life that would be found. Presumably, the discovery of these forms of life would, once and for all, prove the inspired theory of evolution, and accordingly they heralded the "discovery" of what turned out to be imaginary creatures: *Bathybius* and *Eozoon*.

Rather than describe the demise of *Bathybius* and *Eozoon*, I prefer to quote an article written by Stephen Jay Gould, the very articulate professor of biology, geology and history of science at Harvard University.

His essay, "Bathybius meets Eozoon" is reprinted hereunder in its entirety.[1]

Early evolutionists thought these imaginary creatures must exist, so they found them

When Thomas Henry Huxley lost his young son, "our delight and our joy," to scarlet fever, Charles Kingsley tried to console him with a long peroration on the soul's immortality. Huxley, who invented the word "agnostic" to describe his own feelings, thanked Kingsley for his concern, but rejected the proferred comfort for want of evidence. In a famous passage, since taken by many scientists as a motto for proper action, he wrote: "My business is to teach my aspirations to conform themselves to fact, not to try and make facts harmonize with my aspirations ... Sit down before fact as a little child, be prepared to give up every preconceived notion, follow humbly wherever and to whatever abysses nature leads, or you shall learn nothing." Huxley's sentiments were noble, his grief affecting. But Huxley did not follow his own dictum, and no creative scientist ever has.

Great thinkers are never passive before facts. They ask questions of nature; they do not follow her humbly. They have hopes and hunches, and they try hard to construct the world in their light. Hence, great thinkers also make great errors.

Biologists have inspired a long and special chapter in the catalog of major mistakes — imaginary animals that should exist in theory. Voltaire spoke truly when he quipped: "If God did not exist, it would be necessary to invent him." Two related and intersecting chimeras arose during the early days of evolutionary theory — two animals that should have been, by Darwin's criteria, but were not. One of them had Thomas Henry Huxley for a godfather.

For most creationists, the gap between living and nonliving posed no special problem. God had simply made the living, fully distinct and more advanced than the rocks and chemicals. Evolutionists sought to close all the gaps. Ernst Haeckel, Darwin's

[1]Reprinted with permission from *Natural History*, Vol. 87 No.4; Copyright the American Museum of Natural History, 1978.

11

chief defender in Germany and surely the most speculative and imaginative of early evolutionists, constructed hypothetical organisms to span all the spaces. The lowly amoeba could not serve as a model of the earliest life, for its internal differentiation into nucleus and cytoplasm indicated a large advance from primal formlessness. Thus Haeckel proposed a lowlier organism composed only of unorganized protoplasm, the Monera. (In a way, he was right. We use his name today for the kingdom of bacteria and blue-green algae, organisms without nucleus or mitochondria — although scarcely formless in Haeckel's sense.)

Haeckel defined his moneran as "an entirely homogeneous and structureless substance, a living particle of albumin, capable of nourishment and reproduction." He proposed a moneran as an intermediate form between the non-living and living. He hoped that it would solve the vexing question of life's origin from the inorganic, for no problem seemed thornier for evolutionists and no issue attracted more rear-guard support for creationism than the apparent gap between the most complex chemicals and the simplest organisms. Haeckel wrote: "Every true cell already shows a division into two different parts, i.e., nucleus and plasm. The immediate production of such an object from spontaneous generation is obviously only conceivable with difficulty; but it is much easier to conceive of the production of an entirely homogeneous, organic substance, such as the structureless albumin body of the Monera."

During the 1860s, the identification of monerans assumed high priority on the agenda of Darwin's champions. And the more stuctureless and diffuse the moneran, the better. Huxley had told Kinsley that he would follow facts into a metaphorical abyss. But when he examined a true abyss in 1868, his prior hopes and expectations guided his observations. He studied some mud samples dredged from the sea bottom northwest of Ireland ten years before. He observed an inchoate, gelatinous substance in the samples. Embedded in it were tiny, circular, calcareous plates called coccoliths. Huxley identified his jelly as the heralded, formless moneran and the coccoliths as its primordial skeleton. (We now know that coccoliths are fragments of algal skeletons, which sink to the ocean bottom following the death of their planktonic producers.) Honoring Haeckel's prediction, he named it *Bathybius Haeckelii*. "I hope that you will not be ashamed of your godchild," he wrote to Haeckel. Haeckel replied that he was "very proud," and ended his note with a rallying cry: "Viva

Monera."

Since nothing is quite so convincing as an anticipated discovery, *Bathybius* began to crop up everywhere. Sir Charles Wyville Thompson dredged a sample from the depths of the Atlantic and wrote: "The mud was actually alive; it stuck together in lumps, as if there were white of egg mixed with it; and the glairy mass proved, under the microscope, to be a living sarcode. Prof. Huxley . . . calls it *Bathybius.*" (The Sarcodina are a group of single-celled protozoans.) Haeckel, following his usual penchant, soon generalized and imagined that the entire ocean floor (below 5,000 feet) lay covered with a pulsating film of living *Bathybius*, the Urschleim (original slime) of the romantic nature philosophers (Goethe was one) idolized by Haeckel during his youth. Huxley, departing from his usual sobriety, delivered a speech in 1870 and proclaimed: The *Bathybius* formed a living scum of film on the seabed, extending over thousands upon thousands of square miles . . . it probably forms one continuous scum of living matter girding the whole surface of the earth."

Having reached its limits of extension in space, *Bathybius* oozed out to conquer the only realm left — time. And here it met our second chimera. A tale writ larger than life, tailor-made for Hollywood as *"Bathybius* meets *Eozoon."*

Eozoon canadense, the dawn animal of Canada, was another organism whose time had come. The fossil record had caused Darwin more grief than joy. He balked particularly at the Cambrian explosion, the coincident appearance of almost all complex organic designs, not near the beginning of the earth's history, but more than five-sixths of the way through it . . . His opponents took this explosion as the moment of creation, for not a single trace of Precambrian life had been discovered when Darwin wrote the *Origin of Species* . . . Nothing could have been more welcome than a Precambrian organism, the simpler and more formless the better.

In 1858 a collector for the Geological Survey of Canada found some curious specimens among the world's oldest rocks. They were made of thin, concentric layers, alternating between serpentine (a silicate) and calcium carbonate. Sir William Logan, director of the Survey, thought that they might be fossils and displayed them to various scientists, receiving in return little encouragement for his views.

Logan found some better specimens near Ottawa in 1864, and brought them to Canada's leading paleontologist, J. William

Dawson, the principal of McGill University. Dawson found "organic" structures in his microscope slides, most notably a canal system in the calcite, and identified the concentric layering as the skeleton of a giant foraminifer, more diffusely formed but hundreds of times larger than any modern relative. He named it *Eozoon canadense.*

Darwin was delighted. *Eozoon* entered the fourth edition of the *Origin of Species* with Darwin's firm blessing: "It is impossible to feel any doubt regarding its organic nature." (Ironically, Dawson himself was a staunch creationist, probably the last prominent holdout against the Darwinian tide. As late as 1897, he wrote *Relics of Primeval Life,* a book about *Eozoon.* In it he argues that the persistence of simple Foraminifera throughout geologic time disproves natural selection since any struggle for existence would replace such lowly creatures with something more exalted.)

Bathybius and *Eozoon* were destined for union. They shared the desired property of diffuse formlessness and differed only in *Eozoon's* discrete skeleton. Either *Eozoon* had lost its shell to become *Bathybius* or the two primordial forms were closely related as exemplars of organic simplicity. The great physiologist W.B. Carpenter, a champion of both creatures, wrote:

"If *Bathybius* . . . could form for itself a shelly envelope, that envelope would closely resemble *Eozoon.* Further, as Prof. Huxley has proved the existence of *Bathybius* through a great range not merely of depth but of temperature, I cannot but think it probable that it has existed continuously in the deep seas of all geological epochs . . . I am fully prepared to believe that *Eozoon,* as well as *Bathybius,* may have maintained its existence through the whole duration of geological time."

A vision to titillate any evolutionist. The anticipated, formless organic matter had been found, and it extended throughout time and space to cover the floor of the mysterious and primal ocean bottom.

Before I chronicle the downfall of both creatures, I want to identify a bias that lay unstated and undefended in all the primary literature. All of the participants in the debate accepted without question the "obvious" truth that the most primitive life would be homogeneous and formless, diffuse and inchoate.

Carpenter wrote that *Bathybius* was "a type even lower, *because less definite,* than that of Sponges." Haeckel declared that

14

"protoplasm exists here in its simplest and earliest form, i.e., it has scarcely any definite form, and is scarcely individualized." Huxley proclaimed that life without the internal complexity of a nucleus proved that organization arose from indefinite vitality, not vice versa: *Bathybius* "proves the absence of any mysterious power in nuclei, and shows that life is a property of the molecules of living matter, and that organization is the result of life, not life the result of organization."

But why, when we think about it, should we equate formless with primitive? Modern organisms encourage no such view. Viruses are scarcely matched for regularity and repetition of form. The simplest bacteria have definite shapes. The taxonomic group that houses the amoeba, that prototype of slithering disorganization, also accommodates the Radiolaria, the most beautiful and most complexly sculpted of all regular organisms. DNA is a miracle of organization; Watson and Crick elucidated its structure by building an accurate Tinkertoy model and making sure that all the pieces fit. I would not assert any mystical Pythagorean notion that regular form underlies all organization, but I would argue that the equation of primitive with formless has roots in the outdated progressivist metaphor that views organic history as a ladder leading inexorably through all the stages of complexity from nothingness to our own noble form. Good for the ego to be sure, but not a very good outline of our world.

In any case, neither *Bathybius* nor *Eozoon* outlived Queen Victoria. The same Sir Charles Wyville Thompson who had spoken so glowingly of *Bathybius* as a "glairy mass . . . actually alive" later became chief scientist of the *Challenger* expedition during the 1870s, the most famous of all scientific voyages to explore the world's oceans. The *Challenger* scientists tried again and again to find *Bathybius* in fresh samples of deep-sea mud, but with no success.

When mud samples were stored for later analysis, scientists traditionally added alcohol to preserve organic material. Huxley's original specimens of *Bathybius* had come from samples stored with alcohol for more than a decade. One member of the *Challenger* expedition noticed that *Bathybius* appeared whenever he added alcohol to a fresh sample. The expedition's chemist then analyzed *Bathybius* and found it to be no more than a colloidal precipitate of calcium sulfate, a product of the reaction of mud with alcohol. Thompson wrote to Huxley, and Huxley — without complaining — ate crow (or ate leeks, as he put it).

Haeckel, as expected, proved more stubborn, but *Bathybius* quietly faded away.

Eozoon hung on longer. Dawson defended it literally to the death in some of the most acerbic comments ever written by a scientist. Of one German critic, he remarked in 1897: "Mobius, I have no doubt, did his best from his special and limited point of view; but it was a crime which science should not readily pardon or forget, on the part of editors of the German periodical, to publish and illustrate as scientific material a paper which was so very far from being either fair or adequate." Dawson, by that time, was a lone holdout (although Kirkpatrick . . . revived *Eozoon* in a more bizarre form later). All scientists had agreed that *Eozoon* was a metamorphic product of heat and pressure. Indeed, it had only been found in highly metamorphosed rock, a singularly inauspicious place to find a fossil. If any more proof had been needed, the discovery of *Eozoon* in blocks of limestone ejected from Mount Vesuvius settled the issue in 1894.

Bathybius and *Eozoon,* ever since, have been treated by scientists as an embarrassment best forgotten. The conspiracy succeeded admirably, and I would be surprised if one percent of modern biologists ever heard of the two fantasies. Historians, trained in the older (and invalidated) tradition of science as a march to truth mediated by the successive shucking of error, also kept their peace. What can we get from errors except a good laugh or a compendium of moral homilies framed as "don'ts."

Modern historians of science have more respect for such inspired errors. They made sense in their own time; that they don't in ours is irrelevant. Ours is no standard for all ages; science is always an interaction of prevailing culture, individual eccentricity, and empirical constraint. Hence, *Bathybius* and *Eozoon* have received more attention in the 1970s than in all previous years since their downfall. (In writing this column, I was guided to original sources and greatly enlightened by articles of C.F. O'Brien [*Isis,* 1971] on *Eozoon,* and N.A. Rupke [*Studies in the History and Philosophy of Science,* 1976], and P.F. Rehbock [*Isis,* 1975] on *Bathybius.* The article by Rehbock is particularly thorough and insightful. *Isis* is the leading professional journal in the history of science.)

Science contains few outright fools. Errors usually have their good reasons once we penetrate their context properly, rather than judge them according to our current perception of "truth." They are usually more enlightening than embarrassing, for they

16

are signs of changing contexts. The best thinkers have the imagination to create organizing visions, and they are sufficiently adventurous (or egotistical) to float them in a complex world that can never answer "yes" in all detail. The message provided by a study of inspired error is not a homily about the sin of pride, but a recognition that the capacity for great insight and great error are opposite sides of the same coin — and that the currency of both is brilliance.

Bathybius was surely an inspired error. It served the larger truth of advancing evolutionary theory. It provided a captivating vision of primordial life, extended throughout time and space. As Rehbock argues, it filled a plethora of functions as, simultaneously, lowliest form of protozoology, elemental unit of cytology, evolutionary precursor of all organisms, first organic form in the fossil record, major constituent of modern marine sediments (in its coccoliths), and source of food for higher life in the nutritionally impoverished deep oceans. When *Bathybius* faded away, the problems that it had defined did not disappear. *Bathybius* inspired a great amount of fruitful scientific work and served as a focus for defining important problems still with us.

Orthodoxy can be as stubborn in science as in religion. I do not know how to shake it except by vigorous imagination that inspires unconventional work and contains within itself an elevated potential for inspired error. As the great Italian economist Vilfredo Pareto wrote: "Give me a fruitful error any time, full of seeds, bursting with its own corrections. You can keep your sterile truth for yourself." Not to mention a man named Thomas Henry Huxley who, when not in the throes of grief or the wars of parson hunting, argued that "irrationally held truths may be more harmful than reasoned errors."

The preceding details are additionally interesting in that they shed light on the "scientific" atmosphere of the late nineteenth century. Darwin's theories were defended to the bitter end even though support was based on little more than overactive imagination. Speculations were considered to be "scientific" truths; few dared question them for fear of ridicule.

Gould states that "orthodoxy can be as stubborn in science as in religion." How true! We have come to expect unquestioning belief from theologians and their followers, since they openly rely on faith — a stand that rarely yields before logical argument. Scientists, however, are expected to be always objective, open-minded, and willing to follow wherever the evidence leads. To stubbornly deny the obvious, to insist on a fanciful dream, long after convincing evidence has failed to materialize, is a disservice to the advancement of science.

These were not the only serious lapses of Darwin and his disciples. Modern evolutionists tend to forgive or forget some of the positions held by Darwin that proved to be wrong and embarrassing.

For example, Darwin's concept of "gemmules" postulated that reproduction was performed through the unification of components carried within the blood. Gemmules were conceived to be quite small particles generated by organs throughout the human body which were then absorbed into the bloodstream. These gemmules would then combine under certain circumstances and, as a result, the sexual cells of both the male and female would contain gemmules from all parts of the body. They would then combine to form the embryo. What evidence was there that gemmules existed? None.

We know now that gemmules did not exist outside of Darwin's imagination. Many scientists defended this theory, simply because they assumed it to be true. Gemmules were taken quite seriously at the time — they had been advanced by an authoritative scientist and couched in "scientific" terms.

With time, however, it was realized that heredity did not work according to the fantasies of Darwin's imagination. Instead, Gregor Mendel's theory of genes, originally submitted in 1865, and based on his experiments in pollinating peas proved to be scientifically correct. Although his paper was distributed throughout the scientific world, little attention was paid to it and no acclaim came to Mendel during his lifetime; in those years Darwin's magnetism was much too strong to overcome. The scientific community of the 19-th century preferred to continue theorizing with Darwin's hypothetical pronouncements, rather than evaluate the solid, factual data submitted by Mendel. His significant laboratory results were brushed aside by all the "learned" scientists, as though they meant nothing. Instead, Darwin's illusory gemmules theory was paid serious attention and subscribed to as being established scientific fact.

It was only in 1900, sixteen years after Mendel's death, that other scientists working independently rediscovered the basic principles which Mendel had announced 35 years before. It was only then that Mendel's work was fully appreciated and the gene theory was formulated and applied. Later, when science came to understand the functions of the DNA, the theory of genes became only a component of the overall genetic mechanism. The ultimate, confirmed explanation bore little resemblence to Darwin's concept of gemmules.

Eozoon, Bathybius, and gemmules, were embarrassing lapses of faulty scientific approaches by scientists who let their enthusiasm run away with them. When the error became apparent, scientists preferred to bury the subject and keep quiet about the negative results obtained. There is little wonder that less than "one percent of modern biologists ever heard of the two fantasies," as Gould stated.

An earlier evolutionist had developed and Darwin accepted, another theory which most scientists now believe to be wrong. According to this theory (Lamarckism), and as part of the evolutionary process, acquired characteristics are inheritable. This theory has been essentially discredited as being at odds with Mendel's principle. Subsequent understanding from our new knowledge of the DNA and RNA, is that genetic information flows only from the DNA, never to it, and thus acquired characteristics cannot be genetically transmitted. Lamarck's theory, was quite plausible, and readily accepted by Darwin, because it provided an easily explained and readily appreciated rationale for gradual evolution. The idea was that if a finger, for example, is greatly used and thus strengthened and developed, this enlarged finger would be inherited by ensuing generations. If this reasoning were correct, the postulated sequence of evolution becomes more logical and is consistent with the idea that organs develop gradually from one level of complexity to the next. Yet, today we know that acquired characteristics are not inheritable.

One would think that if all these important aspects of the theory were found to be wrong, then the basic foundation on which the theory of evolution was built might need to be critically reconsidered.

For centuries, scientists have tried to find a plausible and elegant theory that would explain to their own satisfaction both the origin of life and the existence of millions of different species. The oft-repeated passages of the Old Testament helped little because they required supernatural processes (as then understood) which could not be tested by any of the means available to science.

Darwin's theory filled an acute intellectual void in the scientific community and responded to their psychological need for answers to the frustrating desire to replace biblical statements with scientific explanations. In their eagerness to explain, many scientists were led by imagination rather than evidence. This zeal to prove a theory naturally put blinders on usually critical thinkers. Most scientists readily fell into line. As nicely put by Gould, "All of the participants in the debate accepted without question the *obvious* truth that the most primitive life would be homogeneous and formless, diffuse and inchoate." Today we know that that is certainly not so. The advances made in science indicate a precise and structured basis for all life-bearing cells and/or organisms. Thus, what was considered "obvious" or "scientific" in the 1860s is not acknowledged as such in the 1980s.

Gould observes that these errors made sense in their own time; the fact that they do not in ours is considered by him to be irrelevant. Yet I believe that they are quite relevant and should serve as a warning to scientists to always be aware that there are still severe limitations to what is known. It is only when we appreciate the extent of our own ignorance that we foster true science. Mistakes, whether classified as "inspired errors" or overzealous anticipation of future discoveries, are still mistakes. As Gould so aptly observes, "great thinkers" can also make "great errors." Thus every statement or conclusion issued by well known scientists need not and should not be accepted without question as representing reflections of objective and scientific truth. There must always be a certain element of doubt, — agnosticism if you will, about any "consensus" however plausible it seems.

Unfortunately, this type of realistic carefulness and scientific humility was not widely exercised during the 19th century and Darwin's theory was virtually acclaimed as the arrival of the scientific Messiah. Still more unfortunately, we continue to consider that theory as law, without having the intellectual courage to question anew each aspect of it as if there were no alternatives. Darwin's theory is not scientific law — it still lacks conclusive proof in spite of its plausibility and popularity.

As Gould points out, it is true that these errors "inspired a great amount of fruitful scientific work and served as a focus for defining important problems still with us." If we clearly appreciate that today's accepted facts may become tomorrow's acknowledged errors, then the direction of our research will be shackled to a lesser degree by obligatory conformance to the trend of scientific thinking of the day. Research scientists must have the intellectual courage to step outside approved norms. The repetition and reemphasis of a concept by the majority of the scientific community does not make it objective truth. We need not be ashamed of our past mistakes; we must be ashamed of not learning the lessons taught by our past mistakes.

Unfortunately, the Darwinian evolutionists seem to have forgotten that the theory of evolution was based, in part, on various embarrassing errors that were valiantly defended by foremost scientists as representing true scientific dogma. In our further search for the "truth," let us always keep in mind gemmules, *Bathybius,* and *Eozoon* as shining examples of unscientific thinking coupled to stubborn orthodoxy.

21

2
Concept of Probabilities

Evolution is the type of theory that greatly depends upon one's healthy imagination. We are asked to evaluate concepts — that means, aspects of problems that require the infusion of our subjective deductive reasoning alone since the underlying processes are unknown.

When applying deductive logic, we tend to ask simply whether it might be *possible* for a certain event to occur. Everything in life is possible. Nothing is impossible since the outer limits of conceptual capacities depend completely upon the imagination of the evaluator. All "possibilities" thus become a direct function of subjective thought.

Is it possible for a human to grow wings and fly? Philosophically, the answer has to be *yes*. However, is it *probable* for such an event to occur? The anser is a resounding *no*.

Science is not usually involved in ascertaining "possibilities;" instead it evaluates "probabilities." Science can trust probabilities because of an objective and scientific tool that can measure it reliably: mathematics.

To logically evaluate evolution, we have to understand the implications of probabilities.

Suppose we have four balls marked 1, 2, 3, and 4. If we throw these balls into the air and line them up in the same sequence they fell, we could possibly obtain 2413. It is obvious that 1234 is not the same as 2413. Even though the component digits are exactly the same, the position of each ball within the whole sequence alters the final value of the entire group.

A new throw might produce a new realignment of the balls, for example: 4132. Again we have a new sequence — a new meaning — composed of the same four digits. How many different values — or combinations — can we get using these four digits? If we write down all possible combinations, we see that only 24 arrangements are possible, namely:

1234	1243	1324	1342	1423	1432
2341	2314	2413	2431	2143	2134
4123	4132	4213	4231	4312	4321
3124	3142	3214	3241	3412	3421

There are only 24 possible combinations when dealing with four digits. In mathematical notation, this is written as 4! (pronounced: four factorial). It is the shorthand form of 4 x 3 x 2 x 1 (four multiplied by three multiplied by two multiplied by one), the result of which is 24. Thus, the simple rule applied to obtain the possible combinations of a given number, is to multiply the number of digits with each one of its lower-valued numbers.

Suppose we had eight digits, such as 1-2-3-4-5-6-7-8. How many combinations are possible? Based on the above rule, we would have

8x7x6x5x4x3x2x1 = 40,320 different combinations.

This means that with eight balls on hand, we could obtain 40,320 different combinations, each one with a different sequence of numbers. The more digits we add, the greater the number of possible combinations.

The above is an exercise in a field of mathematics called combinations and permutations. Another, equally sound, is probabilities, widely used in statistics. It can predict the likelihood of a given event to occur. To understand the underlying principles let us revert to our first example of four balls 1-2-3-4. When the balls are thrown up into the air, what is the probability that they would wind up in the same order of 1234?

From the basic mathematical laws of probability, we develop the following logic:

1) We have seen that with four digits we can obtain a maximum

of 24 possible different arrangements.

2) The sequence 1-2-3-4 is but *one* among 24 possible combinations.

3) Consequently, the probability of obtaining the sequence 1-2-3-4 is one in 24, or

$$\frac{1}{24} = 0.041667 \quad (4.1667\% \text{ of the time})$$

This means that were we to throw these balls a few thousand times, the probability is that only 4.1667 percent of the time would we obtain the sequence 1-2-3-4 (or any other specific sequence.)

In the second example of eight balls, we would get a probability of:

$$\frac{1}{40,320} = 0.0000248 \quad (0.00248\% \text{ of the time})$$

As we see, the larger the number of balls, the larger the number of possible combinations and the smaller the probability of a haphazard occurrence of a specific sequence. Table 1 illustrates the incredible magnitude of the results we obtain by increasing the number of balls.

When we deal with situations of 1000 balls, or 5,375 balls, or 11,000,000 balls, the resulting numbers would be so huge (or small) that we are unable to even mentally comprehend them. Although we can still represent them with symbols, they completely transcend our practical grasping capacity. For all practical purposes, they become essentially meaningless in the context of mathematical probabilities.

Interestingly enough, a scientist at the Lawrence Livermore National Laboratory, California, calculated the permutations for the figure 1,000,000. He obtained a number that had 5,565,709 digits. Considering that a page of this book contains about 2,100 characters, to print such a number would require about 2,650 pages or roughly 12 books similar to this!

Table 1 displays the enormous possible combinations that are obtainable when the number of digits are increased — even by only

Number of digits	Number of Possible Combinations	Probability of occurrence of a given sequence
(n)	$(n\ !)$	$\left(\dfrac{1}{n!}\right)$
1	1	1.00
8	40,320 (4.03×10^4)	2.48×10^{-5}
12	479,001,600 (4.79×10^8)	2.09×10^{-9}
14	87,178,291,200 (8.72×10^{10})	1.15×10^{-11}
15	1,307,674,368,000 (1.31×10^{12})	7.65×10^{-13}
16	20,922,789,888,000 (2.09×10^{13})	4.78×10^{-14}
20	2.43×10^{18}	4.12×10^{-19}
25	1.55×10^{25}	6.45×10^{-26}
30	2.65×10^{32}	3.77×10^{-33}
35	1.03×10^{40}	9.68×10^{-41}
40	8.16×10^{47}	1.23×10^{-48}
50	3.04×10^{64}	3.29×10^{-65}
60	8.32×10^{81}	1.20×10^{-82}
70	1.20×10^{100}	8.33×10^{-101}
75	2.48×10^{112}	4.03×10^{-113}
76	1.88×10^{114}	5.32×10^{-115}
1,000,000	$\ldots \times 10^{5,565,709}$	$\ldots \times 10^{-5,565,710}$

Table 1: Combinations and probabilities of a few selected numbers representing linear, distinct objects.

one additional unit. As we increase the number of digits, the number of available combinations become mind-boggling. Naturally, with every permutation, we proportionately reduce the probability of occurrence, to the extent that it becomes, for all practical purposes, zero — or non-existent.

When these numbers become so enormously large, or small, we are forced to apply a shorthand system used in mathematics; otherwise we would have no room on our paper. These new abbreviated numbers are represented by elevating 10 to a given power. For practical purposes, it simply means that the number in

25

question, if completely written out, would contain as many zeros as the raised small number indicates. Thus, 10^{13} means "1 followed by thirteen zeros" or 10,000,000,000,000.

Table 1 indicates that, for example, if we had 16 balls and threw them up into the air, the chances for them to form the exact sequence 1-2-3-4-5-6-7-8-9-10-11-12-13-14-15-16 (or any other specific sequence), would be 1 in 20,922,789,888,000 throws. Percentagewise that would be so infinitesimally minimal that it can be considered almost negligible. Based on the concepts of probability we can state that the chances to obtain the above sequence in a random throw is almost non-existent.

If we had 75 balls, the possible combinations would be 2.48 x 10^{112}. If written out, this number would read as follows:

24,800,000,000,000,000,000,000,000,000,000,000,000,000,000,000, 000,000,000,000,000,000,000,000,000,000,000,000,000,000,000,000, 000,000,000,000

Frankly this author does not know how to pronounce such a figure, and it is doubtful that anybody else does.[1] Let us clearly keep in mind what this number represents: these are the possible different combinations one can obtain by throwing 75 balls into the air.

By the same rule of mathematics, the probability that a specific sequence of 75 digits could occur haphazardly is 1 in 2.48 x 10^{112} or 4.03 x 10^{-113}. If written out, such a number would read:

0.000,000,000,000,000,000,000,000,000,000,000,000,000,000,000,000, 000,000,000,000,000,000,000,000,000,000,000,000,000,000,000,000, 000,000,000,000,040,3

We can all agree that the degree of probability expressed by this

---

[1]According to Webster's Seventh New Collegiate Dictionary (Published 1967 by G & C Merrian Co. Springfield, Mass.), in the U.S.A. the figure 10^{63} seems to be read as vigintillion. However, in England, vigintillion means 10^{120}.

number is practically zero. It would be a waste of time to even attempt to calculate any larger numbers — they become redundant since they all would result in the same answer: zero.

The preceding explanation is applicable to any series of linear, distinct objects, for example: different numbers. However, we could have another set of facts: a class of objects that are indistinguishable from one another. We could have green balls mixed with carmine balls. What are the probabilities of getting specific sequences?

Suppose we have a quantity of balls, equally divided among four colors: carmine (C), green (G), almond (A), teal (T). How many combinations are possible with the linear sequence CAAA?

We observe that we have four letters of which three are indistinguishable, they are all "A". Whether the first A is in first place or in third place, makes no difference. Even if we move the positions of the As among each other, the final result does not change; it will still read CAAA.

The permutations for such a situation can be obtained on the basis of the general rule:

$$\frac{[\text{TOTAL NUMBER OF LETTERS}]\ !}{[\text{TOTAL NUMBER OF INDISTINGUISHABLE ITEMS}]\ !} \quad \text{or} \quad \frac{n!}{a!\ b!\ldots z!}$$

If we apply this formula to our example CAAA, we get

$$\frac{4!}{1! \times 3!} \quad = \quad \frac{24}{6} \quad = \quad 4$$

This means that we have four possible ways of rearranging CAAA, namely:

CAAA

ACAA

AACA

AAAC

Suppose we have more than one class of indistinguishable items within a group, such as CCAA. What are the permutations in this particular case? We again apply the same general rule stated above, and insert our known values. We obtain:

$$\frac{n!}{a! \times b!} = \frac{4!}{2! \times 2!} = \frac{24}{4} = 6$$

That means there are only six different combinations for the sequence CCAA, namely:

CCAA

CACA

CAAC

ACAC

AACC

ACCA

Let us expand this concept further and work out the permutations for a group of items reading:

CAGTGCAAGGCTTACT

Here we have a total of 16 letters. They contain four each of C, G, A, and T. In this case, inserting the known factors into the formula, we obtain

$$\frac{n!}{a! \ b! \ c! \ d!} = \frac{16!}{4!4!4!4!} = \frac{2.09 \times 10^{13}}{3.32 \times 10^{5}} = 6.3 \times 10^{7}$$

This result indicates that we have 6.3×10^{7} different possibilities or 63,000,000 permutations. In terms of probability we obtain 1.59×10^{-8}. (This result is obtained by dividing 1 by 63,000,000).

Based on this rule, we can now establish a table for a variety of cases.

Number of items n	Number of possible combinations $K = \dfrac{n!}{C!\,G!\,A!\,T!}$	Probability of occurrence of a given sequence $P = \dfrac{1}{K}$
4	24	0.04167 (4.17 x 10^{-2})
8	2.52 x 10^3	3.97 x 10^{-4}
16	6.3 x 10^7	1.59 x 10^{-8}
32	1.0 x 10^{17}	1.00 x 10^{-17}
64	6.7 x 10^{35}	1.49 x 10^{-36}
80	2.05 x 10^{48}	4.88 x 10^{-49}
84	4.80 x 10^{50}	2.08 x 10^{-51}

Table 2: Combinations and probabilities of a few selected numbers representing indistinguishable objects (based on the assumption that the four components C,G,A,T are present in equal amounts.)

Table 2 indicates to us that if we had 84 balls evenly divided into 21 each of carmine (C), green (G), almond (A), teal (T), the possible rearrangements obtainable are 4.8 x 10^{50}. This translates into a probability of occurrence of 2.08 x 10^{-51}. At that magnitude we are dealing with enormously large numbers, which in turn, reflect an essentially infinitesimally small probability.

Mathematicians are exceedingly careful and conservative evaluators of facts. They consider that any probability displayed by figures beyond 10^{-50} is automatically classified as being zero. In fact, even situations expressed by larger magnitudes, such as for example 10^{-40}, have hardly any probability of predictable occurrence. Yet, extending it the full benefit of the doubt, it has been agreed in statistical analysis that 10^{-50} will be considered as the outer limit of a probability of haphazard occurrence of any given event.

It is important to keep in mind that this limit is reached when we have 84 balls made up from equal numbers of the four colored types. The calculations shown in Table 2 were stopped at 84, since all numbers beyond 84 would translate into virtual zero probability and serve no further practical purpose.

An additional concept should be kept in mind. The probability of two independent events occurring at the same time, is covered by the "product rule." This simply means that the individual probabilities are multiplied, so as to obtain the combined probability factor. For example, if one coin is tossed, the chances of getting heads is 1 in 2, or $1/2$. If two coins are tossed at the same time, the likelihood that both will turn out heads is $1/2$ x $1/2$ = $1/4$ or 1 chance in 4.

Let us revert to the examples shown on Table 1. If we threw 76 balls with the left hand and another 76 balls with the right hand, what are the chances that both groups will end up in the same specific sequence? Based on the "product rule" the permutations would be 1.88 x 10^{114} x 1.88 x 10^{114} = 3.53 x 10^{228}. The probability would be 1 in 3.53 x 10^{228} which represents an enormously increased factor, in comparison to the probabilities of each of the components.

Keeping these few mathematical and statistical principles in mind, we can now apply them to evaluate the construction of the cell and its DNA structure.

3
The Cell

To understand whether species might be the end products of evolutionary processes, it is necessary to have a general understanding of the physical aspects of the cell and their functions.

All living matter — plants, fish, birds, reptiles, or humans — is composed of cells, the basic building blocks of life. We have life forms that are composed of only one cell, such as bacteria, viruses, or amoebas. That one cell performs all the functions necessary to sustain and reproduce its own form — it will nourish itself, digest and eject excreta, breathe, function and reproduce. In other words it is an independently functioning complete life-machine.

As we consider more complex forms of life, we observe that the cell continues to function as the building block. We have colonies of cells — groups that coordinate their activities for quite specific purposes and which, acting together, make possible distinct complex species — until we finally reach Man, who is composed of billions upon billions of cells.

Cells are extremely small and can be seen individually only through a microscope. They are nearly uniform in design even though shapes may differ, yet follow the same general blueprint — be it the cell of a leaf, ant, dog, sparrow or human. Microscopes giving an image enlargement of about 200 times allow us to observe the basic elements of the cell: a roundish mass surrounded by a membrane which holds semi-liquid material (called cytoplasm). Suspended in it is a central nucleus contained in turn within its own membrane. Except for a few additional details, that was about all that could have been seen and understood 125 years ago — and that was all that Darwin had in mind, when he referred to the "simple single cell." For many years scientists continued to refer to it as the "simple" cell. How wrong they were!

As science advanced, new insights were gathered, new understandings were amassed and new meanings ensued. We realized that the "simple cell" of Darwin is anything but simple. The cell, complicated in the extreme, is a highly sophisticated mechanism with many sub-mechanisms, arranged intricately to carry out the most awe-inspiring job: the creation and support of life in all its forms. Much of this new information about the cell has been obtained thanks to a new tool — the scanning electron microscope which magnifies to about one million times. But even with these advances in molecular biology and high technology there are still many aspects of the cell which scientists do not fully understand.

With this new tool — and other laboratory techniques — a completely different world opened up. And with it, an utterly different understanding came to light. It was as though a blind man had all of a sudden obtained 20-20 vision. An immensely different view came into sharp focus together with incredibly exquisite details. We then realized that it was a very, very long ways from Darwin's original conception of the "simple" cell. Instead, it was established that the cell is the most complex chemical factory we could imagine, with hundreds of actions and reactions taking place within its confines — all performing at the very same moment. In fact, despite the constant research going on, despite the fact that we are enormously more knowledgeable now than Darwin was during his time, we still do not know the whole "story" of the cell.

With all this complexity, and through studies over many years, microbiologists were able to discern a number of components within the cell, such as for example:

Cytoplasm
Cytoplasmic membrane
Nucleus
Nucleus' membrane
Nucleolus
DNA (Deoxyribonucleic acid) helix
Strands of messenger RNA

Strands of transfer RNA
Strands of ribosomal RNA
Ribosomes (protein producing centers)
Various amino acids
Proteins
Smooth Endoplasmic reticules (traffic lanes)
Granular Endoplasmic reticules (traffic lanes)
Cisternae
Mitochondria (power plants)
Mitochondrial DNA and RNA
Enzymes (repair crews)
Microvill
Plastids
Vacuoles
Tonoplast (vacuole membrane)
Golgi complex
Vesicles
Lysosomes
Centrioles
Microtubules
Microfilaments
Basal body
Cilia
Flagella
Chloroplast
Chromoplast
Chromosomes
Amyloplast
Extracellular space
Desmosomes
Plasmodesmata
Intermediate junctions
Terminal bars
etc.

Fig. 3 — represents a general schematic diagram of some of the component parts in typical cells.

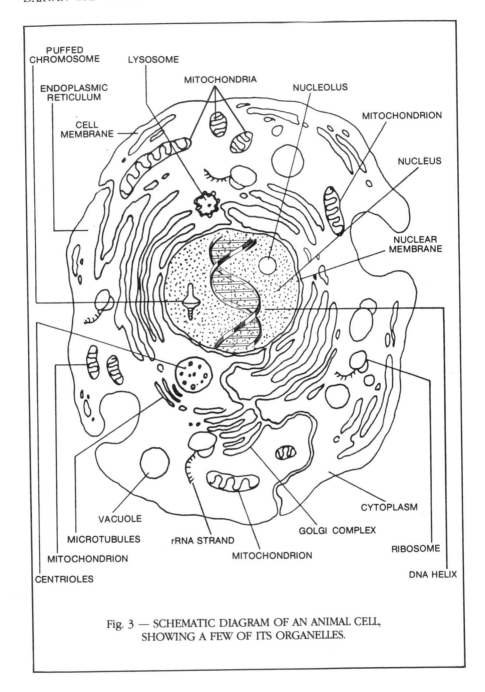

Fig. 3 — SCHEMATIC DIAGRAM OF AN ANIMAL CELL,
SHOWING A FEW OF ITS ORGANELLES.

A detailed description of all the functions within the cell is beyond the scope of this book. A few "inhabitants" of the cell are briefly described, however, hereunder, to impart some sense of the immense complexity built into the cell.

DNA: Within the nucleus of each cell, microbiologists discovered the existence of a long strand of molecules, chemically bonded to each other and forming a chain of deoxyribonucleic acid, or DNA for short. A more detailed description is given in the next chapter.

RNA: Outside of the nucleus are additional long strands of molecules, also chemically bonded to each other, called ribonucleic acid, or RNA. These are in constant motion and move back and forth between the nucleus and its enclosing cytoplasm. Further details are to be found in the next chapter.

Cytoplasm: A jelly like substance called cytoplasm fills the area within the cell walls and contains the nucleus.

Ribosomes: Within the cytoplasm are ribosomes, described as the protein producing factories of the cell. They consist of two sections which together synthesize protein chains from amino acid molecules received from strands of RNA.

Enzymes: Within the crowded cytoplasm, enzymes are actively plying their trade. These too are protein chains, however, they act only as catalysts to help certain chemical reactions take place without actually being part of, or affected by the process.

Mitochondria: Outside the nucleus and within the cytoplasm are mitochondria — the power generating plants of the cell. They oxidize chemicals received through food intake; that means they separate hydrogen to combine with oxygen, producing water molecules. This automatically releases energy, which is stored within the mitochondria as the chemical ATP (aderiosinetriphosphate.) The mitochondria thus both produce and store ATP for use as needed by the particular cell. Such needs could be synthesis of proteins, fats, or sugars for muscular requirements and movements. Cells requiring large amount of energy (such as the flight muscles of birds) contain very large numbers of mitochondria. Individual liver cells seem to contain up to as many as 2,500 mitochondria.

To the surprise of many scientists, it was determined that mitochondria have their own DNA/RNA structure. In other words, each minute organelle of mitochondria is a semi-independent order-giver in its own right, a computer sub-station so to speak. Their type of DNA is based on the same principles as the nuclear DNA. Although the DNA of mitochondria have slightly different procedures, they nevertheless interact with and complement the nuclear DNA activities.

Mitochondria are self-replicating; their DNA divides and reproduces itself. They are generated through division of previously existing mitochondria since the cell cannot create new mitochondria from raw materials. This has very significant implications to evolutionary theory, as explained in Chapter 6.

Plastids: Plant cells contain a prominent group of organelles active in photosynthesis. Their organization is similar to the mitochondria of animals, in so far as they contain their own DNA, RNA and ribosomes, allowing them to replicate independent of nuclear DNA of their cell.

Vacuoles: Fluid-filled spaces, surrounded by a membrane, particularly prominent in plant cells, are called vacuoles. They apparently act as storage areas, where salts, anthocyanin pigments, and waste are segregated.

Endoplasmic reticulum: A system of cytoplasmic membranes consisting of tubes, channels, and sacs, all connected to one another, are collectively known as the endoplasmic reticulum. They are centers of chemical reactions within the cell. In many instances, ribosomes are attached. Cells that produce large amounts of protein invariably contain equally large concentrations of endoplasmic reticula. Their main function is to keep separate the various chemicals generated within the cell so that they do not interfere with each other. In many instances they form troughs through which specific chemicals are channeled without coming in contact with the other chemicals in the cytoplasm. They are the transport lanes of the cell.

Golgi Complex: Complementing the activities of the endoplasmic reticulum, by storing and packaging certain products destined to be exported from the cell, are membrane-lined sacs or bodies called the Golgi apparatus. It was determined, for example, that proteins formed in pancreas cells move through the endoplasmic reticulum to the Golgi complex where they are grouped into sacs (vesicles.) These are then pushed to the outer surface of the cell where they release the protein they carried.

Lysosomes: The same Golgi apparatus secretes enzyme-rich bags, or droplets contained within a membrane, called lysosomes. These enzymes may be likened to repair crews or sweepers of the cell. They break down foreign material, including bacteria that penetrate the cell, as well as injured or deceased cells. When the lysosome membrane is ruptured, the enclosed enzymes are capable of breaking down and digesting the foreign material or defective cell.

Centrioles: Electron microscopy has revealed cylindrically shaped tubes, made up of nine groups of tubules, each one composed of three tubules, called centrioles. Some biologists believe they determine the orientation of the plane of cell division.

Microtubules are long slender tubes made of protein and associated with cellular movement. They act as tracks on which other organelles move; they form the main supportive and propulsive machinery of cilia and flagella. They vary in length and location depending upon requirements of particular cells.

Cilia and Flagella: The function of cilia and flagella, which line the surface of some cells is to propel the cell or move something past it. Most have the same internal structure: nine fibrils surrounding two central fibrils. They act as the locomotive of the cell to push or pull it into a given direction.

There are a number of additional components to be found within the cell, such as basal bodies, extracellular space, desmosomes, plasmodesmata, intermediate junctions, terminal bars, etc. Some of their functions are known while others are not too clear.

This, then, is a partial description of what Darwin called the "simple cell!" What an ironic misnomer! It is interesting to compare the above with the description of a cell as it appeared in old textbooks. For example a 1903 publication, *Animal Life* by Jordan and Kellogg (published by D. Appleton and Co. New York, Pages 3 and 4), described the cell as follows:

"The primitive animal cell consists of a small mass of a viscid, nearly colorless, substance called *protoplasm*. This protoplasm is differentiated to form two parts or regions of the cell, an inner denser mass called the *nucleus*, and an outer, clearer, inclosing mass called the *cytoplasm*. There may be more than one nucleus in a cell.

...the cell may contain certain so-called cell products, substances produced by the life processes of the protoplasm. The cell may thus contain water, oils, resins, starch grains, pigment granules, or other substances.

...Its chemical structure is so complex that no chemist has yet been able to analyze it, and as the further the attempts at analysis reach the more complex and baffling the substance is found to be, it is not improbable that it may never be analyzed."

About 50 years ago, in 1929, H.G. Wells, Julian S. Huxley and G.P. Wells cooperated in writing a textbook, *The Science of Life* (The Literary Guild, New York, pages 41-43), at a time when the DNA/RNA was unknown. Their description of the cell followed contemporary information available then. According to them:

"A cell is a tiny, flat, irregularly-shaped lump of protoplasm. It is not bounded by any visible wall; there is just a simple interface...separating the cell-substance from the surrounding fluid. The outline is constantly changing ... The ground-substance, which is called the *cytoplasm* is a fluid as clear as glass. Somewhere about the middle of the cell is the large, rounded nucleus; floating in the transparent cytoplasm round the nucleus are numbers of smaller bodies of various kinds...

Most conspicuous among those bodies are certain regular globules, more or less numerous, which appear to the observer as brilliant shining spheres. These we now know are tiny droplets of oil... Scattered among these globules, less brilliantly luminous, and much smaller is a host of fine granules. These granules show irregular movements which, like those of the oil-droplets, are probably passive and due to currents in the transparent cell-fluid.

Very different from these granules and droplets are certain snakelike threads which writhe slowly through the cell. These threads are exceedingly fine and their length is variable... The threads are called *mitochondria* and are composed of albumen and a fat-like compound, *lecithin.* Though evidently of importance to the cell their use has not yet been discovered. Lying like a cap over one end of the nucleus, a zone called the *centrosphere* may be distinguished ... it seems to be a region where mitochondria are made; they can be seen wriggling out from it into the cytoplasm.

The nucleus is a relatively large oval or spherical mass which drifts slowly to and fro in the cell...has no visible wall. Inside the nucleus there are usually two mistily opaque bodies of irregular contour, the nucleoli; these bodies are continually changing their

38

size, shape and position. Except for the slowly writhing nucleoli nothing can be seen inside the nucleus but a clear fluid.

This, then, is a simple kind of cell, released from the body and leading a life of its own."

In the 1980s we know that the above descriptions are not complete nor accurate. What a tremendous difference between today's knowledge and the information available to earlier scientists!

This information, published just about 50 years ago, included the statement that "nothing can be seen inside the nucleus but a clear fluid." And yet we know today that the inside of the nucleus is the most important part of the cell — the home of the DNA. In 1929 our scientific knowledge was not advanced enough to observe and understand the extent of the activity taking place within the nucleus. Past generations of scientists cannot be faulted, since they expressed the knowledge level of their time. As science progressed, we learned more. With each advance we shed past imperfect or erroneous beliefs, and replaced them with revised ones. This is the normal course taken by scientific progress — a course that should always be pursued, including in the case of Darwin's theory of evolution.

With this general overview of the complexities of the cell, let us now consider some of the physical activities taking place within the cell.

4

DNA/RNA

In the 1950s scientists started to penetrate and unravel the mystery of life-bearing cells. They discovered the structure of the DNA, how it fit in with other aspects of the cell and how it functioned. The physical construction of the DNA was described by Francis Crick and James Watson, although, it must be pointed out, a great many other scientists contributed to the deciphering and understanding of different parts of the process and of the structure. We are indebted to a whole list of researchers, among whom could be named Wilkins, Hershey, Taylor, Kornbergs, Chase, Woods, Hughes, Ochoa, and Okazaki.

The DNA was discovered to be located inside the nucleus. It represents two elongated twisted strands of alternating phosphate (P) and deoxyribose (D) molecules. These two strands are held together by "rungs" called nucleotides (or bases) consisting of four specific chemical molecules: thymine (T), adenine (A), cytosine (C), and guanine (G).

Diagrammatically this structure may be likened to a ladder that has been twisted around a theoretical vertical axis. The rungs of the ladder are made up of the four chemicals mentioned above, while the two side rails are formed of alternating molecules of phosphate and deoxyribose. (Fig. 4)

These four organic chemicals have the capacity to unite and continue holding on to each other in a very specific manner: T is attracted only to A, but never to G or C. Naturally the reverse holds true: A always unites with T. Similarly, G joins only with C but never

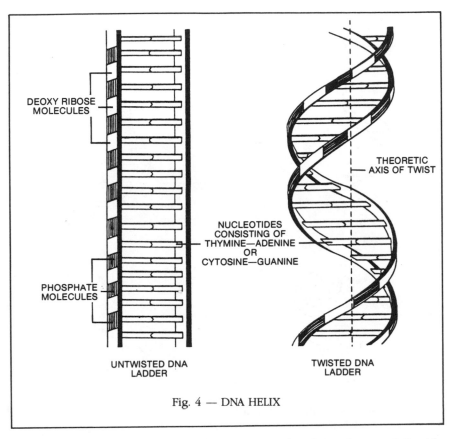

DEOXY RIBOSE
MOLECULES

THEORETIC
AXIS OF TWIST

NUCLEOTIDES
CONSISTING OF
THYMINE—ADENINE
OR
CYTOSINE—GUANINE

PHOSPHATE
MOLECULES

UNTWISTED DNA
LADDER

TWISTED DNA
LADDER

Fig. 4 — DNA HELIX

with A or T. As a result, we have pairings only of T with A, and C with G. Thus limited, there are only four combinations of position and component: T-A; A-T; C-G; G-C.

It was further suggested that the in-between "glue" uniting the molecule pairs consists of hydrogen atoms (Fig. 5.) As a result, we understood that each rung of the twisted ladder (double helix) is composed of a two-part marriage between two compatible molecules. These rungs, may be positioned in any sequential order. We find repeats of the same chemicals or alternating ones and innumerable intermixtures. There appears to be no limit to the numbers of nucleotides that can be constructed within this scheme. In fact, millions upon millions of nucleotides are known to exist in the nuclear DNA structure of the living cells of virtually every species; a tree, or a bee, or a lion has DNA whose strands comprise only these

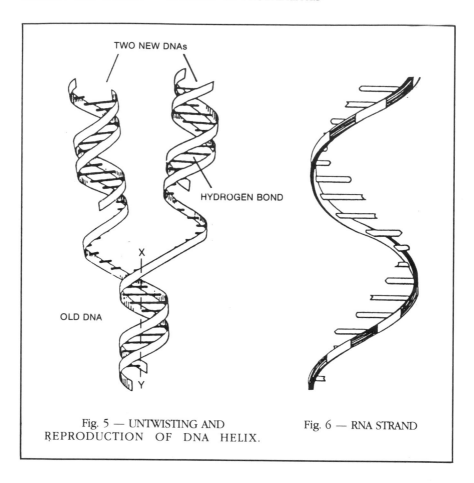

Fig. 5 — UNTWISTING AND REPRODUCTION OF DNA HELIX.

Fig. 6 — RNA STRAND

four types of nucleotides.

The difference in DNA between species resides almost strictly in the sequential positioning of the nucleotides, relative to each other, and in the exact quantities of each type of nucleotide. Every form of life contains its own length of strands and sequence of nucleotides. No two individual plants or animals have DNA spirals that are identical — excepting clones. Such differences in DNA structure are reflected in different growth which, in turn, mean different species.

The surprising understanding that emerge is the fact that the sequence of the nucleotide controls and governs everything else within the cell. The particular alignment of T-A-C-G rungs translates into the several specific amino acids, which in turn generate distinctive protein chains. These then define the exact growth leading to clearly separate forms. Thus the determining key is the sequential positioning of nucleotides within the DNA double helix. That is one of the almost miraculous tools that governs the growth of every single aspect of every one of the 6,000,000 species (or more) believed to exist on this planet. With this realization, science discovered the core of the program that regulates and determines every form of life.

For a given species to reproduce, it has to transfer that precise program to the next generation. How is this achieved? Researchers finally discovered the ingenious system: the split and reconstitution of the DNA. In essence, it works as follows:

1) At a given moment the DNA spiral unwinds its twist, and splits open along axis X-Y (Fig. 5.)
2) The uniting bonds between C and G, as well as between T and A, are broken. This leaves A dangling alone on one side of the rail, and likewise T becomes unattached on the other side of the opposite rail (similarly C and G become disassociated.)
3) When this occurs, an A (that happens to be, for example, on the left rail) is immediately available to unite with any other T molecule in its vicinity, so as to reconstitute a new A-T nucleotide.
4) By the same token, on the right rail, the now separated T molecule is available to pair with any unattached A molecule. It unites with it resulting in a new T-A nucleotide link.
5) Both processes take place simultaneously and at a constant rate. As the DNA spiral is splitting and unravelling on one end, it is immediately being reconstituted, thus creating an identical duplication of the original DNA double helix. Such an action has been compared to opening and closing a zipper.

At the conclusion of this action, we end up with two identical DNA strands. A duplicate program has now been formed — a perfect, or near perfect, copy of the original DNA has been generated. Continuation of the species has been provided for by this transference of its growth program for use by the next generation. The entire process is said to take place within a matter of seconds.

When splitting and duplicating millions of nucleotides in such a speedy manner, can mistakes occur? Would some rungs not miss uniting with their mates? Of course errors can be produced. Improbable as it might sound, this complex mechanism has a built-in repair crew, always on hand, available to promptly repair the damage. This so-called "simple" cell contains different types of enzymes that rush to the rescue. The first group of enzymes pinpoint the incorrect or missed joint, while the next groups of enzymes have the capacity to repair the damage, take out the unacceptable section, insert correct sections, and properly join the sections together. The end result is an exact duplication of the original twisted ladder, corrected or repaired to reflect the same exact sequence as programmed in the mother DNA. When one considers that this work is being performed with precision and on a continuous basis by molecules of enzymes, one must be impressed with the order and inherent organization of the entire system.

These groups of chemical molecules, the enzymes (or catalytic agents), perform additional functions. Some enzymes have the ability to start unwinding the twisted ladder. Others will stop the process — still others start the duplication of the helix, and so on. It is as though crews of workers, each having a specific task perform prodigiously within the microscopic nuclei of the cells.

Essentially, the DNA is a packaged program that can be compared to the punched card or tape system we once used in computers. Small holes were punched into these cards at precisely determined locations. Every position had a meaning. A mispunch would result in an erroneous information being given to the computer. The thousands of cards kept together as a group, used to be stacked in a very specific sequence. When these cards were inserted into the machine, the computer would guide itself according to the coded information it "read" from the holes on the card and in the sequence in which the cards followed each other. Based on this input, the computer would automatically perform the type of action which these cards "ordered" it to undertake. In a sense, the machine was but a robot that could do nothing else than follow orders encoded in the program. If an engineer designed a program to cut a 3-inch gear, this is the only gear that the computer, under that program, could order the machine tool to cut.

That system was similar to the perforated cards used in our Jacquard looms to weave specific designs in cloth. These cards, punched with round holes at very specific spots, were predetermined according to the design the textile engineer created. Every hole, the position of every hole, and every card sequence within the train of cards, has a particular meaning within the context of the overall design. And every design is represented by one — and only one — sequence of properly punched cards. Any mistake in the punching of the holes, or any displacement of one of the cards, would result in a flaw in the final product. The loom would produce only what was dictated by the hole program encoded on the cards.

The DNA works along the exact same principles, only it is millions of times more sophisticated and more perfect. Nevertheless, it represents simply the punch card program of life. It directs the cell as to what protein chain to produce, when to produce it, in what quantities to produce it, when, for example, to stop including the amino acid alanine and start adding the amino acid glutamine. In itself, the DNA has no independent intelligence. It performs as a robot *because* of the purposefulness and intelligence built into the program it contains. It can be compared to our modern floppy discs that carry programs — they too have no "intelligence." They can transfer only the information encoded on them by the programmer — the computer's outside intelligence. All the performers taking part in this drama within the cell, can do nothing but follow the orders encoded within the program.

How is this program transmitted from the DNA located inside the nucleus to the rest of the cell? This entails another remarkable tool: strands of RNA (ribonucleic acid), which are similar to DNA, yet somewhat different.

Instead of being a coiled ladder, or double helix, the RNA is only a single twisted rail — or one side of a ladder split lengthwise through the rungs. It is composed of a string of alternating molecules of phosphate (same as in DNA) and ribose (unlike DNA which has instead deoxyribose.) From this rail stick out the same chemical molecules C,A,G (as found in DNA) except that it holds uracil (U) instead of thymine (T). Uracil has properties similar to thymine as it,

45

too, will bind only with adenine (A). A schematic representation is given in Fig. 6.

Cells contain various RNA strands each performing a different activity; they have been given distinctive names to reflect their function.

As the DNA is sitting comfortably within the nucleus of the cell, it needs a transmission mechanism that will notify the world outside the nucleus. This function is relegated to the RNA. At a given time, a small section of the DNA unwinds and opens up, thus allowing the RNA strand of ribose and phosphate to work its way through and come in contact with the exposed split nucleotides in the opened section of the DNA. As it faces the bared molecules of the DNA, the RNA "reads" the sequential positions of the C-G-A-T components of the split nucleotide and copies that information on its own rail. When the complete message has thus been copied, the loaded RNA strand leaves the nucleus and moves into the cytoplasm of the outer part of the cell. There it contacts one of the protein factories — ribosomes — and transmits the coded message it has just brought from the master program.

The ribosome "reads" the message and attracts the type of amino acids ordered by the new instructions it received. These coded messages are constantly being transferred from the DNA to the production centers of the cell via the RNA, which, because of its activity, has been named mRNA (messenger RNA).

While this activity takes place in one corner of the cells, dozens of other mRNA segments are performing similar messenger functions to other ribosome centers. A continuous movement of mRNA is taking place within the cell, which in turn means continuous production of proteins. Depending upon the message they carry, these mRNA vary in length, some having over 10,000 bases to transmit.

Another group of RNA strands are attached to the ribosome, the rRNA (ribosomal RNA). Biologists are not sure as yet, how this type of RNA works and what exact role it plays within the overall protein production capacity of the ribosome.

A third class is called the transfer-RNA (tRNA). Each of these can attract a single specific amino acid molecule at one of their ends. Since there are only 20 different amino acids within a cell, it follows that we have 20 different types of tRNA, each capable of recognizing a specific amino acid, grabbing a molecule and travelling with it to a ribosome that is calling for that kind of amino acid.

The production of proteins is constantly taking place within the cell. Ribosomes consist of two sections, one larger than the other which together synthesize proteins. In simplified form, (many complex procedures are involved, some still not well understood) the following happens:

1) The mRNA (messenger RNA) brings in from the DNA a coded sequence of nucleotide message.

2) This mRNA seeks and attaches itself to a ribosome. While passing through it, it allows the ribosome to "read" the sequence of C-U-A-G messages inscribed.

3) These four chemicals are read in groups of three, thus forming a word (or codon) understood by the ribosome. Each three-letter word represents the symbol for a specific amino acid. For example the sequence C-C-C means amino acid *proline,* and the sequence G-A-C translates to amino acid *aspartic acid.* One specific mRNA strand might contain 3000 bases, while another one could carry 7000 bases of a different sequence. By reading these bases in groups of three, the ribosome is given exact instructions as to which amino acid to combine into a protein chain.

4) Proteins are long chains of amino acids. Having received an order as to what to create, the ribosome attracts tRNA (transfer RNA) strands that carry the type of amino acid desired. As stated previously, each tRNA carries only one of the 20 amino acids used in the cell. The ribosome factory is now in a position to put together the sequence of amino acids ordered by the particular mRNA strand into a specific length of protein.

5) As each tRNA comes and surrenders its cargo of amino acid to the ribosome, it is then free to return to the cytoplasm to repeat the action. (see Fig. 7)

6) The ribosome continues to "read" along the mRNA thread,

47

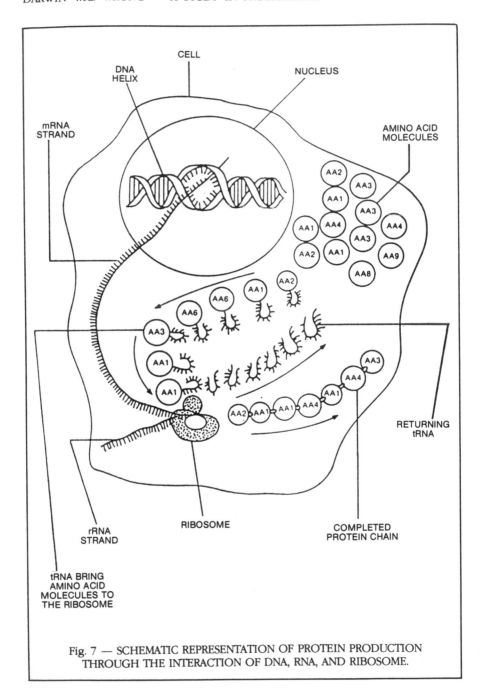

Fig. 7 — SCHEMATIC REPRESENTATION OF PROTEIN PRODUCTION
THROUGH THE INTERACTION OF DNA, RNA, AND RIBOSOME.

receiving the necessary amino acid molecules in the same sequence as was implanted on the message carried by the tRNA. At the end of the line, the newly formed chain of amino acids — now called a protein — detaches itself from the ribosome and wanders away into the cytoplasm.

7) The ribosome having finished its task is ready for a new message from the DNA encoded on a new RNA messenger.

A schematic view is submitted in Fig. 7.

This entire process is continually being repeated inside all cells. If we keep in mind that a human being has a few billion cells, it means that during every second of the day and night, there are billions upon billions of trips being performed by our RNA strands between the nuclei and the ribosomes. We (and all other life forms) are literally aggregations of cells, each teeming with all sorts of internal activity.

Some cells contain more RNA strands than others. Cells that have to produce more protein contain many more strands of RNA — while cells called upon to produce less protein display a lesser quantity of these strands. This is to be expected since the RNA is simply a mechanism that complements the cycle of protein production. The interactions between ribosomes, mRNA, tRNA, rRNA, and a quantity of enzymes are the backbone for a species to grow in a healthy manner, work efficiently and reproduce accurately. All of these main players interact to perform complicated, yet coordinated maneuvers, the sum total of which represents the cause and process of "living."

These simplified details, impressive and implausible as they may be, are only *some* of the actions taking place within the cell. There are myriad additional activities taking place — some known and understood, others not. The cell is an extraordinarily complex, yet amazingly organized machine performing with precision in all its minutest details. These activities seem to be universal in their applications and purposes.

We observe an exact chain of command:

From DNA to RNA to ribosome to protein

It is always unidirectional, always starting at the DNA and flowing downwards. So far as can be determined, it never acts in the reverse direction. Thus amino acid "AA" cannot "dictate" back to the DNA whether it should add to its nucleotide chain an additional 10,000 links so as to issue permanent orders for the inclusion of additional "AA" amino acid molecules into a given protein chain. There is no allowance for the "system" to add — by its own — more or different nucleotides to the already existing package in the DNA. The implanted program must remain as is with no expansion taking place, if that particular species is to be reproduced. Once a program is set to produce species "X", it cannot rearrange the millions of nucleotides by means of its own internal mechanism so as to regenerate a different sequence — one that would be completely purposeful to produce species "Z".

Within this enormous complexity and perfection, certain important characteristics stand out:

a) Immense numbers of nucleotides.

b) Absolute purposeful sequencing of nucleotides, in relationship to each other, so as to translate into a meaningfully performing end-product: a given species.

c) Utmost precision in the entire mechanism to transmit the message of the programs, as encoded in the sequence of nucleotides. These actions are performed on time and directed to the proper order-receiving centers.

d) Capacity to reproduce itself and transmit, at the same time, the same program to the next generation. We thus have a system for the perpetuation of each specific program — or species.

These aspects are most important since once clearly understood, they become the cornerstone of our entire understanding of the principles guiding the existence of each species on earth. We must constantly remind ourselves of these details; they are the key to our determination as to whether evolution did take place or not.

Let us not forget that scientists still do not know the reason why and how the organelles behave the way they do. A great many questions remain unanswered. For example:

Each cell in our body contains a copy of the same DNA helix which sends out the proper chronological messages to construct protein chains. Yet a liver cell receives different orders than a skin-cell. How does the DNA know that it is located in a liver cell and thus should send only those orders that pertain to liver functions? What forces the DNA to open the proper section so that the RNA read the necessary message applicable to a liver cell? What controls the sequence of messages being sent? In other words, what mechanism determines the order in which specific sections of the DNA are opened?

The DNA is the master program that directs all the activities within the cell. Is there a super-program that directs the DNA? Or does the DNA contain its own control mechanism directing the actions of the rest of the helix? When the RNA reads the nucleotides of the opened DNA helix, how does it know whether it should read the left side or the right side of the DNA-rail? Even though the two sides are complementary, it makes a significant difference as to which sequence is read, since a different sequence would cause the ribosome to produce a different type of protein.

The mitochondria procreate independently from the DNA. How do the mitochondria know that the exact moment has come to reproduce, because the cell is about to split? How does the DNA notify the hundreds of mitochondria in that specific cell that it is about to split so that the mitochondria should perform the same act at the same time? During mitosis (cell splitting) all mitochondria in that particular cell must reproduce at the same time. What type of a synchronized and coordinated signal do they get or give each other which forces all of them to reproduce simultaneously?

Additional questions could be asked, for which microbiologists do not yet have the answers. Research continues and additional discoveries and better understandings can be expected. Yet, faced with this immense complexity, few words can appropriately express the feelings of a thinking person; perhaps "flabbergasting awe."

So as to get some general idea of the magnitude of the numbers of nucleotides involved, it is interesting to consider the following figures:

GAGTTTATGCTTCCATGACGCAGAAGTTAACACTTTCGGATATTTCTGATGAGTCGAAAAATTATCTTGATAAACGAGGAATTACTACTGCTTGTTTA

TCAACTACCGCTTTCCAGCGTTCATTCTCGAAGAGCTCGACGCGTTCCTATCCAGCTTAAAAGGAGTAAAAGGCGGTCGTCAGGTGAAGCTAAATTAAGC

AACGATTCTGTCAAAAACTGACGCGTTGGATGAGGAGAAGTGGCTTAATATGCTTGGCACGTTCGTCAAGGACTGGTTTAGATGAGTCACATTTGTT

TGAACTGAGTACTAAAGAATGGATAATCACCAACTTGTCGTAGCCTGAGTCTCATCATTAGGTGCGAGAAAATTTACAGTGTTGTTCTCTTAGAGATGGTAC

TACTGAACAATCCGTACGTTTCCAGACCGCGTTTGGCCTCTATTAAGCTCATTTGGATTTAACCGAAGATGATTTCGATTTTCTG

TCGCTCCCATAGGATGTTTCAGGTCGCATGGTATTTGCGTTCGGAGTTGCGTCGCTCGCTCCGCCAGTCATCGTTAGGTTTGAAACAATGAGCA

TTCCTGCTCCTGTTGAGTTTATTGCTGCCGTCATTGCTTATTATGTTCATCCGTCAACATTCAAACGGCCTGTCTCATCATGGAAGGCGCTGAATTTAC

CAGTCATTCTTGCGAGTCACAAAGGACGCGCA;TGCGTCCATTTGCGCTTGTTAAGTCGCCGAAATTGGCCTGCGAGCTGCGGTAATTATTACAAAAGG

GCAGAAGAAACGTGCGTCAAAAATTACGTGCGGAAGGAGTGATGTAATGTCTAAAGGTAAAAACGTTCTGCTCGCGGGGACGTTAATCATGAGCG

TTAAATAGGAGTTCATTCCCCGGCTTCGGGGACGTTAATTTTAACAACTGGTGATGTATGGTTTCCTTGCTGGTCAGATTGGTCGTCTTATTACCATTCAACTA

ATGTCTAATATTCAAACTGGCGCCGAGCGTATGCCGCATGACCTTTCCCATCTTGGCTTCCTGCTCGCGGTTGCCGGTGAGAGCTTCCTCAGCGGTCGTATTGGCTC

TACAGATGTCATCTCAGTTATCGTCCCGTGCGTTATGGTGAACAGTGGATTAAGTTCATGAAGGATGGTGTTAATGCCACTCCTCTCCCGACTGTTAACCAA

TTTTACTTTTTATGTCCCTCATCGTCACGTTTACGAATCCCTAAAATAACCATAGTCCCAATTAGCACGGTTCTTTTCGCCGTACCAGTTATATTGGTCATCA

GATATCTATAGTTTATTGGGACTTTGTTTACGAATCCCTAAAATAACCATAGTCCCAATTAGCACGGTTCTTTTCGCCGTACCAGTTATATTGGTCATCA

CGTATTTTAAAGCGCCGTGG---ATGCCTGACCGTACCGAGGCTAAATCCCTAATGAGCTTAATCAAGATGCTCGTTATGGTTTCCGTTGCTGCCATCT

TCGTCGAACGTCTGGATTATTACAGTTATCTCACACCATCTTCAGCAGTAAACCGCTCTTCGAGTCAGAGATCCTCCTCCTTCGCCGTCGTCAGGTTTACAAAAC

TATGCTAATTGCATACTGACCAAGAACGTGATTACTTCATGCAGCGTTACCATGA-GTTATTTCTTCATTTGGAGGTAAAACCTCATATGACGCTGACA

ACTTGTGCTGGTCTTTTGACCGGATTGCTGCAAACCAGTCAAGGAGTAGTTGTAGTATCGGTCTAACTCGGCGTACTGTTCATTCCTGCCA

ACAGACCTATAAACATTCTGTGCCGCGTTTCTTTGTTCCTGAGCATGCCACTATGTTTTACTCTTGCTCGACTAAAGAG

GGAAGTATCTTAAAGTGCGCCGCCGTCAACGGGTGTATGTTTTGTCCCAGCGGTCGTATAGCCGATATTCCATGACTTA

ATGTTTCCGTTCGGTGATTCGTCTAAGAAGTTTAAGATTGCTGAGGGTCAGTGGTATCGTTATGCGCCTTCGTATGTTTCTCCTGCTTATCACCTTCT

TTGACTTGCTGACTTTGTGACCAGTTAGTACCAACGCTTATTCATGCGCAGGAACGTTAGTGGTCTTCCGCCAAGGACTTACTTACCCTTCGGAAGT

GTTGCAGTGGATAGTCTTACCTCATGTGACGTTTATCGCAATCATTCAATCATGACTTCGTGATAAAGATTGAGTGTGAGGTTA

TTTCAGACTTTGTACTAATTTGAGGATTCGTCTTTTGGATGGCGCGAAGCGAACCAGTTGGGGAGTCGCCGTTTTTAATTTTAAAAATGGCGAAGCCAAT

TATTTCTGCCACAATTCAAACTTTTTTCTGATAAGCTGGTTCCTCACTTCGTTACTCCAGCTTCTTACGACAACCTAAAGCTACA

GGACTAATCGCCGCAACTGTCTACATAGGTAGACTTACGTTACTTCTTTTGGTTGGTAATGTCGTAATTGGCAGTTTTATATTGCAACTGCT

TTGTTTCAGTTGGTGCTGATATTGCTTTTGATGCCGACCCTAAAATTTTTGCCTGTTTGGTTCGCTTTGAGTCTTCTTCGGTTCCGACTACCCTCCCGAC

```
TAACGGCCGCATGCCCCTTCCTGCAGTTATCAGTGTGTCAGGAACTGCCATATTGGTGGTAGTACCGCTGGTAGGTTTCCTATTTGTAGTATCCGT
AACGTCTACGTTGGTTTCATGGTTTGGTCTAACTTTACCGCTGGTCTAACTAAATGCCGCGGATTGGTTTCGCTGAATCAGTTATTAAAGAGATTATTTGTCTCC
AACTGGCGGAGGTTTGTTAAATCTGTACCGCGGTGGTCGTTCTCGTCTCGTTATGGCGGTCGTTATCGTGGTTTGTATTTAGTGGAGTGAATTCACCGA
AAAGCCGCCTCCGGTGGCATTCAAGGTGATGTGCTTGCTACCGATAACACATACTGTAGGCATGGGTGATGCTGGTGTATTAAATCTGCCATTCAAGGCTCTA
CTTCACGGTCGGACGTTGCATGGAAGTTCTTCAGGAAATGGTCGAAATCGTTATCGTGCTTTGTTTTGATCCCGCCGGAGTAGTCCAATCCTTGTA
TGCCGTTTCTGATAAGTTGCTTGATTGGTTGGACTTGGTGGCAAGTCTGCCGCTGATAAAGGAAAGGATACTCGTGATTATCTTGCTGCTCATTTCCT
GGTCAACGTAAAATCATTCGAGAAAAACTAAGAGTTTAGGCCGCAGTTGGTATGGTCGTCCTTCGTAGTGTCGTGCGCGAATTCAGTGGGTTCGTAATTCGAG
ACAATCAGAAAGAGATTGCCGAGATGCAAAATGAGACTCAAAAAGAGATTGCTGGCATTCAGTCGGCGACTTCACGCGCAGAATACGAAAGACCAGGTATA
CCTTTGGACGACAACGAACCTTTCTAACCACAAAAGGTATTATCGTGCTTGCGTGTCAGTATTTACCAATGACCAAATCAAAGAAATGACTCGCAAGGTTAGTGCTGAGGTTG
GAGATTATGCGCCAAATGCTTACTCAAGCTCAAACGGCTGGTCAGTATTTATAGGAAACGTCATCGCGGTATTTCTTCGCGGTATGGCTTAATTGTCT
GGTCTTCGTCGTAGTCACTGCTGTAATCTTATAGGAAACGTCATCGTTGCCGATACTGGAACAATTTCTGGAAAGACGGTAAAGCTGATGGTATTGGCTCTAATTGTCT
TGTGGTTGATATTTTCATGGTATTGATAAAGCTGTTGCCGATACTGGAACAATTTCTGGAAAGACGGTAAAGCTGATGGTATTGGCTCTAATTGTCT
TAAGTCTTCCCATTATTCTTGCTTGGTATTTTTCGGAGGTTCTAAACCTCCGTACTTTGTATGTTAACCCTCCCACAGTTAGGACTGCCAATAAAGGA
GTCACGCTGATTATTTTGACTTTGAGCGTATCGAGGCTGTCTAAACCTGCTATTGAGGCTGTGGCATTTCTACTCTTTCTCAATCCCAATGCTTGGCTT
CGGCAGTTGTATGTAAAGCTTGAGTTGCGGGACGTAATAGCTTGAGTTTCGTCTTCTGTCTTAGAGAAGGTTCTGAACTACGCCAATAGGTAGACGAATACC
CATAAGGCTGCTTCTGACGTTCGTGATGAGTTTGTATCTGTTACTGAGAAGTTAATGGATGAATTGGCACAATGTCTCCCCAACTTGATA
CCCGCAAGTCGTCGGTCGAACGTTTGACGATGTATAATTACCCCAAAAAGAAGGTATTAAGGATGAGTGTTCAAGATTGCTGAGGCCTCCACTAAGATATCGGCTAGA
TCTTAAGGATATTCGCGATGAGTATAAATTACCCCAAAAAGAAGGTATTAAGGATGAGTGTTCAAGATTGCTGAGGCCTCCACTAAGATATCGGCTAGA
GATTAGCCAGCAGTCGGTTGCACTCCACAGTTTTTGCTATTTGGTCATTTTGGTAGTCGTACTCGGACAGCGTAAGCGTAAGTAGTTGCGACTTATCGTTTCGG
AGGCGTTTTATGATAATCCCAATGCTTGCGTGACTATTTTGCCGTGATATTTTCGTGATATTTTCGTGATATTTTTATGACTATCGTCAGC
CGATGGACATCCTTCACAGGCGTATTTCACGTGGCGTACCTTTACTTCTGCCGTGATAATCGACATGTATGCCCATGGTTACAGTATGCCCATGGTTACAGTATGCCCATGGTTACAGTATGCTCAGC
GTTGACCCTAATTTTGGTCTGGGTATATTGACCATCGAAGTTTGACCATCGAAATAGCTTGCAAAATAGCTTGCAAAATACGTGGCCTATGGTTACAGTATGCCCATCGCAGTTCGCT
TGTATCTTTGGTTGTCGGTATATTGACCATCGAAATAGCTTGCAAAATACGTGGCCTATGGTTACAGTATGCCCATCGCAGTTCGCT
GGCTAAATACGTTAACAAAAGTCAGACATTGAGGTGCCACCTGTCTAAACACTCGTAAAGGTCTAGGAGTCAAAGTAGGGCTTCAACGCCGAGTAAGACTTGTCGAAGAACCC
CGAACCATTCAACCTAATTCGTGAGGCACCTGTCTAAACACTCGTAAACAGTAACACTCGTAAAGGTAGGGCTTCAACGCCGAGTAAGACTTGTCGAAGAACCC
TGGGTTACGACGACGCCGTTCAACCAGATATTGAACGCAAAAGAGAGATGAGATTGAGGCTGGGAAAAGTTACTGTAGCCGACGTTTTGGC
ACGTCCAACCTATGCGTTAGTAAAAATAGCTTCGCGCGTATTTAAACTCGTCTAAACAGCAGTCCAACGCGG
```

Fig. 8 — DNA NUCLEOTIDE SEQUENCE OF øX174 (ON PAGES 52 AND 53)

GENETIC CODE of an extremely small bacterial virus, the bacteriophage designated øX174, is given by the sequence of letters on the opposite page. The letters stand for the four nucleotides cytosine, guanine, adenine and thymine, which are linked end to end to make up each strand of the normally double-strand DNA molecule. The genetic message embodied in each strand of DNA is represented by the particular sequence of nucleotides, and one of which may follow any other. In the øX174 virus the DNA molecule, which has only a single circular strand for part of its life cycle, consists of approximately 5,375 nucleotides; the nucleotides are grouped into nine known genes, which are responsible in turn for coding the amino acid sequences of nine different proteins. . . The complete nucleotide sequence for the DNA in øX174 was worked out recently by Frederick Sanger and his colleagues at the British Medical Research Council Laboratory of Molecular Biology in Cambridge. About 2,000 pages of this type would be required to show the nucleotide sequence for the DNA in the chromosome of a typical single-cell bacterium; roughly a million pages would be needed to similarly display the genetic code embodied in DNA molecules that make up chromosomes of a mammalian cell.

(From *The Recombinant-DNA Debate,* by Clifford Grobstein. Copyright © 1977 by Scientific American, Inc. All rights reserved)

---

1) An extremely small bacterial virus (øX174) was determined to have 5,375 nucleotides (Fig. 8)

2) Single cell bacteria are known to have about 3 million nucleotides (all aligned sequentially in a very specific order, mind you!)

3) A human mitochondrial DNA has slightly more that 16 thousand nucleotides.

4) A mammalian cell (which includes our own species) is estimated to have approximately 3 billion nucleotides in its DNA!

Imagine 3 billion links that have to be in *very precise order without any mistakes!* We can but ponder these figures in utter amazement and infer the awesome sophistication and intelligence that must have gone into setting up such a system! Any thinking person who appreciates the overwhelming majesty of these complexities might well be struck dumb by their implications.

5
The Genetic Code

The master program, the DNA, contains only four chemicals: cystosine (C), guanine (G), adenine (A), and thymine (T) tied to each other in the form of nucleotides. With these four units, the DNA is able to send innumerable messages to the rest of the cell. How is this done?

It was discovered that with these four chemicals (for notational convenience, read "letters") the system "spells" out only three-letter words — called *codons* (sometimes referred to as *triplets*). On the basis of this "language" the ribosomes know exactly what proteins to create, how much is ordered, and the sequence in which it is wanted.

In view of the fact that we have three-letter groups where each letter could be any one of four letters, it means that the maximum possible codon combination can only be 64. Thanks to the brilliant laboratory work of such research scientists as Nirenberg, Khorama, Holley, Leder, and Matthei, the genetic code was finally broken. It was established that each of the 20 amino acids in the cell is coded by a three-letter "word" — a codon.

This incredible systematized perfection has been depicted in the form of a table — the genetic code — as shown in Table 9. It is the equivalent of the periodic table of elements which gave us the atomic equivalence of all the elements.

THE RNA GENETIC CODE

First Letter	Second Letter				Third Letter
	U	C	A	G	
U	PHE	SER	TYR	CYS	U
	PHE	SER	TYR	CYS	C
	LEU	SER	**	**	A
	LEU	SER	**	TRP	G
C	LEU	PRO	HIS	ARG	U
	LEU	PRO	HIS	ARG	C
	LEU	PRO	GLN	ARG	A
	LEU	PRO	GLN	ARG	G
A	ILEU	THR	ASN	SER	U
	ILEU	THR	ASN	SER	C
	ILEU	THR	LYS	ARG	A
	MET*	THR	LYS	ARG	G
G	VAL	ALA	ASP	GLY	U
	VAL	ALA	ASP	GLY	C
	VAL	ALA	GLU	GLY	A
	VAL*	ALA	GLU	GLY	G

Table 9: The dictionary of the genetic code as found in the RNA. The letters of the codons appear on the outside and should be read in the same sequence as they appear in the codons.

*These combinations translate into START messages.

**These three codons translate into STOP messages.

The twenty amino acids read through the RNA Genetic Code are:

ALA	= alanine	LEU	= leucine
ARG	= arginine	LYS	= lysine
ASN	= asparagine	MET	= methionine
ASP	= aspartic acid	PHE	= phenylalanine
CYS	= cysteine	PRO	= proline
GLN	= glutamine	SER	= serine
GLU	= glutamic acid	THR	= threonine
GLY	= glycine	TRP	= tryptophan
HIS	= histidine	TYR	= tyrosine
ILEU	= isoleucine	VAL	= valine

After this genetic code was graphically arranged, five of the codons (UAA, UAG, UGA, AUG, and GUG) seemed to make no sense. With time, and more research, an amazing fact was established: these were the punctuation marks in the genetic code. The first three codons imparted the message of STOP while the last two read START. In other words, this incredible system has, incorporated in its structure, orders as to when to start performing a certain meaningful activity and when to stop it!

It was further discovered that the codon AUG also orders the production of the amino acid methionine, while GUG also doubles to give the order for the amino acid valine. It is still a mystery as to why AUG and GUG are sometimes read by the ribosomes as orders to pick up the mentioned amino acids, and at other times, as an order to "start" reading the sequence that follows.

On the other hand, it was also realized that this code contains a number of synonyms — that is, two or more codons call for the same amino acid. Thus the amino acid proline (PRO) can be coded by four different combinations of nucleotides; namely: CCU, CCC, CCA, CCG.

One thing is certain, however: nothing is haphazard in this utterly logical system. Everything in the code has a meaning and everything is arranged with precision. We can only imagine the awe and amazement of those who discovered, and first appreciated the intricacies and sophistication of the DNA/RNA mechanism.

The following example will illustrate the workings of the genetic code. Let us consider that a given section of the DNA reads as follows:

A T G T T T A A A C C A G T T T A A

This sequence will be inscribed by the mRNA as:

A U G U U U A A A C C A G U U U A A

because every T in the DNA becomes a U on the RNA. The ribosome that receives this message from the mRNA reads it in groups of three or:

AUG   UUU   AAA   CCA   GUU   UAA

This, translated via the genetic code shown in Table 9, says:

AUG — start reading
UUU — first attract a molecule of amino acid *phenylalanine*
AAA — then attach a molecule of amino acid *lysine*
CCA — then attach a molecule of amino acid *proline*
GUU — then attach a molecule of amino acid *valine*
UAA — stop producing this sequence.

With this ingenious system, an extended chain of amino acids can be built. There is virtually no limit to the length of the message that could be sent. For example, UUU codes for phenylalanine (PHE). If we had nine Us in a row it would mean an order to create three consecutive molecules of phenylalanine, in the same protein chain. The pattern of this amino acid chain is determined by the sequence of the nucleotides in the mRNA. Any error in the order of the nucleotides, would result in the creation of a different amino acid, which in turn would change the characteristics of the protein chain within which it is located. Thus, the DNA program, with its precise sequential ordering of nucleotides determines the kinds of proteins the cell produces at any given moment. Precision is essential and is achieved by this incredible nearly computer-like program inherent to the double helix of the DNA.

This genetic code appears to be universal in application; the cells of all plants and animals, including men, obey the same instructions, for, so far, no exception has been discovered to the rule. Until it is proven differently, we can consider that the genetic code is the same for all the 6,000,000 or more species presumed to live on this world.

Once the DNA/RNA was understood, and the implications grasped, Darwin's pronouncements became oversimplified postulates when compared to the mathematical precision and intelligence instilled in this awe-inspiring universal system governing life.

6
Purposefulness

Previous chapters have brought out some of the incredible intricacies of the component parts of the cell and the precision of their activities within an overall pattern.

Two aspects are particularly thought provoking.

STOP/GO: In the previous chapter 5, describing the genetic code, we observed that the codons UAA, UAG, UGA, AUG and GUG were the punctuation marks of the system. The first three were read by the cell as STOP while the last two were understood as GO signals. Thus, the generation of protein chains (which, in the final analysis initiate and sustain growth) takes place only after the codons AUG or GUG are read by the ribosome, and proceed for all the subsequent codons that follow, until a UAA, UAG or UGA message reaches the template of the ribosome. At that moment the ribosome stops construction of that particular protein chain. The process is then repeated as additional GO — STOP signals are received by the protein manufacturing centers of the cell.

The fact that this system includes a STOP — GO signal has significant implications. It indicates a predetermined purposefulness of action, a knowledge of an expected future necessity within an enormously complex, yet perfect, system. Purposefulness is clearly a reflection of sophistication or intelligence. These are not characteristics that we can attribute to unthinking chemical atoms and molecules. This aspect alone, should have alerted us that some form of "intelligence" has been at work to provide so perfect a system.

There is an additional fact that becomes apparent. If the system did not have "STOP — GO" signalling capacities, there would be no beginning and no end to the creation of different proteins of given lengths. Under a continuous system, the cell would generate one never-ending protein of almost infinite length — which, in turn, would result in a non-species or one endless growth. That means "STOP — GO" codons are essential to the proper growth of a species. This again means that predetermining thought must have preceeded the establishing of the DNA/RNA complex; it reflects the presence of "intelligence." How did unknowledgeable molecules know that they needed to incorporate a "STOP — GO" signal within their system so as to generate a meaningful end product?

The laws of chemistry and physics do not, so far as we understand them, provide for inanimate molecules to haphazardly decide on their own, what coding system to use nor what type of punctuation system to incorporate, and how to react on the orders thus encoded.

Mitochondria: Chapter 3 reviewed highlights of the various components found within the cell. Among these are mitochondria — the power-generating centers of the cell. These small cylindrical suborgans have their own DNA and RNA organization. Because of this, they are self-replicating along very nearly the same process as the entire cell. The main DNA in the nucleus controls everything in the cell — except the mitochondria, which seem to be going their own way, although they cooperate functionally with the entire cell. This means that new mitochondria arise only by the division of previously existing ones. The cell cannot create new mitochondria by synthesizing them from existing raw material.

A surprising aspect is that different types of cells have different quantities of mitochondria. Cells that spend large amounts of energy contain a great many more mitochondria than cells with lesser energy needs. Liver cells, for example, are said to contain up to 2,500 of these organelles. These facts have significant implications.

Since the general DNA program does not control the generation of new mitochondria it means that each one of these powerplants is master of its destiny and procreates, based on existence of a previous mitochondrion. This apparently indicates that liver cells have always had 2,500 mitochondria so as to provide 2,500 units in each new

61

generation of cells. If this is correct, then going back into time, earlier generations of liver cells must have always been liver cells — and hardly anything else but liver cells, In fact, they must have started as liver cells from the very beginning of that species and included the requisite numbers of mitochondria to perform the energy job expected from liver cells. Ultimately this points to purposeful design by the intellectual equivalent of a genetic engineer who knew what a liver was, how a liver cell was supposed to perform, and how many powerplants were necessary in each liver cell so as to generate the type of energy needed. Such an evaluation is logical, and would fit into the master plan of a Genetic Engineer — a larger organized intellect that had long before mastered and used the complexities of the cell.

If we cannot accept this as a possible, even likely, alternative then we are almost forced to infer that cells in and of themselves may generate as many mitochondria as they feel are needed, and that, as additional energy requirements are felt, mitochondria create promptly additional units to meet the demand. This would imply a sense of evaluation of the situation, plus a trigger that starts the reproduction mechanism of the various mitochondria in that particular cell. Although such a situation is a theoretical possibility, it is not likely to be what actually takes place. It would imply that as the embryo forms, all cells are initially equal — that they all have the same number of mitochondria. As the embryo develops further, cells would become specialized, so that liver cells would be drastically restructured to provide many more mitochondria than cells destined to become skin cells. It would also mean that mother-mitochondria do not split when the entire cell divides, but only after a demand for energy is felt. This is not consistent with what we understand to be the actual functions of the cell.

On the contrary, based on the evidence we have so far, liver cells will always lead to liver cells having the same quantity of mitochondria as were present in the liver of the first specimen of that species.

These two aspects — an advanced "STOP — GO" system and self-replicating mitochondria complex — are telling evidences that purposefulness played a crucial part in cell development.

No chance groupings of however many chemical molecules there are would lead, without direction at some stage, to these amazing complexities and strictly regulated routines within the cell — routines that lead to very specific results. It reflects a level of intelligence far higher than any we are familiar with — certainly far superior to our own level of intelligence and knowledge. We have yet even to understand how all the components of a cell interact, much less invent a new cell system. We cannot even make a working copy of a living cell of any kind.

As shown in Chapter 3, different cells may have forty or more different component parts — each one of which has its distinctive function. None of these functions appear redundant but all are rather necessary for proper functioning of the cell. We cannot conceive that chemical molecules could get together and decide that they needed lysosomes, and microvills, and Golgi apparatus, and endoplasmic reticula so as to perform properly as a team. We cannot conceive that chemical molecules could reach decisions as to what type of organelles were necessary, how many of them would suffice, and how to manufacture them. Forethought or, at least, a mental blueprint is almost mandatory. Nor can we conclude that chemical molecules have enough perseverence, even when applied over a span of millions of years, so as to translate such mental blueprints into physical organelles.

All of these aspects reflect an enormous purposefulness; this, in turn, is a direct expression of design — of intelligence.

7
What Does It All Mean?

Until now, debates about evolution were essentially exercises in imaginary concepts — mental gymnastics. It started, we were told, with a fortuitously motivated simple cell, added "millions of years" of stark, barren void and inferred natural processes by means of convoluted logic to reach imaginary conclusions. Based on nebulous "facts" we reached "solid conclusions" to which we allowed ourselves — almost by self hypnosis — to swear allegiance. Such debates were almost by definition inconclusive because discussions pivoted around hypothetical situations lacking evidence. We were continually exposed to contests between differing imaginations. He who had a more vivid imagination and a more glib tongue would prevail.

The bottom line turned out to be always the same: debates concerning amorphous possibilities that *might* or *might not* have led to the end result: the functioning human beings we know today. In the end they all deteriorated into a tug-of-war between differing faiths.

Luckily all of this blurry exercise in imagination and/or "faith", came to an end with understanding of the DNA/RNA. We now have a precise mechanistic tool to translate every basic action within the cell.

In chapter 2 we had observed that with 84 balls we had obtained 4.80×10^{50} possible combinations, or a figure with 50 zeros! The probability of haphazard occurrence of any given combination was calculated to be 2.08×10^{-51}. Statisticians agree that such figures reflect virtual zero probability. Since the number of nucleotides under consideration is beyond the 84 mark, any number beyond this point has in effect a zero probability. At that stage, it is not even worthwhile to calculate the exact mathematical result. Any arithmetical calculation will represent such an outrageously small probability factor that it becomes zero, many times over. Any prescribed combination of nucleotides simply has no chance of random occurrence.

This means that any viable DNA having over 84 nucleotides is automatically beyond the range of random occurrence. Since *all* the DNAs of *all* the species we know have DNAs with more than 84 nucleotides, it follows that none of the species on this earth could have been the results of random mutations of nucleotides!

The arguments and conclusions could stop there. However, for lovers of mathematics inclined to be more precise, let it be mentioned that the above statements refer only to the DNA itself. The same probability considerations have to be applied to the interactions of the tRNA, mRNA, rRNA, the ribosomes, mitochondria, etc. For those readers who like mathematical brain teasers, the following problem should be a challenge:

Given a species whose DNA strand has 11,000,000 nucleotides, what are the probabilities of occurrence of the following events to have taken place simultaneously but haphazardly:

a) Given 22,000,000 molecules of phosphate and deoxyribose holding on to each other in an alternating fashion, along two separate rails.

b) Given 11,000,000 C-G-A-T nucleotides aligning up in the DNA in a *specific* sequence.

c) Given 11,000,000 hydrogen atoms acting as bonds between C and G as well as between A and T.

d) Given 2,500,000 uracil molecules taking the place of each thymine molecule, when forming the RNA strand.

e) Given additional 2,000,000 phosphate and ribose molecules, alternately tying to each other to create RNA strands.

f) Given 200 mitochondria to perform in the cell.

g) Given 2,000 additional molecules of phosphate and

deoxyribose holding on to each other in an alternating fashion, inside each mitochondrion.

h) Given 1,000 C-G-A-T nucleotides aligned in a very specific way within the mitochondrial DNA.

i) Given 500 nucleotides for the mitochondrial RNA.

j) Given 250 ribosomes, each built of two sections.

Shall we stop here, or should we continue enumerating all the other physical parts necessary within the cell that would have to cooperatively organize themselves in one spot during a random meeting of molecules?

To evaluate the chances for so many independent events to occur simultaneously, each event has to be computed separately, and its specific probability factor calculated. Then, applying the "product rule" described on page 30, these factors have to be multiplied with each other. The arithmetical answer would be a superastronomical figure. It would be futile and a waste of time to even consider the mathematical probability of molecules becoming sufficiently organized, by random mutation, to result in any part of these intricacies in the cell — and then perform according to the rules they just laid down themselves.

Surely scientists should be convinced from their studies of the various component parts of the cell that there is amazing complexity, perfection, purposefulness, meaning, sequence, and order existing or implied within every cell. With this new insight, we have a new and unexpected tool; every aspect of growth can now be expressed in precise mathematical and engineering language — a language that leaves little to the imagination and replaces blurry, wishful thinking.

We now know that the growth of five fingers, for example, is the result of the orders issued by millions of nucleotides aligned in a very *specific sequence*. A new human species growing permanently eight fingers per hand would have a DNA with different sequence of nucleotides, again numbering in the millions. We further know that there is a direct and precise relationship between a given portion of the DNA program and the growth of particular parts of the body. The one is tied directly to the other. The one cannot exist without the other. A growth — no matter of what shape, form, or size — *cannot* exist without a corresponding alignment of millions of nucleotides, all of them strung along in a precise, predetermined order. One must underline again the precise sequential order of millions upon millions of nucleotides that are involved. This program is the cause for the growth of any part of any life-machine. Change the sequence of the nucleotides (even a few) and you destroy the program — thus the characteristics of that species. If we have 6,000,000 species on this planet (and some people believe there are more) then we have 6,000,000 distinctive and, literally, specific programs.

Now we can relate our arguments to absolute numbers. Within how many million nucleotides is the program for a nose, a hand, a paw, or a high-cheek bone inscribed? The answer will be precise. What are the exact nucleotide sequences for each one of these growths? Again the answer will be very, very precise sequences. What are the probabilities for these numbers and sequences to occur randomly: The answer will again be precise.

We now know that for the smallest bump to grow on a skin, it has to receive a proper order from its controlling central: the DNA. If the nucleotides within the DNA are in such a sequence so as to order the growth of the bump, the new growth will ensue. To a very great extent, we do not have to conceptualize anymore how an insect with six legs *might* have evolved into one with 100 legs. The growth of these legs depend completely upon the nucleotides of their DNA. Consequently, our debate and evaluation can now be centered within the world of the DNA/RNA — an incredibly huge world!

It also means, that to understand any aspect of any species, we have to evaluate that section of its DNA program that controls the growth of that particular aspect. Since they are directly tied to each other, we can now generate comparative studies of DNA/RNA sequences which will show us how to code groups of nucleotides so as to achieve a desired growth. Microbiologists are presently deciphering cause and effect relationships of the DNA programs.

In the past, we used to state: "a fish with gills moved onto dry land, and after millions of years developed lungs and discontinued gills." That was a hazy, unscientific generality — a cliché for which the proferred biologic and paleontologic "evidence" was irrelevant and inconclusive. We used it for 125 years as it was convenient to the

67

rhetorical purposes of evolutionists.

Let's analyze this oft-repeated gem of "scientific" logic. How a fish with gills survived the first twenty minutes on dry land is unknown; how it discovered that land-existence necessitated a separate organ working on different principles of atmospheric oxygen, is also not understood; how it managed to grow the proper organ (i.e. lung) to fit inside the body for the proper purpose, is enigmatic; how it persevered for a few million years to continue perfecting its mental blueprint of the lung, is also problematic; how it managed to phase out the growth and functions of the gill and simultaneously improved the development of the lung, is mysterious; how it rearranged its own DNA nucleotide sequence each time it made an anatomical change, is incredible. Despite all these unknowns, enigmas, and theoretical concepts, we are asked to have "faith" in these farfetched stories of evolution. Of course we must consider that both the male and female of the species jumped together out of the water so as to continue procreating on land. We must also assume that the same immense changes were taking place simultaneously in two separate bodies of both partners!

Today, we have a completely different measuring stick. We can translate every single aspect of growth into precise mathematical language. Today we know that fish of species "F" with one type of gill needs, perhaps, 1 billion nucleotides within which is encoded a unique sequence defining the fish. The gill portion of the program may be encoded within an identifiable DNA section of, say 200 million nucleotides[1] — again in a *very specific sequence*. For fish "F" to become a land animal of species "S", it might need 100 million nucleotides to grow a lung, aligned in a completely different sequence than the 200 million nucleotides of species "F". The difference between the two are enormous.

We can now ask: what are the probabilities of occurrence for a DNA to discontinue all *by itself* 200 million specific nucleotides and

[1]Undoubtedly, critics will jump at the opportunity to point out that there is no factual proof at this time to consider that the gill mechanism is defined by 200 million nucleotides. That is true enough; these figures have been used as examples of probable magnitudes. At the present stage of the debate we are only interested in the concept rather than the exact figures. Whether a gill is represented by 100 million nucleotides or only 500,000 or even 10,000 is unimportant since the conclusion would be the same. We established the fact that any situation displaying 10^{50} permutations is considered having zero chances. This would be equivalent to 84 nucleotides (see Table 2). Thus, any number larger than 84 will continue to have zero probability. Whether we have 10 thousand or 200 million nucleotides, the conclusion remains the same.

replace them with 100 million (or any other number) of differently aligned nucleotides?

The previous chapter gave us an emphatic answer: zero.

What is the mathematical probability for a specific sequence of DNA helix of 200 million nucleotides to incorporate *by itself,* an additional 50 million nucleotides in a completely different meaningful sequence?

The answer is another emphatic: zero.

Let us be clear on an important point: fish of species "F" may vary between individuals and from generation to generation in, for example, scale coloration or fin size. However, there will not be differences displayed by whole new organs or by varied systems of organs. Gills and lungs are not the same organ, nor do they perform along the same principle. To grow these two dissimilar organs necessitates different sequences in their DNA nucleotides. How will fish "F" arrange to change the sequence of 100 million nucleotides so as to become "S"? We have no scientific knowledge as to how this can be achieved haphazardly.

There is an additional consideration that ensues. If we subscribe to the concept of gradual incremental change, as submitted by Darwin, we would in effect imply that the DNA is continually changing at some gradual incremental rate. A physiological or morphological change cannot exit without a corresponding nucleotidal change in its DNA. This raises two substantial questions:

1) During this proposed evolutionary incremental alteration, which part is the first to change? Did the physiology first change and then *instruct* the DNA to realign itself to reflect such a change for the future generation? Or, did the DNA first rearrange its nucleotidal sequence which then ordered the physiology to change? Darwin had no knowledge about the existence of the DNA — thus he did not take such factors into consideration when formulating his theory of evolution.

2) In either of these two events, the net result would be that the

nucleotides have to be realigned so as to reflect the physical change of the species — no matter how insignificant that change might be. How does a DNA add or subtract or rearrange its nucleotides at will?

If we admit, for argument, that a DNA helix is free and willing to add additional nucleotides whenever it desires, we reach an impasse that raises further questions:

Suppose we have a DNA with 10 million base pairs. It needs to add, for example, 100 additional nucleotides in precise order so as to reflect a given change in the morphology of that species. Any change of a given organ would be defined as requiring encoding somewhere between base pair 1 and base pair 10,000,000. A change in a given organ usually affects other organs (such as blood vessels, muscles, tissues, nerves, and/or performance capabilities of other member organs.) Does that mean that the DNA would split open at, say, base pair 5,355,760, incorporate 40 new nucleotides, and then repair the junction? The same procedure presumably takes place after base 7,445,700 for the introduction of 36 additional bases; after base 8,400,000 for 15 new pairs, and again after base 9,122,000 for the introduction of the remaining 9 new nucleotides? Does a DNA helix have the capacity to open up at specific spots so as to add nucleotides, on the basis of a meaningfully aligned new inclusion — an action that has to maintain intact the purposefulness and survivability of the species?

Or shall we consider that the addition of 100 nucleotides takes place at the beginning of the sequence, or at the end of the sequence of 10 million nucleotides? If that were the case, these 100 new members of the program could not properly interact at the spot at which their change was to be reflected. Consequently, they could not be introduced at the beginning or the end of the helix. Obviously it would mean that the DNA would need the ability to insert new bases only at those spots along the helix that would encode for the precise change involved. This, again, implies knowledgeable purposefulness. Of course, each and every addition had to be performed in such a manner so as to coordinate with existing codons and not interfere in the proper triplet counts. If one of these triplets were broken up, all the ensuing codons would misread and the species expire.

Many more questions arise, all leading to a vicious circle of logic.

Does a DNA helix have the capacity to add nucleotides at will? So far as we know, the DNA cannot. If it did, all we had to do would be to isolate a DNA, place it in a proper medium and add quantities of C—G—A—T—P—D chemicals. In due time these loose molecules should end up as additional rungs of an expanded DNA helix. Certain tests were performed which indirectly, indicated that DNA chains do not attract molecules indiscriminately, nor do they add nucleotides at will.

Laboratory experiments were performed in which the double helix of different species were isolated and split. The strands were then broken down into smaller pieces. When such DNA segments belonging to separate individuals of the *same* species were placed together, perfect sections of DNA were reconstituted. However, when DNA pieces from unrelated species (such as insects and humans) were mixed together, no double helix was formed. DNA pieces derived from species having a relatively closer relationship (such as humans and monkeys) would form certain sections of a double helix, but these usually proved unstable and came apart upon heating.[1]

In each of the three cases, we observe that the same chemicals were placed in contact with each other: C-G-A-T-P-D. If there had been an easy and normal way for the DNA to add nucleotides, the samples in the experiments would have had ample opportunity to use the available raw materials, arranging and rearranging them into new nucleotides. And yet this did not happen. They reconstituted themselves only according to previously established programs and along functionally compatible sections. They did not improvise and add additional bases, even though they might have done so.

Obviously this indicates to us that the DNA does not have the independent capacity to add nucleotides at will. Once a given program is established, it remains fixed in its sequence. The living proofs are today's insects who survived in exactly the same form for hundreds of millions of years.

Accordingly, any theory which requires incremental evolutionary changes involving the introduction of additional nucleotides into an existing DNA program is quite apparently untenable.

---

[1]See *Darwin to DNA, — molecules to humanity,* by G.L. Stebbins, Pages 319-320.

In the final analysis, we reached the point in our understanding that allows us to explain biology in terms of mathematical probabilities and the principles of mechanical engineering. We now have a measuring device of great precision — a precision once possible only within the physical sciences and mathematics.

In mathematics, numbers have very very specific meaning. The number 5 is precise and means one thing — it differs from the number 6 which has a different meaning. Figures are not amorphous, hazy concepts that can be glossed over and stretched out of their intrinsic value through generalizations. A strand of DNA with 6,375,876 nucleotides is not the same thing as a strand with 7,444,837 nucleotides.

Microbiology provided us with an opportunity to evaluate the processes that might have been followed when the first plants or animals appeared. The sequence of those events became clear, since they followed (to a great extent) the procedures used by a mechanical engineer who designs particular machines. His building blocks are usually pieces of steel shaped in the forms of levers, cams, shafts, and gears. By arranging and rearranging these in predetermined ways, relative to each other, he can cause the machine to provide a given effect. For this machine to constantly perform as anticipated, it requires instructions and a prime-mover. The human operator can manually push buttons and turn shafts as often as needed. If the designer is more sophisticated he will use a computer, write a proper program, and load it onto a floppy disc. This software will subsequently issue orders and activate the entire train of gears, levers, and shafts.

The mechanical engineer relies heavily on two specific tools when designing his machine: the laws of physics and the laws of mathematics. From physics, he extracts the knowledge of cause and effect in the material world. From mathematics, he takes and uses objective logic and precision. If he learned his lessons well and applied them correctly, his machine will work.

The same principles could have been, might have been and, I shall argue, probably were applied by some original genetic engineer (or engineers) who was much more knowledgeable in his skill to design life-machines than we are at present. First he determined the type of effects and products he wanted; then he decided what causes would result in the desired effects. Subsequently he designed, if you

72

will, the type of floppy disc that would repeat the program in an untiring manner. He used mathematical precision to the fullest and displayed an enormous mastery for handling very large groups of numbers in an elegant and efficient manner.

Realistically, a species is nothing but a robot. It performs, grows, and reproduces as it does *because* it can do no other. It is programmed to grow along a very specific way; it cannot change its own program (unless it is a human being with intelligence who just discovered the inner workings of the DNA/RNA program.) Instead of levers and gears, the original genetic engineer used limbs, organs and senses. Instead of floppy discs and related hardware, he designed the marvelously complex DNA/RNA system. Instead of steel, his raw materials were chemicals. Instead of a program based on electrical impulses, he used atoms and molecules. Instead of using the simple binary system, he used four units (C-G-A-T) grouped into triplets, thus generating an enormously more sophisticated capability than our binary system (which becomes a primitive tool in comparison to the DNA language.) Underlying all of these components is the intertwining thread of utter mathematical precision.

We now *know* that species *can* be created. Mathematically speaking, we realize that the DNA nucleotidal sequences are not the products of random occurrences. Consequently, species *must* have been created as individually functioning units in themselves. Paleontologists have been unable to disprove it — on the contrary our fossil finds suggest such a situation.

This conclusion is not based on any religious or metaphysical concept — it is based strictly on scientific facts and logic.

73

8
Natural Selection And Mutations

Darwin's foundation for his evolutionary theory lies in his claim that "natural selection" promotes progressive changes, thus rationalizing the production of different organs and species. Part of the mechanism to achieve this metamorphosis is attributed to mutations — which, by implication, are chance occurrences.

Darwin's own words, on this subject, as stated in his *The Origin of Species,* are instructive:

> "Natural selection will never produce any structure more injurious than beneficial to that being, for natural selection acts solely by and for the good of each. No organ will be formed...for the purpose of causing pain or for doing an injury to its possessor.
>
> Natural selection tends only to make each organic being as perfect as, or slightly more perfect than, the other inhabitants of the same country with which it comes into competition."

Basically, Darwin infers that chance in nature — thus nature itself — is a plant and animal breeder that not only *improves* species, but also spawns additional millions of species. Yet the proposed tool for these changes — mutation — does not achieve the desired effects Darwin read into it. Today we understand more clearly what mutation means because our new knowledge of the DNA/RNA gave us a completely different perspective.

Up to now, the concept of mutation has been misused to

generalize and visualize aspects that were hardly understood or known. The word "mutation"was the magic password pronounced to gloss over immense areas of ignorance. A given species was supposed to have changed (or evolved) into a completely different species by means of individually imperceptible but continuing mutations. Each change was theoretically expected to improve or alter a certain physical aspect of the species. Again, theoretically, each significant change should have resulted in in-between species, or missing links.

In practice, we know that mutations do exist in nature. They are usually classified as freaks, oddities, abnormalities. We know for example, that such mutations may result from exposure of reproductive cells to radiation. It is generally agreed that the effect of mutation is almost invariably negative.

Now that we know how the DNA/RNA works, we can easily understand why mutations have destructive influences on the cell and not positive nor constructive effects.

Suppose we have an RNA sequence that reads:

AUG UUU AAA CCA GUU UAA

Applying the genetic code, this message translates into:

AUG = start reading
UUU = attract amino acid PHE,
AAA = attach amino acid LYS,
CCA = attach amino acid PRO,
GUU = attach amino acid VAL,
UAA = stop production.

Now let us suppose that the fourth letter (U) of the above sequence were destroyed — for some reason or other. Since the system would continue to "read" three letters at a time, it would take in the next letter of the sequence so as to complete the triplet or codon. We would then get a rearranged sentence that reads:

AUG UUA AAC CAG UUU AA-

The message would accordingly translate into:

AUG = start reading
UUA = attract amino acid LEU (Instead of PHE)

AAC = attach amino acid ASPN (Instead of LYS)
CAG = attach amino acid GLN (Instead of PRO)
UUU = attach amino acid PHE (Instead of VAL)
AA? = continue producing (by adding the next base to AA-)

As is seen, the destruction or mutation of a *single* nucleotide would change the meaning of the entire program that follows the point of the accident. The protein chains generated would be completely different than what the original program was expecting to create. The result would be a meaningless form, that, most probably, would end that line of plant or animal. Codons reading STOP and GO (AUG, UAA) would be destroyed so that protein chains would continue endlessly, creating giant chains which, in turn, would generate — if they generated anything — monstrous growths.

Similarly, if two nucleotides were deleted, added to, or substituted for, it would affect all the millions of codons that follow the point of the accident. The message read would be completely different.

If three consecutive nucleotides were destroyed, the chances are that the species would probably continue to survive but would have some sort of shortcoming. In such a case an entire codon would be missed, but the subsequent triplets would continue to be properly used.

For example, we know that sickle-cell anemia disorder is the result of a mutation of a single amino acid. Instead of having the three nucleotides necessary to order the inclusion of glutamic acid within a certain protein chain, they are substituted by nucleotides reading valine. This simple substitution is enough to alter the capacity of the red blood cells to carry oxygen, thus resulting in the anemia disorder. Interestingly the difference between glutamic acid and valine amino acids is only one nucleotide.

Valine is coded on the RNA strand by the codons GUA or GUG. Glutamatic acid, however, is coded by sequences GAA or GAG.

That means, a replacement of a single "U" by an "A" nucleotide is sufficient to create an imbalance in the program. It is certainly amazing to realize that a single nucleotide out of 3,000,000,000 nucleotides present in a human DNA, is sufficient to generate a serious problem!

If entire groups of codons were to be destroyed, there is no telling what the results would be. It would depend completely upon the nature of the missing triplets, and the type of growth they control. The chances are that the species could not survive. One thing is certain: any interference with the existing millions of codons. will translate into a meaningless result — meaningless within the context of that particular program. The species will expire, or at least, will continue to limp as an aberration.

Ultraviolet rays, radiation, and certain chemicals cause mutations. For example, it was determined that nitrous acid (HNO_2) is a powerful mutagen. It can transform C (cytosine) into U (uracil). Thus whatever sequence contains a codon with C is replaced with U, which in turn, generates a completely different sequence of amino acids or protein chains. Other chemicals are known to have similar effects on cells.

For a real mutation to be beneficial it would have to destroy that particular codon whose absence from the program would enhance certain aspects of it. Which ones are these? We don't know. And at any rate, how does one enhance the value of an existing perfect sequence of nucleotides? The evidence continually points to all species functioning at maximum efficiency within their original limits — that means unchanged and unchanging DNA programs.

There is an additional interesting observation. The theory of evolution teaches that mutations and "natural selection" forces are at work to alter a given species from a specific state into a more complex and advanced stage. (see Darwin's statements given on page 74). This process is supposed to be active both for microevolution as well as for macroevolution. Why is it that mutations are not active the other way around? Why are we not observing a change from a perfect complex species to a much simpler form of life? Since this is supposed to be a haphazard process, theoretically speaking, mutations should have stood the same chance of going in one direction as in the other. Yet our observable facts, as depicted through paleontology, reflect an ascendency of complexity. There is a steady movement from the simple to the more sophisticated forms of life.

Translated into our new DNA/RNA language, it means that at the beginning of life on earth, we started with let us say 3 million nucleotides (i.e. single cell bacteria) and proceeded to 3 billion nucleotides (i.e. mammalian cell.) This occurred by adding nucleotides in meaningful sequences.

If this change in the numbers of nucleotides was strictly a function of random occurrence, then we should have encountered, mathematically speaking, the same haphazardness in *reductions* of nucleotides, from one level to a lower one. Yet we did not. In fact, it should have been easier to *subtract* nucleotides rather than *add* them to the DNA chain. On the contrary, all our observations indicate that, as time passes, the complexity of the life-machine increases. Obviously this occurrence could not be random since it displays itself in one direction only. There had to be a specific mechanism that was geared to act in one sense only.

How does one improve a sequence of 2 billion meaningfully aligned nucleotides by destroying a number of them? Invariably any destruction must result in unbalancing an already functioning program. To infer that the haphazard destruction of 1 million nucleotides will, all of a sudden, create a different *perfect* species is wishful thinking. Random destruction of nucleotides via any method (which does not even choose the particular sequence to be annihilated) is bound to have only negative effects.

This being the case, Darwin's suggestion that species evolve into other species via incremental mutations, is now so farfetched that it should not be considered in a serious vein any longer. These theoretical changes, translated into the DNA/RNA understanding prove to be untenable. Species cannot change into other species; but even if they could (*a la* Darwin), such changes, no matter how minimal, would mean a rearrangement and/or an addition of millions of nucleotides, all of them in a precise *meaningful sequence*. Mathematical probabilities tell us that there is no chance what-so-ever for such a situation to occur and still end up with a cogent, vibrant new species.

As a result, those magic concepts labelled "mutation" and

"natural selection" were a generalization to gloss over aspects about which we were ignorant. Our new knowledge of DNA/RNA permits explanations in a different language with a completely different meaning.

As Stephen Jay Gould once wrote:[1]

"Natural selection is the central concept of Darwinian theory — the fittest survive and spread their favored traits throughout populations. Natural selection is defined by Spencer's phrase "survival of the fittest," but what does this famous bit of jargon really mean?"

This famous bit of jargon really means nothing — not after we understood what the DNA/RNA is and how it functions within the cell.

Unfortunately this concept of "mutation" coupled with "natural selection" has become so deeply ingrained that a number of our scientists have suffered loss of objectivity. Some assume that any discovery *must* be forced to fit Darwin's theory of evolution. A typical example is displayed by a professor of science in his book on the DNA. After clearly describing the incredibly complex performances of the DNA/RNA system, he interpolated:

"From the beginning of life about several billion or so years ago, mutations have been produced in an unending stream, and they are largely responsible for evolution. The millions of species of plants and animals which have appeared are the products of mutations which have accumulated in the DNA messages of these organisms and made them different. For the individual species, mutations are a kind of insurance against a rainy day. It may never have to use the mutations but there is no way of knowing which one of the thousands of mutants appearing at random can save the species from extinction."[2]

[1] *Ever Since Darwin,* pg. 40 (W.W. Norton & Co., New York, 1977).

[2] Edward Frankel, *DNA, the ladder of life,* (McGraw-Hill Book Company, New York, 1979) on pages 141-142.

The logic displayed, the conclusions presented as fact, and the sweeping generalizations are appalling. It is hardly credible that a professor of science can take the liberty of instilling this type of "truths" to his students — the future scientists. Let's analyze this statement:

(a) *"Mutations have been produced in an unending stream."* How do we know that? What statistical data do we have that proves it to be really so? This is a categorical statement, that implies knowledge. Since this seems to have proceeded for billions of years, there must be some accumulated data in this professor's file. Yet, we know that mutations are normally considered to be mistakes in an original program — not improvements.

(b) Mutations *"are largely responsible for evolution."* That must be a wonderful thought. A cynic would exclaim: no wonder we are such a messed-up society — we all are misfits, or mutations of an earlier perfect human being! How do we *know for a fact* that mutations are largely responsible for evolution?

(c) *"The millions of species of plants and animals which have appeared are the products of mutations which have accumulated in the DNA messages of these organisms and made them different."* How does a DNA helix with 5,375 nucleotides become a meaningfully functioning program with 11,000,000 nucleotides? Just by "ordering" molecules to get in line? Did this professor ever calculate and evaluate the probability factor of 11,000,000?

(d) *"For the individual species, mutations are a kind of insurance against a rainy day."* Even if it pours on that day, species cannot decide when to cash in on this wonderful "insurance" policy discovered by this professor. Science did not know — till now — that mutations were guarantees for perfect survival. That must be something new! How can 100 mistakes generate one perfection in a different shape and form?

(e) *"It may never have to use the mutations.."* In other words,

80

mutations (destruction of nucleotides) are aspects which an animal or a plant decide to use or not, whenever they feel like it? How would that be performed in a scient manner? As far as we know no cockroach, no tomatoe, no cucumber, no eagle can order a mutation of its DNA at will. The only one who probably performed along the lines "taught" by this professor must have been Dr. Jekyl when he turned himself into Mr. Hyde.

This scientist is in other respects a knowledgeable person, yet his evaluation capacity suffers because of evolutionist teachings he absorbed in his younger days. For the sake of the survival of Darwin's theory, he inverts his logic and submits concepts that are unscientific. Obviously Darwin's theory must be made to survive — by hook or by crook, and if evolutionary theory does not fit the DNA, too bad for the DNA!

If we perpetuate this type of misinformation in our science textbooks under the guise of "science", is it a wonder that we cannot see the tree for the forest?

Summing it up, and contrary to the oft-repeated evolutionist claims, a random mutation is not an enhancing factor — it is almost invariably a destructive one. It interferes with the exquisitely fine balance and purposefulness of the hundreds of millions of nucleotides within a given program. To propose and argue that mutations even in tandem with "natural selection" are the root-causes for 6,000,000 viable enormously complex species, is to mock logic, deny the weight of evidence, and reject the fundamentals of mathematical probability.

The DNA/RNA system is telling us very clearly: given the billions of nucleotides necessary to define a specific species, no haphazard change has any chance to end up into another meaningful program — notwithstanding Darwin's imagination.

9
Fossils And Punctuated Equilibria

Fossils are relics of plants or animals that lived on this planet during ancient geological eras. They have been preserved in rocks consisting of, or derived from, the sediments in which they were buried. In a greater sense, they serve as substitute eyewitnesses to past life on Earth, allowing us marvelously detailed descriptions of their physical structures. Fossils provide the evidence from which we deduce the kind of animals and plants that became extinct and those that survived up to the present time. The study of tens of thousands of specimens from all parts of the world, has supplied an extraordinary picture of life during Earth's younger days. Geology and paleontology have contributed a profound understanding of the mosaic of our past — a past that extends back about four and a half billion years when, we now believe, the Earth was formed.

New and continuing discoveries of fossils have always been a source of excitement, especially to evolutionists. These fossils were expected to reflect "living proof" — so to say — of the various stages and paths life took through the millions of years of its evolution. With every new find, a determined effort was usually made to pinpoint the proper niche it filled in the overall pattern of evolution.

If enough samples from successive strata were collected, they should have given us the precise incremental branchings in the tree of life. Such progressive "improvement" through millions of years, would have provided the clearcut proof so confidantly expected by everyone: scientist and layman alike. In the final analysis, fossils probably constitute the only source of historical proof available to us.

They provide the best evidence on the exact forms and sophistication. in the design of thousands upon thousands of earlier life forms.

Table 10 summarizes the generally accepted geological time scale of our planet. Note that, for a paleontologist, a hundred million years is a modest time span, for it represents only slightly more than two percent of the four and a half billion years Earth has existed. Most of this span of time, or about seven-eighths, is designated by paleontologists and geologists as the Precambrian era, which simply means all time before the Cambrian period.

Rocks of the Cambrian period (currently understood to have begun about 570 million years ago,) are the oldest that provide a display of fossils in any really meaningful number and variety. Indeed, it gives us the impression that a sudden explosion of life-forms took place then. Substantial quantities of many different fossils have accumulated; among the life forms first encountered in Cambrian rocks are jellyfish, corals, trilobites and other crustaceans, sea lilies, starfish, sponges, anemones, octopuses, clams, and snails. The diversity of form and number of available specimens is truly impressive.

In contrast, the geological strata deposited before the Cambrian period contain few fossils. Although some representative forms of life have been found, they are by no means as abundant, as complex, or as varied as those of the Cambrian period. We encounter much simpler forms, namely single-cell blue-green algae, stromatolites (another form of algae), and fungi. The variety does not seem to be too pronounced, although paleontologists may have been unable to locate fossils of many other unicellular form of life, because these mainly consist of soft tissues that rarely become fossilized. Nevertheless, those records we do have clearly indicate that only very simple life forms were present before the Cambrian period.

The evidence leads us to conclude that life — even though much less complex and developed than during the Cambrian — was present for about 3 billion years earlier. These conclusions are well known and generally accepted by paleontologists. Our attention will therefore focus on these two geological times (Cambrian and Precambrian) as they suggest very important events in the development of life. The boundary between the two is especially significant.

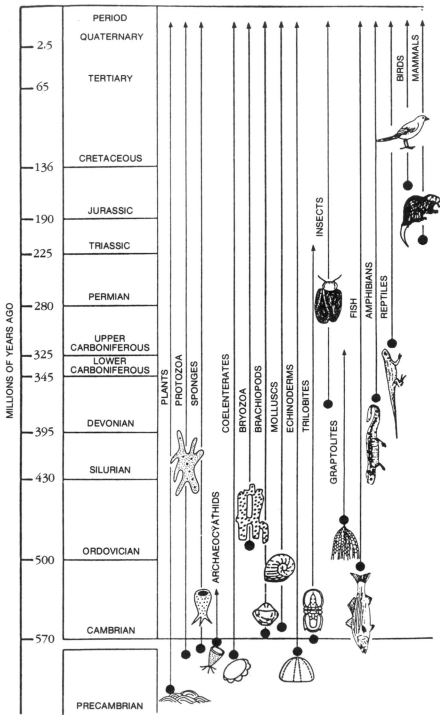

Fig. 10 — GEOLOGICAL ERAS (MODIFIED FROM RANSOM)

84

During the Precambrian era the single-cell life forms observed, were of the prokaryotic type (cells that lack distinct nuclei.) Then, and quite abruptly (in geological terms), we witness the presence of a large variety of new life-forms, much more sophisticated and complex in design and construction. All these newly emerging life-forms were built out of eukaryotic cells (those with distinct nuclei) — radically different in structure than the prokaryotic predecessors. This difference in construction is important; it has been described in greater detail as follows:[1]

"By definition, the prokaryotic cell has a minimum of internal organization. It possesses no membrane-bound organelle components, its genetic material is not enclosed by a nuclear membrane, nor is its DNA complexed with histones. Indeed, histones are not found in this cell. Its sexual reproduction involves neither mitosis nor meiosis. Its respiratory system is closely associated with its plasma membrane. Typical prokaryotic cells include all bacteria and the blue-green algae. All other cells are of the eukaryotic type.

"An eukaryotic cell has a considerable degree of internal structure with a large number of distinctive membrane-enclosed organelles. For example, the nucleus is the site for informational components collectively called chromatin. Reproduction involves both mitosis and meiosis; the respiratory site is the mitochondrion; and, in plant cells, the site of the conversion of radiant energy to chemical energy is the highly structured chloroplast.

"Although in prokaryotic cells no nucleus per se is observed, a fibrilar area can be detected on the interior side of the plasma membrane which is associated with an extremely involuted double-stranded circle of DNA. It has been estimated that in a single bacterial cell 2 μm long, its DNA, if stretched out as a single fiber, would be over 1000 μm long, 500 times the length of its own cell body.

"In eukaryotic cells, the nucleus is a large dense body surrounded by a double membrane with numerous pores which permit passage of the products of nuclear biosynthesis into the surrounding cytoplasm. Internally, the nucleus contains

[1] Eric E. Conn and P K. Stumpf, *Outlines of Biochemistry*, (John Wiley & Son Inc.) 1976.

chromatin or expanded chromosomes composed of DNA fibers closely associated with histones."

Thus, structurally speaking, we observe two distinct building blocks, two types of cells whose construction differ substantially.

The time region separating the beginning of the Cambrian period from the end of the Precambrian era seems to be most intriguing as it gave birth, all of a sudden, to a new and sturdier variety of cell. This new type was robust enough to be used for the construction of all sorts of new and complex species. In fact virtually all life forms are built only from eukaryotic cells with only bacteria and certain algae continuing to be built with prokaryotic cells.

What happened at that moment, geologically speaking, when the Precambrian ended and the Cambrian period began? How did eukaryotic cells come into being just then? Is it the reason for the virtual explosion of all sorts of complex life-forms?

These warrant more detailed consideration of two major events:

1) The appearance of the first cell during the Precambrian,

2) The sudden explosion of complex life forms in the Cambrian.

Cellular life, as recognized to be the basic blueprint and fundamental necessity for all types of life forms on this planet, did exist during Precambrian eons — 2 to 3 billion years ago. That means that the enormously sophisticated and complicated DNA/RNA system was at work at least that many billion years ago.

Life, as we know it, is based on the cell (either eukaryotic or prokaryotic). This unit, in turn, cannot exist and reproduce unless and until it contains a DNA/RNA program with all its marvelous appurtenances. Then — and only then — does it become "life."

That means, for life to have started on Earth, the concept of the DNA/RNA complex had to be perfected and ready to go. The very first living cell on Earth had to contain this supersophisticated internal mechanism, in functioning form, at the very beginning of its existence. Such a cell would have necessitated a DNA double helix with thousands of nucleotides, ribosomes, RNA, an established genetic code, including "STOP/GO" signals, and a perfected system of splitting the DNA. But then, it is implied, enzymes must have been on hand capable of determining how and when to perform within the general scheme. Various amino acid molecules must have been present and ready to interact with other components of the cell. In short, the entire enormous system of the DNA/RNA must have been perfected ahead of time to the point where all its parts were integrated within the same purposeful program.

These requirements for the beginning of life is intellectually uncomfortable to the evolutionists. Should they infer that there were separate evolutionary paths followed by the original molecules of thymine, adenine, cytosine, guanine, phosphate, deoxyribose, ribose, and uracil? Can molecules get together, agree, and standardize on a highly organized sequential procedure so as to create life? Can they create all by themselves this immensely sophisticated complex called the DNA/RNA system?

We usually marvel how an ant came to be, or a giraffe was formed, or a bison evolved from a previous ancestor. In reality we are misdirecting our awe in the wrong direction. Instead, we should realize that the most important wonder, the most incredible revolutionary step, is the appearance of the first functioning cell, complete with an operating DNA/RNA system, sometime after the formation of the Earth. From then on, presumably, everything that ensued was simply a rearrangement and expansion of the same theme: the basic building blocks of life. By analogy, consider the performance of an engineer who is called upon to construct a building. We marvel at his ability to build a 75 floor structure — yet, in reality he is hardly a noteworthy innovator. The real genius was the one who invented mortar and brick. Each new building represents only a rearrangement, with embellishment, of these two construction materials — eventually it becomes routine to erect newer forms. With each new structure there is, undoubtedly, a display of greater sophistication, but nevertheless it is a repetitive performance.

Similarly with DNA; once the cell was invented, all subsequent forms of life were simply exercises in the rearrangement of chemical molecules based on the system operating in that first cell, which appeared some 3 billion years ago. Consequently, the first cell with the first DNA/RNA was the most imposing wonder of our planet.

Assuming the Darwinian principles of evolution to apply, we should expect molecules to continually arrange and rearrange themselves and finally hit upon a working system for the first cell. But doesn't that imply a spirit of purposefulness in molecular reactions? Must we infer that molecules have intelligence and know what they want to achieve and when to stop? Darwin and his contemporaries knew nothing about the DNA/RNA system; this aspect of cellular life was completely unknown during his time. As a result, evolutionists felt they needed only to explain how *ONE* cell came about — underlining the concept of *one*. But we now know that a single cell contains *millions* upon *millions* of meaningfully aligned nucleotides (here we underline the concept of *millions*). The conclusions to be drawn when evaluating manipulations of items in the order of 1,2,3. . .etc., are completely different than when evaluating 3,000,000 or 5,000,000. . .etc.

We are, thus, led to choose between two possible explanations for the beginning of life:

Alternative 1 — There was an "evolutionary process" (*a la* Darwin) that took place 3 billion or more years ago when a few molecules aggregated auspiciously. With time they added newcomers to their club and "millions of years" later ended up with a supersophisticated working mechanism — the DNA. At the moment the molecules finally perfected the complex DNA/RNA system, "life" started. Can we seriously entertain such a scenario?

Alternative 2 — There was an earlier source of outside intelligence (quite superior to even modern man) that put molecules to work, on the basis of a predetermined program. The preparatory work for such a development could have taken place on this planet or the expertise imported from some other planet or solar system.

Admittedly, the very concept of the possible existence of other or superior intelligence is abhorrent to the scientific community. It is an option which is rarely even considered and hardly ever enters seriously into the minds of research scientists as a *possible* answer to our unanswered questions. Our scientific education prepares and attunes us to the concept that all channels of thought are fertile ground for hypotheses and theories — except the existence of outside intelligence superior to our own. After all, did not Eiseley state: "Of man elsewhere and beyond, there will be none forever?"[1] The finality of this statement matches the intellectual blind-spot sickness we have imposed on our deductive processes.

The dilemma persists — we still must decide as to whether the DNA/RNA complex resulted from a fortuitous beginning on Earth followed by an evolutionary process of adding rung by rung to the double helix — or whether a superintelligence contributed to the establishment of the system we call "life".

As stated, the first and sudden appearance of thousands of more advanced forms of life at the outset of the Cambrian period has been widely noted. We see no corresponding earlier ancestors during the immediately preceding Precambrian era.

If we accept the logic of evolution, we should have had a multitude of similar species — less-developed — which in time turned into, for example, a trilobite. Surprisingly, we observe scarcely anything of the sort. The fossil records lacks traces of incremental advances from blue-green algae to trilobite. It is as though suddenly, at a given Cambrian stage, trilobites sprouted in various oceans around the world with no connections to earlier forms of life.

Even though the trilobite is here used as an example, the same holds true for practically all the other metazoan species whose many fossils are found in Cambrian rocks. They appear in surprisingly well-formed shapes.

These facts greatly troubled Darwinian evolutionists. In fact Darwin himself had observed this situation, as stated in his *The Origin of Species:*

> "To the question why we do not find rich fossiliferous deposits belonging to these assumed earliest periods prior to the Cambrian system, I can give no satisfactory answer.

> ...Nevertheless, the difficulty of assigning any good reason for the absence of vast piles of strata rich in fossils beneath the Cambrian system is very great.

[1] Loren Eiseley, *The Immense Journey,* (Vintage Books edition, Page 162).

...The case at present must remain inexplicable; and may be truly urged as a valid argument against the views here entertained.

"The abrupt manner in which whole groups of species suddenly appear in certain formations, has been urged by several paleontologists — for instance, by Agassiz, Pictet, and Sedgwick — as a fatal objection to the belief in the transmutation of species. If numerous species belonging to the same genera or families, have really started into life at once, the fact would be fatal to the theory of evolution through natural selection. For the development by this means of a group of forms, all of which are descendants from some one progenitor, must have been an extremely slow process; and the progenitors must have lived long before their modified descendants."

Even though the paucity of Precambrian fossils did raise many doubts, these were usually set aside by such excuses as that paleontologists did not have enough samples that were truly representative of the Precambrian, or that earlier forms simply lacked the hard parts that would fossilize. It was felt during Darwin's time (about 1850) that geologists had not dug deep enough and persistently enough to discover the predicted "progenitors" that *had* to be found, if the theory of evolution was to be proven. Once again, there was an accepted conviction that predictable forms of Precambrian fossils *had* to be found — shades of *Eozoon* and *Bathybius.* Darwin was not too shy when he wrote:

"Most of the arguments which have convinced me that all the existing species of the same group are descended from a single progenitor, apply with equal force to the earliest known species. For instance, it *cannot be doubted* that all the Cambrian and Silurian trilobites are descended from some one crustacean, which *must* have lived long before the Cambrian age, and which probably differed greatly from any known animal." (emphasis added)

Why could it not "be doubted"? On what scientific fact was this statement of Darwin erected? On nothing else but wishful prediction. That should not have been sufficient to graduate a "theory" into the realm of "fact." Unfortunately, this type of conclusive reasoning, based on non-existent evidence, pervaded various aspects of Darwin's evolutionary theory.

It is true that paleontological field work had been scant before the 1850s. But since then (about 130 years), a great many fossils have been collected and classified — and still the answer is the same: no earlier forms leading up to the Cambrian fauna. These are established facts, acknowledged now by the vast majority of Darwinian paleontologists, including Gould and Eldredge.

If the fossil record accurately reflects what happened, how do we explain the sudden appearance of such complicated forms?

First, we can apply the findings and, in Darwin's own words, conclude that this "...fact would be fatal to the theory of evolution through natural selection..."

Secondly, we can logically infer that the sudden appearance of complex life forms, such as a trilobite, out of nowhere — so to say — without antecedents, indicates to us (like it or not) an act of "creation." The sudden appearance of hundreds of new species, implies logically that an "intelligence" was present at a given time, and put together, out of certain known and tested building blocks (i.e., DNA/RNA), the forms of life observed in the early Cambrian period.

The mute story told by our fossils should have been objective enough and sufficiently weighty to move scientists to become agnostics in their faith of evolution. Yet, it did not, because, intellectually they could not even consider alternatives to evolution.

Instead, many scientists submitted all sorts of explanations to account for the void — excuses would be a more apt word to use. All these proposed theories had a common denominator: they all depended upon wishful thinking, bias, and hopeful expectations — exactly as displayed by the well-meaning dreamers of 130 years ago, now proven to be so fundamentally wrong in their assertions.

Among the paleontologists trying to fit the facts to the theory have been, recently, Gould and Eldredge; they call their new theory "punctuated equilibria."

Before discussing this new theory, let us review some statements offered by one of our truly brilliant paleontologists:

"...the Precambrian fossil record is little more (save at its very end) than 2.5 billion years of bacteria and blue-green algae. Complex life did arise with startling speed near the base of the Cambrian... Paleontologists have spent a largely fruitless century trying to explain this Cambrian "explosion" — the steep rise in diversity during the first 10 to 20 million years of the Cambrian period...

"All paleontologists know that the fossil record contains precious little in the way of intermediate forms; transitions between major groups are characteristically abrupt. Gradualists usually extract themselves from this dilemma by invoking the extreme imperfection of the fossil record — if only one step in a thousand survives as a fossil, geology will not record continuous change. Although I reject this argument... let us grant the traditional escape and ask a different question. Even though we have no direct evidence for smooth transitions, can we invent a reasonable sequence of intermediate forms, that is, viable, functioning organisms, between ancestors and descendants? Of what possible use are the imperfect incipient stages of useful structures? What good is half a jaw or half a wing? The concept of "preadaptation" provides the conventional answer by permitting us to argue that incipient stages performed different functions. The half jaw worked perfectly well as a series of gill-supporting bones; the half wing may have trapped prey or controlled body temperature. I regard preadaptation as an important, even an indispensable concept, and recently defended it... in discussing the evolution of a decoy "fish" on a clam's rear end. But a plausible story is not necessarily a true one. And, in any case, the issue is not, can preadaptation save gradualism in some cases, but rather, does it permit us to invent a tale of continuity in most or all cases? I submit, although it may only reflect my lack of imagination, that the answer is no...

"The essence of Darwinism lies in a single phrase: natural selection is the creative force of evolutionary change.

"Indeed, if we do not invoke discontinuous change by small alteration in rates of development, I do not see how most major evolutionary transitions can be accomplished at all. Few systems are more resistant to basic change than the strongly differentiated,

92

highly specified, complex adults of "higher" animal groups. How could we ever convert a rhinoceros or a mosquito into something fundamentally different. Yet transitions between major groups must have occurred in the history of life."

The above words clearly describe the dilemma of Darwinism. If we did not know the author, we would conclude that a logical and methodical mind was submitting truly scientific arguments *against* the theory of evolution, as the points mentioned are well taken. Yet, these thoughts were expressed by none other than the evolutionist Gould.[1]

Niles Eldredge, a curator at the American Museum of Natural History, New York City, also had some pointed remarks in his article *An extravagance of Species (The diversity of fossil trilobites poses a challenge to traditional evolutionary theory).*[2]

"Trilobites, including the ones from Bolivia that I studied, pose some fundamentally important evolutionary puzzles, puzzles whose solutions demand changes in evolutionary theory.

"Apart from their dominance, the calmoniid trilobites are a fascinating lot. Derived from a garden variety, run-of-the-mill simple form, the sixty or so species known to date diversified into one of the more spectacular radiations of the entire 400-million-year history of trilobites. A few retained the general ancestral simple form. But most modified the old form, and some became, even by trilobite standards, downright bizarre. I have calmoniids with spines added to the front, or to the sides and middle of the head, or around the margins of the tail. I have others up to seven inches long — quite a length for a trilobite, most of which are less than one and a half inches long.

"But I am totally at a loss to explain strange structures like the pair of enormous, horn-like spines on either side of the head of *Deltacephalaspis.*

"But we are left to explain the most striking fact about these

---

[1] With permission from Natural History, Vol. 86, No. 6; copyright the American Museum of Natural History, 1977.

[2] Reprinted with permission from Natural History, Vol. 89, No. 7, Copyright The American Museum of Natural History, 1980.

fossils — their diversity. What does all this variety suggest? How and why did ancestral trilobites evolve into so many kinds of descendants, so anatomically varied?

"Standard evolutionary theory focuses on anatomical change through time by picturing natural selection as the agent that preserves the best of the designs available for coping with the environment. This generation by generation process, working on small amounts of variation, is thought to change slowly but inexorably, the genetic and anatomical makeup of a population.

"If this theory were correct, then I should have found evidence of this smooth progression in the vast numbers of Bolivian fossil trilobites I studied. I should have found species gradually changing through time, with smoothly intermediate forms connecting descendant species to their ancestors.

"Instead I found most of the various kinds, including some unique and advanced ones, present in the earliest-known fossil beds. Species persisted for long periods of time without change. When they were replaced by similar related (presumably descendant) species, I saw no gradual change in the older species, that would have allowed me to predict the anatomical features of its younger relative.

"The story of anatomical change through time that I read in the Devonian trilobites of Gondwana is similar to the picture emerging elsewhere in the fossil record: long periods of little or no change, followed by the appearance of anatomically modified descendants usually with no smoothly intergradational forms in evidence.

"If the evidence conflicts with theoretical predictions, something must be wrong with the theory. But for years the apparent lack of progressive change within fossil species have been ignored or else the evidence — not the theory — has been attacked. Attempts to salvage evolutionary theory have been made by claiming that the pattern of stepwise change usually seen in fossils reflects a poor, spotty fossil record. Were the record sufficiently complete, goes the claim, we would see the expected pattern of gradational change. But there are too many examples of this pattern of stepwise change to ignore it any longer. It is time to reexamine evolutionary theory itself.

"There is probably little wrong with the notion of natural selection as a means of modifying the genetics of a species through time, although it is difficult to put it to the test. But the predicted gradual accumulation of change within species is seldom (if ever) encountered in our practical experience with the fossil record.

"The problem appears to be this: focusing attention purely on anatomical (and underlying genetic) change ignores a fundamental feature of nature — the existence of species. Species are reproductive communities. They are held together by a network of parental ancestry and descent and separated from other, similar networks of parentage. They are coherent entities in space and — and this is the crucial part — through time as well. Species have origins, histories, and extinctions. They may or may not give rise to one or more descendant species during the course of their own existence.

"But natural selection *per se* does not work to create new species. The pattern of change in so many examples in the fossil record is far more a reflection of the origin and differential survival (selective extinction) of species than the inexorable accumulation of minute changes within species through the agency of natural selection."

These are the words of a knowledgeable scientist, known for his evolutionist convictions. Yet, he too realizes that the fossil record clearly points out that *"something must be wrong with the theory."* He admits that "there are too many examples... to ignore it any longer," and that "It is time to reexamine evolutionary theory itself." He further concedes that "natural selection *per se* does not work to create new species."

After reading these objective evaluations submitted by Gould and Eldredge, one would have expected them to proceed to the next linear logical conclusion. Instead, these two knowledgeable and brilliant scientists cooperated in submitting a completely new theory — one which amends the evolutionary theory, but still remains within the conceptual family of logic displayed by Darwin. Thus, although obviously aware that evolution is contrary to the evidence, they were

95

unable to break with traditions instilled into them through their past educational exposure to Darwinism (a situation similar to the one displayed by Loren Eiseley — Chapter 19).

Gould's and Eldredge's theory of "punctuated equilibria," as expressed by Gould,[1] maintains the argument approximately as follows:

"The history of most fossil species includes two features particularly inconsistent with gradualism:

1) *Stasis:* Most species exhibit no directional change during their tenure on earth. They appear in the fossil record looking much the same as when they disappear; morphological change is usually limited and directionless.

2) *Sudden appearance:* In any local area, a species does not arise gradually by the steady transformation of its ancestors; it appears all at once and "fully formed.""

With this as premise the theory postulates that evolution was still a fact but did not take place through imperceptibly small, consecutive, and gradual changes over extended periods of millions of years, but rather, jumped from plateau to plateau, from complete forms to complete forms. Accordingly there were spurts of changes, in very rapid succession, that took place all of a sudden. Between these incredible jumps, were periods of equilibrium (or static rest) punctuated again by another explosion of newer forms of life. Although the rate of change is presumed much faster than the creeping changes envisaged by Darwin, Gould and Eldredge maintain that the process is still consistent with evolutionary theory.

At this point, let us recall Gould's own pronouncement: "But a plausible story is not necessarily a true one." In this particular case, the story is not even plausible!

It is difficult to understand the immense leap in logic expressed by the theory of "punctuated equilibria," especially as it gives us no mechanism to turn single cells into complex life forms. Is it a last

---

[1] *Evolution's Erratic Pace,* Natural History, May 1977, Page 14.

ditch effort to bolster a weakened structure of Darwin's legacy? Why should we abandon sequential scientific thought processes based on observable facts and data, and take refuge in imaginary mental somersaults? Why should we choose the most complicated explanation, while refusing a straight-forward simple solution dictated by established facts? The most urgent aspect of mankind is not to see to it that the theory of evolution be vindicated at all costs. Instead it should have been a search for truth through a process of science: accumulation of established facts which *alone* will lead the way to final conclusions (no matter how unpleasant these might be!)

This tendency to see the problem but miss the answer reminds one of the oft-repeated joke about a methodical zoologist testing the reflexes of a flea. He decides to measure the distance a flea would jump when all its six legs are functional. Placing it on a table, he gives it an order: "jump, flea." The flea, after a certain lapse of time, jumps 12 inches. The scientist cuts off one of the legs and orders again: "jump, flea." Sure enough, after a certain hesitation, the flea jumps; the distance is measured and dutifully entered in a data book: "fleas with five legs, jump 10 inches." This process continues; each time a leg is cut off, the order is renewed, and the flea jumps shorter and shorter distances, which are carefully inscribed in the data book. Finally the last leg is cut off, "jump, flea" order is pronounced — but something funny happens, the flea does not jump. Additional "jump, flea" commands are given, each time in a louder voice — no result. After ten minutes of this exercise, the scientist makes his last entry in the book: "fleas with no legs develop a hearing impairment; they become deaf."

One gets the impression that some evolutionists use this type of inverted logic to reach the most imaginative conclusions, while linear logic is overlooked.

Gould and Eldredge agree that in one sequence we have only prokaryotic cellular life. In the next sequence above we encounter complex animals, such as trilobites or brachiopods, all characterized by sophisticated organs, shapes and functions, built with eukaryotic cells. Trilobites, for example, had compound eyes with thousands of individual lenses in each eye!

How do we get from a simple, prokaryotic, blind, single-cell animal to a functioning crustacean with prismatic lenses (among many another complete organ) in one giant leap? We now learned that there is only one way we can transform a single cell into a trilobite — eyesight and all. By expanding the DNA program of its cell — by adding millions upon millions of additional nucleotides, in very specific sequences, so as to translate the program into a meaningful end result: a trilobite.

Furthermore, the concept of "punctuated equilibria" holds that the rate of change from species to species (macroevolution) or within species (microevolution) was much faster than the slow, gradual progression envisioned by the Darwinists.

Whether the rates of change were speedy or very slow, is almost irrelevant. The basic fact remains: changes occurred. The resultant forms required the addition or rearrangement of DNA nucleotides. And therein lies the crux of the problem: how does a relatively short strand of DNA add to itself untold millions of nucleotides — let alone do it in a meaningful sequence?

On the basis of our understanding of the DNA/RNA mechanism, whether the rates were slow (*a la* Darwin) or fast (*a la* Gould and Eldredge) does not change the need for additional tens of millions of nucleotides for the new DNA program.

In a sense, the concept of "punctuated equilibria" is tautological. In essence it submits a factual observation: since the rate of evolution is not a slow, creeping one, it is a very fast, sudden one! This concept is quite interesting from yet another aspect; it even implies the concept of creation. In the final analysis, a very sudden change is tantamount to an act of sudden creation.

We have established that a single cell bacteria requires about 3,000,000 nucleotides so as to function and reproduce as a unicell species. A human cell contains about 3,000,000,000 nucleotides in a very specific sequence. We may assume that the cell of a trilobite was somewhere in between. Shall we extend it the benefit of the doubt and guesstimate it to have 500,000,000 meaningfully aligned nucleotides? (The argument would still be valid were it eventually established that a trilobite had, for example, as few as 20 million or as many as 920 million nucleotides). How will we get from 3 million to 500 million? What is the probability that 497 million nucleotides would align themselves — all by themselves — into a very, very specific sequence? Certainly Gould and Eldredge would agree that the probability is nil.

If we follow the evolutionary model of the Darwinian school of thought, alterations occurred on a step by step basis, i.e., by adding probably a few nucleotides at a time. Naturally, every successful increment had to be a meaningful program in its own right, and had to be implanted into the DNA so as to continue to translate into a viable species at *each* additional step! Otherwise the evolving species would have limped to extinction. After "milllions of years" 497 million additional nucleotides would have been accumulated. However, let us not forget that at every increase we had to have a functioning species, different from its predecessor, but nevertheless distinguishable as a new species. Thus, thousands of intermediary species should have been present in our fossil record until we reached the trilobite stage. Yet, none have been found. We may infer that trilobites did not follow a slow incremental process of evolution.

If we accept "punctuated equilibria," we must conclude that, all of a sudden — without advance preparation — a prokaryotic cell found the means to add to its DNA program 497 million additional nucleotides in one grand swoop as well as to provide a membrane around its nucleus and convert itself into a eukaryotic cell. Of course, these 497,000,000 molecules aligned themselves in the only unique sequence that would translate into a functional trilobite! Probably thousands of aborted attempts died out — still their remains are not to be found in our fossil record! Does that make sense? Not the wildest imaginative person can concur.

The only possible explanation that makes scientific sense, is to consider the infusion of outside predetermining intelligence, having the knowledge and capacity to manipulate the DNA/RNA technology.

Trilobites are certainly not the only class of animals that appeared abruptly on Earth. Almost all known species follow the same route. Bats made a sudden appearance about 50 million years ago in the shape as we know them today. Flying reptiles showed up 180 milllion

99

years ago, complete with wings and all. Winged insects appeared suddenly some 300 million years ago, and their descendants continue in the same form today. There are hundreds upon hundreds of other examples. Obviously such repeated displays of abrupt appearance followed by unchanging persistence are difficult to fit into the Darwinian theory of evolution.

While postulating all these recent variations and themes, many scientists failed to see the connection between their views on evolution and the immense significance of the DNA/RNA mechanism in species variation. Instead, seemingly oblivious to a world of relevant detail, they jump from wishful thought to wishful conclusion.

This approach is evident in a recent book edited by Ernst Mayr and William B. Provine. *The Evolutionary Synthesis,* published by Harvard University Press in 1980, is a compilation of papers prepared and submitted at a conference on evolution. The authors almost constitute a listing of who-is-who in the evolutionary disciplines:

Mayr — Provine — Lewontin — Darlington — Weinstein — Carson — Hamburger — Churchill — Stebbins — Gould — Ghiselin — Adams — Dobzhansky — Rensch — Boesiger — Limoges — Ford — Burkhardt — Allen.

It is significant that not once was the subject of microbiology discussed in 487 pages of the book; not once are the initials DNA mentioned. Only in a final summation on the conference, is there one short paragraph on microbiology; on page 400, we find:

"Molecular biology, on the other hand, seems new. And molecular biologists and historians have produced a sizeable literature on the origins of molecular biology. Ranging from Watson's Double Helix (1968) and Stent's coming of the Golden Age: A View of the End of Progress (1969) to Olby's Path to the Double Helix (1974), the literature examines the revolution in molecular biology from many angles. One of the very first publications on the historical analysis of molecular biology contained the recollection of almost every major participant (see Stent and others, 1966). Yet, until now, the evolutionary synthesis has received almost no attention from the scientists who participated in it."

That conference was supposed to include the various disciplines necessary for a comprehensive review of evolution. Yet, it is certainly difficult to understand how an objective overview could virtually ignore the significance of thirty years of meaningful research on the inner functioning of the cell.

Evolutionists seem so narrowly confined within their own specialties that the implications of new and relevant research in others are overlooked and ignored. Ironically, Mayr himself pointedly referred to that shortcoming, when he stated in the book's prologue:

> "Historiography of science must avoid two great dangers. Chauvinism exaggerates the importance of whatever field or country a given scientist represents and tends to belittle the contribution of others. Butterfield (1957) has called the second danger the "whiggishness" of science writing — that is, the application of the hindsight of modern understanding in the evaluation of past events, combined with a suppression of all inconvenient phenomena.

> "No one can entirely avoid either of these shortcomings; sometimes they even provoke illuminating controversy. Yet all of us must keep a careful watch for manifestations of both pitfalls so that we can correct misleading statements before still other inaccuracies are added to the all too rich repertory of myths in science."

Unfortunately, that "chauvinism" and "whiggishness" continued to exist and were flagrantly displayed in the very same book, whose prologue warned against it.

To some extent this is not too surprising, as scientists, no matter how learned, have not accustomed themselves to evaluate evolution in terms of the DNA/RNA and to translate every situation into microbiological terms. There is still too much of an ingrained tendency to discuss evolution within a vicious circular pattern of theoretical pronouncements, without opening it to the cross-currents of newer disciplines and newer interpretations.

Evolutionists are remiss in their thinking when evaluating sequences of events. If they get accustomed to translating every single growth into a DNA concept, they will realize the scientific and mathematical impossibility for haphazard changes to result in perfect species.

It is fervently hoped that brilliant scientists such as Gould and Eldredge, will objectively rethink the subject matter in a cool and detached manner and follow the path pointed out by logical evaluation of established facts. Emotional ties to past prejudices or preferences have no room in truly scientific studies.

We reached the point in our evaluation where we have to make a choice: will it be the DNA/RNA reality or evolutionist theories?

The DNA is real — we see it — we know that it exists and that it functions. That is solid science.

As for the theory of evolution, it continues to be the figment of the imagination of some well-meaning advocates who prefer to ignore the significant story told by the DNA/RNA reality, by mathematical probabilities, and the fossil world. It continues in existence despite the meaningful lack of solid evidence, usually demanded from any other scientific theory.

In the final analysis, after everything is said and done, true scientists will have to opt for the DNA/RNA reality.

10
Trilobites

Trilobites have attracted unusual attention since, although highly organized and of complex structure, they are among the first or earliest fossils we have found. Their remains are located, in abundance, in rocks going back nearly 600,000,000 years. They have become a classic example in evolutionary debate and pose serious questions which the "punctuated equilibria" theory has tried to answer.

These marine creatures have been well preserved in fossilized form. Thousands upon thousands of specimens have been collected and studied; they have been found, worldwide, in rocks ranging from the earliest Cambrian to Permian or until the end of the Palaeozoic era, (about 230 million years ago), at which time they became extinct. Scientists are nearly as perplexed for their sudden disappearance, as they are for their sudden appearance on this planet. It is for the latter, however, that trilobites are more important and thought provoking. They mark the frontier between the single-cell existence of the Precambrian era and series of sudden explosions of fully formed complex life forms we encounter from then on in sporadic spurts.

Scientists wonder at the enormously sophisticated and complex organs displayed by trilobites. The distinguishing feature is their most advanced vision made possible through compound eye lenses — the first known use in nature of optical receptors and nerves to create a sensory perception effect. (see Chapter 11). This in itself, is an event of momentous importance. Here we observe complicated eyesight, in good functioning order. All life-forms which preceded the trilobites were blind — so to say; then, suddenly, complex eyesight! What is equally significant is that the very same prismatic principle survives today, in basically the same form, among insects. Suddenly there appears a compound eye lense system which serves its purpose so well that it persists essentially unchanged for nearly 600,000,000 years! Why did "evolution" not improve the original blueprint of the compound eye? Or does evolution "know" when an organ is functioning perfectly and efficiently so as not to require any further improvements? The sudden introduction of a sophisticated optical system and its unchanged application for half a billion years implies an event and mechanism quite different from what we understood to be good evolutionary theory. Do we postulate that evolution "knows" when an organ is imperfect, at which time it runs to the rescue by adding millions of additional nucleotides to the DNA of that species? Of course those new nucleotides have to be introduced only at *the* precise location of the DNA strand that controls the growth of the compound eye. Such evaluating capacities are usually associated with intelligence. In the case of compound eyes, are we not seeing the results of more intelligence than chance mutation and relentless "natural selection?"

Taxonomically speaking, trilobites belong to the phylum Arthropoda, animals with jointed appendages and segmented bodies. Their nervous system was highly developed, with ganglia and nerve cords leading to a developed brain. They possessed a heart, arteries, and veins, along with gills. Naturally, digestive and reproductive systems were present to complete the picture. Although these few facts are summarized here in one small paragraph, the implications of the sudden appearance of each one of these fully-formed organs, is profound. Each represents, metaphorically, a huge world of biology in its own right. These are entire systems that are completely integrated with each other and complement each other. Each one of these organs require millions of nucleotides to define them and order their growth; each would presumably require experimental antecedents leading to the stage of perfection. And yet, virtually all we find before the trilobites, are single cell primitive life-forms.

Although giant trilobites (28 inches) have been found, the average size is one or two inches. The preserved fossils that are usually found are their dorsal shields — carapaces — which were

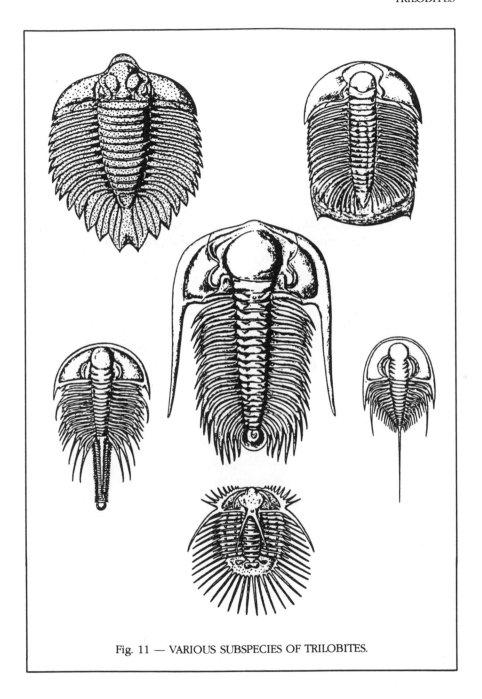

Fig. 11 — VARIOUS SUBSPECIES OF TRILOBITES.

made of chitin. Fig. 11 depicts a few types of trilobites collected from various parts of the world. They had hard body shields and undoubtedly molted several times during growth. It follows that this early form of life had already perfected a system that allowed the hardened carapace to split open, so as to allow the soft body within to extricate itself from the old exoskeleton. The naked body was soon covered with a newer soft exoskeleton which then hardened through chitinization. The process repeated itself as the trilobite grew bigger. This molting process is the same mechanism that has survived 600 million years and is still in use today in a great variety of modern animals.

We know that a complicated internal structure exists within such animals so as to implement every step of the process. Innumerable interconnected activities take place during molting. Through studies made on modern insects and arthropods, we know that the process is stimulated by the ecdysone hormone secreted by two glands in the thorax. These glands, in turn, are stimulated by another hormone secreted by specialized neurosecretionery cells in the brain. At the same time, their bodies contain separate antagonistic hormones which neutralize ecdysone, acting as a controlled check-and-balance system. We thus witness a stop-and-go mechanism to perform this part of the molting process.

Imagine how impossible growth must have been before evolution "created" the mechanism to periodically replace the outer hard shield as the species grew. Baby trilobites must have suffocated within their tight carapaces; they must have had stunted growths waiting a number of million years for evolution and mutations to come to their rescue and arrange their DNA so as to molt. One can almost hear the sigh of relief expressed by the first specimen that finally was able to shed its tight corset and grow to full maturity. But, if millions of years of trilobite generations had no capacity to molt, would they not have died out in such a restricted incarcerating surroundings?

The entire molting process, although very complicated, is enormously interesting. A typical molting procedure is explained by Villee-Walker-Barnes in their textbook *General Zoology:*[1]

[1]From *General Zoology*, Fifth Edition by Claude A. Villee, Warren F. Walker and Robert D. Barnes. Copyright © 1978 by W. B. Saunders Company. Reprinted by permission ol CBS College Publishing.

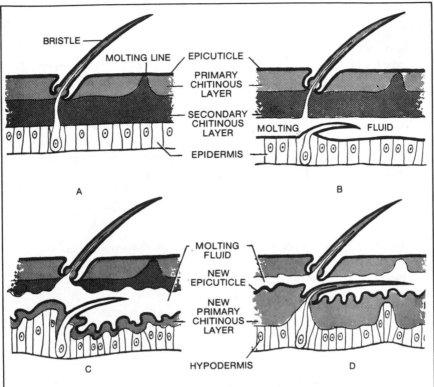

Fig. 12 — THE MOLTING PROCESS

Molting in an arthropod. A, The fully formed exoskeleton and underlying epidermis between molts. B, Separation of the epidermis and secretion of molting fluid and the new epicuticle. C, Digestion of the old secondary chitinous layer and secretion of the new primary chitinous layer. D, Just before molting. (Modified from Wigglesworth.)

(From *General Zoology* 5th Edition, by Claude A. Villee, Warren F. Walker and Robert D. Barnes)

"All arthropods periodically shed their chitinous exoskeleton as a part of growth and metamorphosis. The actual shedding of the old and hardening of the new skeleton, which may take a few seconds (daphnia) or several hours (lobster), is only the obvious culmination of the elaborate process of molting. Before shedding occurs, the new skeleton is preformed and materials of the old skeleton are salvaged.

"The exoskeleton is formed of three layers. The outermost is a thin, flexible, colorless epicuticle composed of wax and cuticulin, a lipoprotein containing a large amount of fatty material. The middle layer is the primary chitinous layer composed of chitin and cuticulin, sometimes impregnated with calcium carbonate or other salts. The inner secondary chitinous layer is made almost entirely of chitin and protein. The epidermis lies beneath this as a single layer of cells with numerous filamentous extensions into the two chitinous layers.

"The first step toward a molt is a separation of the epidermis from the old skeleton by the secretion of a molting fluid. Glandular cells in the epidermis add enzymes to the fluid capable of digesting protein and chitin but not cuticulin. While the epidermis lays down a new epicuticle the molting fluid begins to erode the old secondary chitinous layer.

"Formation of a new skeleton and salvage of the old go on simultaneously. All the secondary chitinous layer and some of the primary layer are ultimately digested, although the amount of cuticulin in the latter may prevent its digestion. If growth is to take place at the next molt, the epidermis with its new epicuticle grows and becomes wrinkled in the confines of the old skeleton. It begins to secrete a soft, pliable, primary chitinous layer.

"At the time of molting the new epicuticle and primary chitinous layer are complete, although they are still soft and flexible. The molting fluid with its digested products is completely absorbed into the body. The old epicuticle and much of the primary chitinous layer remain as a loose covering. At various places, especially along the back, the old primary layer is thin so that after the secondary layer is digested away a line appears along which the old skeleton will break.

"The arthropod must then swell up to burst the old exoskeleton. It may contract the abdomen, forcing blood into the head and thorax, or it may swallow water or air. Once the old exoskeleton has been split open the organism extricates itself, shedding not only the covering of the body and legs but also the lining of the foregut, hindgut, and in the labiates the lining of the tracheal system. If the arthropod grows during the molt it must swell rapidly to stretch the wrinkled new exoskeleton out to its full size. Most arthropods swallow water or air to do this and may increase their volume 100 per cent. Even if the organism is not growing at some particular molt, it may be necessary to compress some parts of the body in order to force blood into others to achieve whatever metamorphosis is taking place. A newly emerged adult moth, for example, contracts the abdomen to force blood into the wrinkled wings and expand them to full size. After the skeleton is adjusted to its new size and shape, the epidermis secretes enzymes which oxidize and harden the epicuticle and primary chitinous layers. Usually the primary layer, which is pale at first, darkens during this process. In the crayfish and many other hard-shelled forms, calcium carbonate is deposited as an additional stiffening agent. The crayfish had previously absorbed much of this lime from the old skeleton and stored it on the sides of the stomach between epidermis and chitinous lining as the gastroliths. After the molt these concretions are exposed to the digestive fluids and dissolve rapidly, providing an immediate supply for the new skeleton.

"The final event of molting occurs later. The epidermis secretes the secondary chitinous layer as a permanently elastic portion of the exoskeleton. The desired flexibility of any part of the exoskeleton is achieved to a considerable extent by the thicknesses of the two chitinous layers. Where rigidity is required, the outer layer is thick; where a tough but flexible skeleton is required, the inner layer is thick; and where great flexibility is wanted, both layers are thin.

"The molting process has been extensively studied in the crustaceans and insects and in both cases has been found to be under endocrine control. Arthropods have also been shown to elaborate other hormones, related to metabolism, reproduction and pigment changes. As the glands secreting these hormones are discovered and studied, it is becoming apparent that arthropods have an endocrine system similar in many respects to that of the vertebrates. Both are intimately related to the brain. In both kinds of animals antagonistic hormones are known, and in both some of the glands have reciprocal actions on each other to produce a controlled check-and-balance system. All evidence suggests, however, that the arthropod and vertebrate endocrine systems evolved independently.

These are but a few superficial details about the molting process. One cannot help but be impressed with the degree of sophistication and complexity implicit in molting — yet it was a working system 600 million years ago! Imagine the purposefulness and architectural capacities that were introduced to obtain these desired effects! Imagine the millions upon millions of nucleotides necessary to program the growth of specific protein chains resulting in this particular growth effect! Those are facts. On the other hand we are asked to apply creative imagination; we are told to make believe that starting with a single-cell existence, hundreds of millions of chemical molecules got together and lined themselves up in a predetermined sequence so as to generate a DNA helix that would order molting! No antecedent life-form, no half-developed or one-quarter developed forebears were found. Chitin, ecdysone hormones, antagonistic hormones are not exactly swimming in a loose stage in rivers or lakes — not even in "warn little ponds." If they did, they would probably dissolve in water. To create the hormones requires special types of manufacturing centers. Such centers are useful only if they fit a given blueprint, a particular plan, put together with predetermining purposefulness. Such centers function only as part of a larger whole (in cooperation with all the rest of the physiological and morphological systems of the trilobite) in excreting the type of hormones that will perform a specific result at a given moment.

Each aspect of the mechanism works only because it is properly incorporated and programmed within its DNA. We must again translate the nucleotidal sequence of the DNA helix into physical growth and ask the same question (over and over again):

What is the mathematical probability of these hundreds of millions of molecules becoming aligned through chance?
The answer of course is zero.

The same reasoning applies for each of the other organs of the trilobite. Respiration, reproduction, circulation, and digestion entail complex systems each reflecting millions of nucleotides meticulously arranged. Each one of these is a world of intricately interwoven biological systems. To conclude that all of this took place as the result of haphazard "mutations," coupled with "natural selection" over however many millions of years one may care to postulate, is to extrapolate quite unrealistically beyond the evidence we have. So far

110

as the fossil record can show, trilobites appeared *suddenly,* fully formed, and functioning well enough to persist essentially unchanged for the ensuing 320 million years.

This physical perfection cannot be assigned to any haphazard "mutations"or "natural selection."

11
The Eyes

Although Darwin postulated a number of concepts couched in a logic that seemed plausible, he was bothered with certain aspects. These were simply too baffling to him to make sense when applying his own theory. The eye was one of the organs that troubled Darwin. He expressed his uneasiness in *The Origin of Species;*

> "To suppose that the eye with all its inimitable contrivances for adjusting different amounts of light, and for the correction of spherical and chromatic aberration, could have been formed by natural selection, seems, I freely confess, absurd in the highest degree.

> "If it could be demonstrated that any complex organ existed, which could not possibly have been formed by numerous successive, slight modifications, my theory would absolutely break down."

To start with, Darwin was out of order, when, in effect, he challenged non-evolutionists to prove him wrong. This is not the usual way to go about it. Evolutionists should provide convincing evidence that they are right — not the other way around. As a result, they have now taken the position that evolution is an established fact, (which it is not), and anybody who is not in agreement, should step forward and submit proof to "demonstrate that any complex organ could not possibly have been formed by numerous, successive, slight modifications. . ." Such an approach would place the cart before the horse. First the Darwinian school of thought had the obligation to submit convincing evidence that the eye is the result of "numerous, successive, slight modifications." This, most agree, has not been provided.

In a letter to Asa Grey in February 1860, Darwin wrote:

"To this day the eye makes me shudder."

However, these doubts were apparently shortlived, since in April 1860, he again wrote Asa Grey, announcing:

"I remember the time when the thought of the eye made me cold all over, but I have got over this stage of the complaint."

This suggests that in a mere two month's time, Darwin was able to solve the immense problem on how evolution generated the mammalian eye. The solution was simple:

"...natural selection has converted the simple apparatus of an optic nerve merely coated with pigment and invested by transparent membrane, into an optical instrument as perfect as is possessed by any member of the Articulate class." (The Origin of Species).

This is a beautiful but meaningless statement — one of those pronouncements that have hypnotized scientists during the past 125 years. How does an optic nerve convert into a perfect optical instrument? The answer probably depends upon the degree of imagination the reader can display. How many millions of nucleotides does it need?

Darwin meant that "millions of years ago" a cell had a light sensitive spot. A few "million years" later, through natural selection, the surface skin at that spot became depressed, creating a small pit. Additional "millions of years" later, the depression continued to grow and generated a lens to cover the depression — and, presto, there was the first sight! Or was it? Well, not exactly, since further "millions of years" had to elapse to give a chance to this new organ to organize itself. It had to generate and be connected to, blood vessels, tear glands, retina, tendons, rods, cones, fovea, ganglion cells, bi-polar cells, optic nerve, cornea, iris and sclera, (see Fig. 13a and Fig. 13b.) Obviously a few "million years" more of mutations, combined with "natural selection," would create all of these components at which point evolution would present us with 20/20 vision! Artists have had a

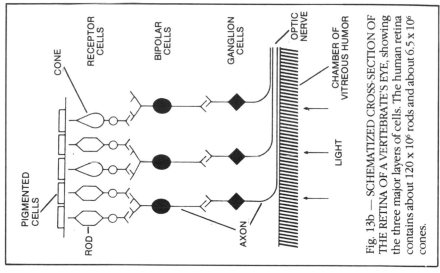

Fig. 13b — SCHEMATIZED CROSS-SECTION OF THE RETINA OF A VERTEBRATE'S EYE, showing the three major layers of cells. The human retina contains about 120 x 10⁶ rods and about 6.5 x 10⁶ cones.

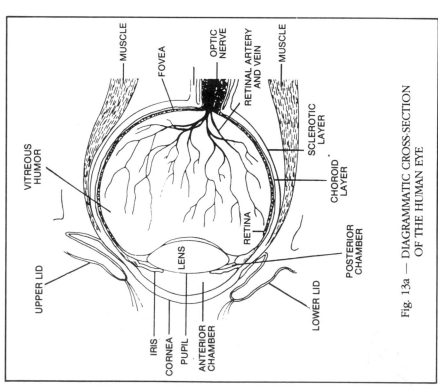

Fig. 13a — DIAGRAMMATIC CROSS-SECTION OF THE HUMAN EYE

114

grand time demonstrating their imagination through their textbook illustrations of the supposed step by step evolution of the eye mechanism.

At this point, we should remind ourselves, that a human eye has (and needs) about 130 million light-sensitive rods and cones to cause photochemical reactions which transform light into electrical impulses. Some 1,000 million of these impulses are transmitted *every second* through the optical nerve system into the brain. How many rods and cones can evolutionary thinking generate each million years? For as long as *all* the component parts were not in place and were not functioning in unison, there was no sight. This means that despite these "millions of years" of blindness, the system was continually pushing to develop and improve — obviously because it "knew" that perseverence would be crowned with success a few million years hence! As soon as vision was achieved, evolution stopped any additional mutations from taking place!

This theory should now be reassessed in the light of our DNA/RNA understanding. The slightest depression of the skin is encoded in the DNA helix. Every step depicted by evolutionists implies an immense addition to the DNA program — steps that cannot be glossed over.

To understand the incredible complexity of the eye mechanism, it is necessary to study the saliant parts of the structure.

The simple eye is a basic sensory organ found in all vertebrate animals, including man. A complex mechanism, it contains a great many subsections, which, when working in unison, results in vision. Fig 13a submits a schematic view of a human eye.

The important reality that stands out is the fact that every part of the chain has to be available and functioning properly to have vision. It can be compared to a television receiver with all the various connections, condensors, wires, and other electronic gadgets that, when put together, produce a picture. If you take one of these items out, you have destroyed the usefulness of the entire unit. In other words, we do not reduce the efficiency of the unit — we simply reduce the whole unit to scrap metal. The eye performs the same way. To have sight, we must have a retina, proper tendons, a cornea, a lens, a fovea, a disc, vitreous material, an optic nerve connection, rods and cones (outer segment, inner segment, cell bodies,) receptor cell bodies, bi-polar cells, ganglion cells, and optic nerve fibres. (see Fig. 13a). What is more, if we did not have a brain ready and available to receive these impulses, the eye would be useless. Also, if we did not have a ready made and available nerve system to connect the optic nerve on one side to the brain on the other side, the eye would have been useless. This means that we have a complete mechanical system that works in unison as one unit *provided* all its component parts are in place and functioning. Thus all three systems had to develop at the same time and be completely functional.

The next question to be answered is: which came first, the eye with all its intricate parts, or the nerve system to transport the impulses, or the brain to be ready in receiving the impulses? If we consider that the brain was there first, then we have to ask ourselves how it generated the nerve system to tie into the optic nerve and then to the eye? If the eye came first, then what good was it until there was a brain ready to "see" the picture? How about the arteries and veins that feed blood to every part of the eye? If they were not there at the very beginning, the eye would die. How about the various muscles to control movement? And so on, and so on.

The obvious answer is that the whole system came into being at precisely the same time. The whole system was created with all its appurtenances exactly in a manner and shape that would properly perform the expected result. It is not possible, under any stretch of the imagination, that all these parts of the optical mechanisms could haphazardly become functional through random mutations. It takes intelligence, foresight, and planning to determine that bi-polar cell, ganglion cells, and receptor cells are necessary and have to be put in the exact spot where they will function, and yet exist in parallel with all the other "appurtenances" of the body, such as nerves, blood cells, and muscles.

As though all these extraordinary aspects and minute engineering features of the eye were not sufficient, we observe that "nature" has provided a yellow filtering pigmentation behind the lens which screens out ultraviolet rays, potentially harmful to our retinas. Experiments have shown that without such a filter man's eyes would be damaged and vision hampered. In order to forestall this occurrence, we amazingly observe that the human eye is endowed with a built-in filter for the specific purpose of taking care of the ultraviolet problem.

This naturally raises the question: At what stage of our evolution was the necessity felt for an anti-ultraviolet filter? Theoretically, we must consider that our early mammalian ancestors did not have such a filter; and, again theoretically, we must assume that they went blind in early childhood when looking at the sun and thus destroying their retinas, nor could they have known why they lost their vision. Somehow or other (and nobody understands how) the blinded system, all on its own, decided it was time to protect the eye.

It found an extraordinary elegant, simple, and perfect device to screen out incoming ultraviolet light. Of course, again theoretically, it is to be assumed that the entire system of the eye, with all its parts, must have experimented with various filters before deciding on the one type that would perform properly. At least this is the trial and error method used by modern scientists to develop their discoveries and bring them to the point of satisfaction.

All of this takes for granted that the early mammals who did not have the built-in anti-ultraviolet filter, were capable of surviving for hundreds of thousands of years in a blind form, so that eventual generations finally generated the proper mechanism for future eyes to be protected from the sun's harmful radiation! This is certainly a difficult, if not impossible, chain of events to picture.

As if this also was not enough, tests have now shown that not all eye structures in the animal world are protected by a yellow pigmentation in the eye lens. A number of animals do not have this filter and, what is more, do not seem to need it at all. Professors M. Kreithen and T. Eisner of the New York State College of Agriculture and Life Sciences at Cornell, N.Y., studied the eyesight of pigeons. They concluded that pigeons do not have the filter, but can see in daylight without damage to their eyes. This means that, in the animal world (at least the pigeons), there is a slightly different eye structure based on different principles and constructions which protect them from the harmful effects of ultraviolet rays. Thus, contrary to what has long been assumed, vertebrates are not necessarily blind to ultraviolet light. Other studies have shown that hummingbirds, lizards, toads,

117

and newts are behaviorally responsive to ultraviolet light. This partially explains how some of these animals can apparently orient themselves with regard to the position of the sun, even when the sky is overcast.

If some vertebrates can sense ultraviolet light, why have man's eyes developed without that capacity? We do not know; possibly man, having an elaborate brain, has the independent capacity of making specific decisions. Other vertebrates that are endowed with much less "thinking" capacity, need other impulses to trigger behavioral actions. Possibly ultraviolet rays activate certain receptors which then act as "order-givers" for given activities to be performed by these less-developed animals.

This might possibly explain another mystery in nature. Horseshoe crabs usually live in shallow waters. During a monthly highest high tide they swim ashore and mate. The female lays eggs which she immediately buries in small holes on that part of the sandy beach washed by the highest of the high tide waves. She then returns to the sea. The incubation period of the egg is exactly four weeks, which means the young horseshoe crabs dig out of the sand at the next monthly high tide, when the waters again wash that section of the beach. They are then immediately swept into the sea by the receding waves, thus reducing the chances of being devoured by land predators. This implies a very intelligent reliance on time schedules, based upon the periodicity of high tides. In turn, it suggests that the crab has to know when the monthly highest high tide occurs, so as to swim ashore at the right moment. How does a horseshoe crab know that such a high tide will take place on any given night?

Research conducted a few years ago by Chapman and Lall (Univ. of Maryland) suggests an answer. Horseshoe crabs have four eyes of two types: two lateral compound eyes, and two dorsal simple eyes. The functions of these latter eyes has heretofore not been understood. The monthly highest high tide occurs at full moon, that is when the sun, earth and moon are so aligned as to exert the maximum gravitational pull on the waters. This, of course, is also when the moon reflects to Earth a maximum of sunlight, including ultraviolet light. The tests performed by these two scientists indicated "that the dorsal ocelli mediate positive phototaxis under near-u.v. stimulation but not under visible light stimulation."

118

These studies indicate that the horseshoe crab is equipped with dorsal eyes which capture ultraviolet light from the moon, which in turn, activates a behavioral mechanism within the crab to force it to swim ashore for reproductive functions.[1] Does the ultraviolet light deflected by the moon to Earth penetrate deep enough into water to be captured by the photosensitive ocelli of the crab? Calculations made by Chapman and Lall indicated that the light of the moon may be detected by these crabs at depths to 20 meters (about 60 feet.)

Many baffling problems remain unanswered. Although we know relatively little about the functions of different animal's eyes, we know enough to appreciate that different species have different arrangements of the same organ, each uniquely suited to the needs of that species.

Fish have single-lens eyes, similar to the human eye. But a South American fish has eyes that are divided into two — an upper half and a lower half — in other words, bifocal lenses. These fish, known as Anableps, (nicknamed the four-eyed fish) thus have the capacity to see well both in water and in air — all at the same time. They usually swim along the surface of the water seeing in the water with their lower lens, while the upper section of the eye, out of the water, observes prey and predators that happen to roam above the surface. Thomas O'Neill in *National Geographic,* of March 1978, described them as follows:

"Built-in bifocals provide the key to Anablep's remarkable dual vision. A speckled band of pigmented tissue and two iris flaps visible just above it divide each eye at the waterline, in effect creating two pupils, one for above water and one for below. Viewed from above, the iris flaps resemble projecting fingers inside the bulging eye.

"Because the refractive natures of water and the surface of the eye, or cornea, are almost identical, light reflected from underwater objects passes straight through the cornea, to be bent

[1]In a 1956 article entitled *Factors controlling the diurnal rhythm of activity of Periplaneta americana* (Journal of Experimental Biology, 33, 224-34), J.E. Harker reported that the output of the ocelli of a cockroach influenced its circadian rhythm. When light registers on the eyes, a message is sent to the suboesophageal ganglion which, in turn, activates and regulates the biological clock through neurosecretion.

and focused sharply on the retina by the lens, which has a higher refractive index. Air, on the other hand, has a lower refractive index than the cornea so that the light is bent twice — once by the cornea and again by the lens.

"Anableps, using its unique egg-shapped lens, sees both images clearly. The part of the lens aligned with the lower pupil is rounded like a typical fish lens, so that an image of a swimming insect larva will be focused on the retina. The less rounded upper part, more like the human lens, compensates for double refraction when objects in the air are viewed. A mosquito can thus be clearly seen.

"The four-eyed fish will lunge into the air to ambush flying insects or dip beneath the surface to catch swimming creatures. More commonly, however, it cruises the shallow water near a shoreline and captures crustaceans, algae, and insects that are trapped in the surface film.

"Scientists have determined that Anableps relies mostly on its aerial vision, which can detect smaller objects at greater distances than the aquatic sight system. But the fish often dives to feed or escape predators. When on the surface, Anableps repeatedly bobs its head to moisten its "upper eyes."

How amazing that this particular fish, acting in two different media — water and air — has the proper optical equipment to perform its function! Every aspect of the eye is a marvelous engineering achievement in construction, perfection, and coordination with other organs. The more we learn of the secrets of nature and the architecture of thousands of parts in millions of species, the more we are impressed with the degree of perfection and great variety. The same questions are prompted: did these species produce the eyes they needed because of a function they were supposed to perform in life, or were they endowed with the type of eye to start with so as to perform the type of life they were supposed to live? However the question is posed, the "theory of evolution" provides fewer convincing answers than a "theory of pre-determining intelligence." The precision and perfection to the minutest detail, the elegant method used within the particular species, indicates to us that a blueprint existed before construction began. Evolutionists however, believe that no outside intelligence is necessary to explain this mastery and sophistication of construction in each organ. Thus, they consider that the bifocal lenses of Anableps are the result of "millions of years" of mutations and "natural selection." The awe-inspiring perfection and variety of architecture speaks against such a point of view.

The same type of bifocal vision is used by a number of fish living in deep waters (about 3000 feet). Not much light penetrates down to such depths, so that the eyesight of fishes must be extra-sensitive to utilize the faint sunlight that does reach those levels.

Accordingly many deep-sea fish have an elongated eye with two retinas (Fig. 14). One senses near-by objects, the other captures light from far objects. These fish also have unusually good depth perception — a necessity at those depths where food is scarce.

This type of eye contruction is much different than the eyes of other fish. As a result the DNA sequence of nucleotides will be different too. How shall we visualize the step by step changes that must have taken place for example, between eye structures described in Fig. 13a and Fig. 14?

The preceding descriptions referred to the simple eye of vertebrates, i.e. eyes with a single lens. However, we know that insects, composed of hundreds of thousands of different species, have eyes of a completely different kind: the *compound eye*. Instead of a single lens, compound eyes have hundreds, and in some, thousands upon thousands of separate little lenses, each working as an optical receptor. The eyes of vertebrates have muscles attached to the eyeball which allows them to rotate it within a certain arc in order to observe a greater area. Insects, do not have this possibility as eye muscles are not involved. The compound eyes of insects and crustaceans, instead of muscles, have a quantity of lenses placed at different angles around a half-sphere so as to receive the light rays coming from a much larger arc of vision.

The compound eye is made of ommatidia, which are individual lenses positioned in different directions along a semicircular arc. Each

121

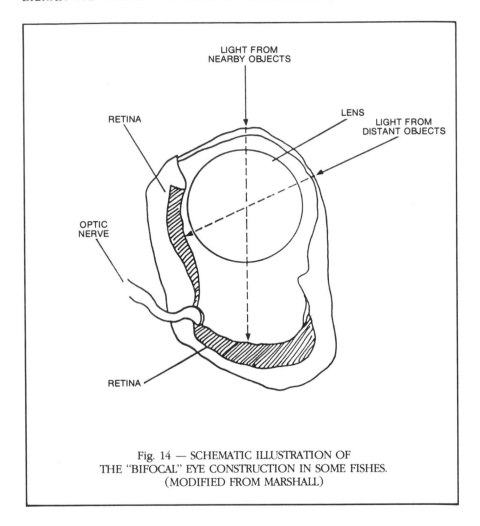

Fig. 14 — SCHEMATIC ILLUSTRATION OF
THE "BIFOCAL" EYE CONSTRUCTION IN SOME FISHES.
(MODIFIED FROM MARSHALL)

ommatidium extends downward so as to direct the incoming light onto receptor cells of another organ — the rhabdom. Light received by these rhabdoms are then guided to the optical nerve, which in turn transmits impulse signals to the brain of the insect. With this ingenious system, the animal obtains vision around the arc of the eye through thousands of these miniscule lenses, without having to rotate its eyes. (Fig. 15a and 15b.)

The single-lens eye of vertebrates (including man's) is equipped with a round iris that opens or closes depending on the intensity of

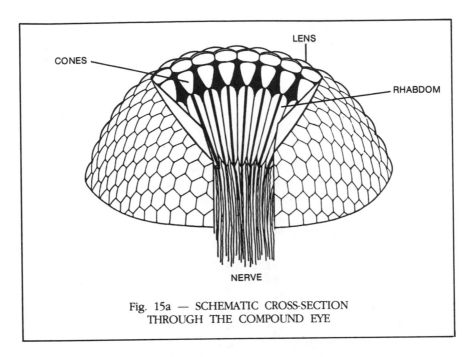

Fig. 15a — SCHEMATIC CROSS-SECTION
THROUGH THE COMPOUND EYE

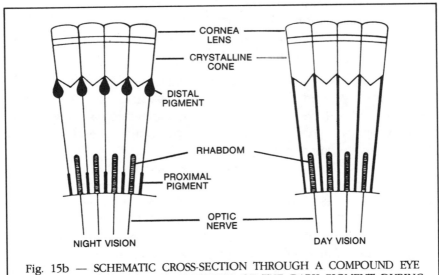

Fig. 15b — SCHEMATIC CROSS-SECTION THROUGH A COMPOUND EYE
SHOWING THE DIFFERENT POSITIONS OF THE DARK PIGMENT DURING
DAY AND NIGHT VISION.

123

the light received, and accordingly controlling the amount of light entering the lens. The compound eye, however, achieves the same result through a different method. At the bottom of the cone-shaped ommatidia is a black pigment with the ability to raise or lower its level — just like the mercury of a thermometer. The higher it moves up the wall of the cone, the greater an area it darkens, the less light penetrates to the optic nerve. The lower its level, the more light will hit the optic nerve. Thus, diurnal insects would display a larger pronounced black surface, while nocturnal ones would require more light which means lower levels of this black filter.

One thing is certain: we are faced with enormously complicated mechanisms that perform exquisitely. Consider, if you will, the number of prisms displayed in each eye of different insects. For example:

The ant has 400 lenses in each eye,
The common housefly about 4,000 lenses,
The honeybee about 6,300 lenses,
The swallowtail butterfly about 17,000 lenses,
The beetle *Mondella* about 25,000 lenses,
The sphingid moth about 27,000 lenses, and
The dragonfly about 30,000.

The numbers are almost unreal; imagine the small size of a dragonfly's eye and divide that miniscule space into 30,000 cones, each one with a perfectly shaped lens, functioning in unison with each other and a nerve system tied to the brain — and all of it in harmony with other organs!

Naturally the question arises: how and why did each insect species develop the same system of vision, but yet generated different amounts of lenses? Why did the dragonfly evolve into having 30,000 lenses, while the common housefly decided to stop at 4,000? Does that mean that the dragonfly existed so many more millions of years longer than the housefly so as to grow additional facets? If we wait another ten million years, does it mean that the housefly will grow 10,000 lenses additional to its present 4,000 units? Today we know that this will not happen. It takes millions of nucleotides all precisely aligned, to translate DNA orders for the creation of 4,000 lenses. It would take additional millions of nucleotides again precisely aligned, to create the growth of 30,000 lenses. These additional nucleotides cannot rearrange themselves at will so as to grow meaningful organs through chance meeting. Again we must ask:

What is the probability that 1,000,000 nucleotides can align themselves by chance in a very specific sequence — one that will translate itself into the growth of 26,000 additional lenses, ommatidia, rhabdoms, and pigment cells? The answer is zero.

The trilobite, one of the first complex life-forms found on this earth (see Chapter 10), first appeared 600,000,000 years ago, complete with compound eyes. Depending upon the subspecies, they sported 100 to 15,000 lenses in each eye. These species survived for about 320 million years, and for all these millions of years, their eye structure did not change. Except for minor variations, trilobites maintained the same form with which they were endowed from the first moment of existence. Why did the trilobite's eye not "evolve" and improve during 320,000,000 years? Could it be that "evolution" was satisfied with the end product and did not feel the necessity for further improvement? Obviously so — but then would that not imply an evaluating capacity and intelligence? How does a trilobite "know" that it could have a superior vision if it only could add another 5,000 lenses to its eye? When is "satisfactory" vision satisfactory?

Up to about twenty years ago most zoologists would have stated that the general descriptions given above for the simple and compound eyes, were in effect, the only basic eye structures to be found in the animal world. At the point when scientists thought they "knew it all," two completely different eye mechanisms were discovered: reflective simple eyes and reflective compound eyes — systems based on mirror optics.

Michael F. Land in *Scientific American* (Dec. 1978) describes the details:

"Over the succeeding centuries mirrors also became important components of optical instruments such as the astronomical telescope, but no one suspected that reflective surfaces might provide the basic optical mechanism of certain animal eyes. In the past few years some remarkable examples of eyes based on mirror optics have become apparent, among them the simple eyes of scallops and the compound eyes of shrimps, crayfishes and lobsters.

"None of these animals is particularly exotic, and indeed the anatomy of their eyes had been described many times. Why then was the role of mirrors in forming the visual image overlooked in view of the wealth of anatomical and optical talent that has been devoted to the study of the eyes of invertebrate animals? The reason may be that until fairly recently mirrors of optical quality, as opposed to shiny bits of tissue, were considered a biological impossibility. The logic was simple: the surface of a mirror is polished metal, and organisms do not make metal surfaces. Since the late 1940's, however, methods of making high-quality mirrors have changed. Instead of consisting of a single layer of silver or aluminum they are made up of multilayered stacks of very thin films of alternating high and low refractive index. This turns out to be the way living organisms have made mirrors all along! Technological progress has therefore removed a major mental block to the concept of animal mirrors."

Strange as it seems, for many centuries, untold anatomical dissections of these animals failed to reveal the true structure of their eye. Why not? Although the evidence was always there to be seen, the beholder was too unknowledgeable to realize and understand what he was looking at. Because of a certain level of ignorance, zoologists were unawares that scallops, shrimps, and lobsters had a different optical system. This is yet another indication that our interpretation of facts depends largely upon our level of knowledge.

The new discovery indicated that multilayer mirrors can be made from a great many materials provided they have different refractive indexes. Scallops, for example, take advantage of the pronounced difference between the refractive indexes of guanine (1.83) and cytoplasm (1.34). Many compound eyes use the refractive difference between chitin (1.56) and air (1.00). Behind the lens of the scallops, these layers of material act as a reflector in the form of a concave mirror. In this construction the images thus formed by that mirror are focused in the rear section of the retina *behind* the lens. They are then captured by the distal photoreceptor cells in the eye. (Fig. 16a-16b-16c).

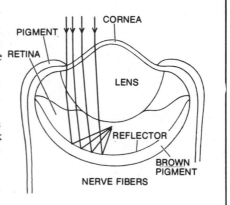

Fig. 16a — CROSS SECTION THROUGH SCALLOP EYE suggests that its optics are unusual. Unlike the lens eyes of vertebrate animals, which have a clear zone between the lens and the retina across which light rays are focused, the lens of the scallop eye is in contact with a crescent-shaped retina. Behind the retina is the extremely thin mirror. . .and then a thick layer of dark pigment. The diagram. . .represents the paths of light rays within the eye. The rays, which are only weakly re- fracted by the lens, pass through the retina to the hemispherical reflector, which focuses them back to the distal photoreceptor cells in the upper layer of the retina. Because the light must pass through the retina once before it is detected, the scallop eye does not have good contrast acuity.

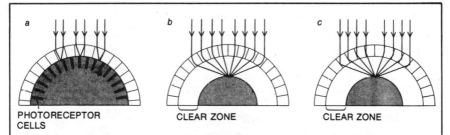

Fig. 16b —THREE TYPES OF COMPOUND EYE are observed in diurnal insects, nocturnal insects and crustaceans of the suborder Macrura (lobsters, shrimps and crayfishes). The eyes of diurnal insects (a) are made up of a hexagonal array of lenslets, each of which has its own set of photoreceptor cells. The eyes of nocturnal insects (b) are also made up of a hexagonal array of lenslets, but (because each lenslet has a radial gradient of refractive index) they bend light continuously so as to focus the multiple rays entering the array at a single spot on the retina, thereby enhancing the brightness of the image under nighttime conditions. Unlike the eyes of diurnal insects, the superposition eyes of nocturnal insects have a clear zone between the lens array and the retina across which the light rays are focused. The eyes of the macruran crustaceans (c) consist of a square array of mirrorlined plugs, which act to superpose light rays on a single spot on the retina. Because these eyes superpose light and also have a clear zone, anatomists postulated incorrectly that they shared the optical mechanism of nocturnal-insect eyes. The fact that in such crustaceans the image is formed by an array of mirrors was not realized until 1975.

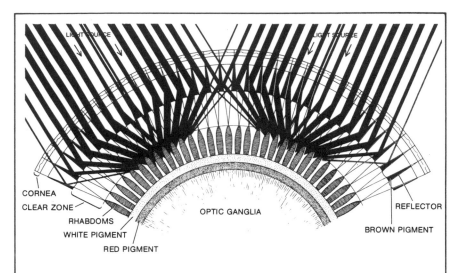

Fig. 16c — SUPERPOSITION OF RAYS in the eye of the macruran crustaceans is diagrammed, showing the effect of illumination with beams of light from two directions. In each case the rays are focused at a single spot on the retina, where they are detected by photoreceptor cells.

(Fig. 16a, 16b, and 16c — ARE TAKEN FROM *ANIMAL EYES WITH MIRROR OPTICS*, BY MICHAEL F. LAND, COPYRIGHT © 1978 BY SCIENTIFIC AMERICAN, INC. ALL RIGHTS RESERVED)

Shrimps, lobsters, and crayfish have compound eyes. Yet it was discovered that they too have mirror eyes, although the principle applied in their physiology differs from that used by scallops. As described by Land:

"In the reflecting compound eye the mirror surfaces are in front of the photo-receptors rather than behind them, and the image is erect rather than inverted. Moreover, instead of consisting of a single mirror the surface of the eye is divided into a square matrix of small rectangular plugs with reflecting sides, giving rise to an array of mirrored facets. The geometry of the array has the property of focusing light onto the surface of a sphere whose radius is about half that of the eye itself.

"There is one feature of all eyes of the reflecting compound type that immediately and reliably distinguishes them from those of the refracting compound type: the reflecting eyes have square

128

facets whereas the refracting eyes have hexagonal facets."

Any thoughtful scientist who studies these incredible details cannot escape the sophistication of the various optical systems used in the animal world — it is indeed impressive.

The theory of evolution tells us that through mutation and "natural selection" a light sensitive cell converted itself into a complex vision-mechanism over a period of untold millions of years. These constant improvements (initiated by mutation) persevered during those eons and finally generated one of the most intricated and complex of organs: the eye. Except for these self-serving generalities, evolutionists have not demonstrated a single verifiable intermediate step of the postulated process that led to such marvelous and purposeful organs. We are expected to accept the concepts on "faith."

One thing is certain: if we rely on evolution, then for millions of years the original species and its continuous offshoots must have been blind. Yet they obviously survived in such a dark world until "evolution" came to their rescue, and — after "millions of years" — created a most complex eye. At that moment the species "saw the light" and could go hunting for their prey. The tenacity of "evolution" must have been prodigious; to continuously push towards the creation of a system that would be perfected only "millions of years" hence, must be considered to be the biggest miracle on earth. Naturally it implies a mental blueprint, or a specific purpose, known ahead of time by this vague concept called "evolution." It must have "known" what it wanted to achieve after "millions of years" of perseverance and until final success was achieved — at which point evolution stopped evolving! None of this mental gymnastics makes sense, unless and until convincing evidence can be shown. Instead of evidence, we have been offered hazy generalities which are forced-fit into a blurrier theory. The moment we postulate, step by step, the possible events that could logically have taken place, we realize there is no possibility such complexities and perfections could occur by chance.

Let us revert to Darwin's original statement:

"To suppose that the eye with all its inimitable contrivances for adjusting different amounts of light, and for the correction of spherical and chromatic aberration, could have been formed by natural selection, seems, I freely confess, absurd in the highest degree."

For once, Darwin was right: natural selection expectations are absurd in the highest degree!

12
Amazing Zoology

The animal world provides innumerable examples of aspects which evolution cannot satisfactorily explain.

Decoy-fish: In the waters off Oahu, Hawaii, lives the relatively rare decoy-fish. This member of the scorpion fish family uses its dorsal fin as a lure to attract other fishes on which it preys. Whenever potential prey is in sight, the decoy-fish's dorsal fin goes up and displays the shape of a smaller fish, complete with a dark spot resembling an eye. The fin membrane is notched between the 1st and 2nd spin and resembles the mouth of a fish. On raising the lure, its gill movements stop, its breathing abates, a deep red coloring flushes through the top part of the dorsal fin while the part attached to the body turns into a transparent band, from all appearances separating the fish from its lure. While the fish itself remains motionless, it moves the decoy fin from side to side, causing the "mouth" to open and shut. The victim approaches the lure, beguiled into believing that it perceives a small fish. As soon as it is near enough, the decoy-fish snaps the prey in one quick move. Once this action is satisfactorily concluded and the displayed lure is no longer required, the bright colors on the fin fade away, the fins are retracted and folded down onto the back of the fish. (Fig. 17).

We observe a tremendous ingenuity, a sense of purposefulness and an exquisite rendition of architectual details.

Based on evolutionist concepts, this fish must have evolved from some sort of an ancestor that had no such decoy capacity, nor the

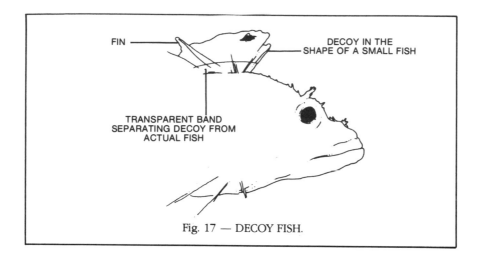

FIN

DECOY IN THE
SHAPE OF A SMALL FISH

TRANSPARENT BAND
SEPARATING DECOY FROM
ACTUAL FISH

Fig. 17 — DECOY FISH.

physical appurtenances to create the desired illusion. We are asked to believe that in its hazy past, a given fish felt the necessity to be endowed with a lure mechanism. To explain such an action, evolutionists use a number of amorphous code words, such as "survival of the fittest," "natural selection," "mutations," etc. No matter what trend of thought is chosen and applied to the case at hand, we cannot visualize a step-by-step growth of this type of a lure.

No matter how we contort our logic, we cannot reach a cogent, logical explanation for such a growth mechanism when applying evolutionist theories. The existence of all the subparts making up this lure, had to be incorporated within the DNA program, in the form of millions of nucleotides, aligned in a very, very specific sequence. There is no possibility for a given fish to change its own DNA so as to achieve a very *purposeful* display of its physiology. Nor are mutations, expressed in haphazard fashion, capable of ending up with such an enormously sophisticated mechanism.

We cannot conceive that such a growth on the back of the fish came about by the simple "desire" of the fish. We cannot conceive that the growth was an incremental one — as this would imply a purposefulness which knew ahead of time what type of lure effect it wanted to create. We cannot conceive that "mutations" or "natural selection" forces were *smart* enough to stop their push for growth, at the moment of perfection — that too would infer a logical evaluation of perfection; in other words: intelligence.

Construction of a dorsal fin resembling a fish with eye and mouth, with a separation of pigment shading different than the basic fish — a true decoy — does not result from chance. It has purposefulness which has to be encoded within the DNA as one complete blueprint — to have any meaning at all, and be genetically transferable to insure generations of decoy-fishes.

Trigger-fish: The distance from mouth to eyes in the trigger fish is unusually great. It feeds partly on crabs which naturally defend themselves with their claws as soon as they are grabbed. If the fish's eyes were close to the mouth, its chances of being hurt by the crab's claw would be great. It is surprising to observe this physical arrangement and distance between the eyes and the mouth to coincide with its method of feeding. We can again discern a purposefulness in construction with forethought of the impending result.

The trigger fish has yet another unusual defense mechanism. As the name implies, it can trigger its first dorsal fin, which is shaped like a long sharp spike. When this fish senses danger, it raises the spike to an upright position. Further, there is a lock at the base of this dorsal fin that prevents the spike from being forced down. Unlocking is accomplished by means of a smaller spine farther down the back that is tied by a tendon to the first spine. In other words, if the smaller spine is pushed down, the larger one falls flat on the back of the fish. However, a predator has no means of triggering the unlocking device — instead it is driven away by the sharp upright spike.

Neither the trigger-fish nor evolution, could possibly have anything to do with the creation of such an ingenious device. Such a physical leverage mechanism incorporated within the anatomy of this fish requires knowledge. The trigger-fish has no possibility to order such a meaningful growth on its back, nor can evolution persist over millions of years of constant mutations to eventually generate such a meaningful morphology. Again, a tremendous predetermining intelligence was necessary to design such a purposeful effect — and to create the necessary DNA program that would order the growth of such a blueprinted mechanism.

Surgeon fish: A similar device is found in the surgeon-fish, a reef dweller. A sharp movable spike is located on the side, at the narrow point between body and tail. When danger threatens, the fish releases the spike, extending it at right angle from the body — just like a switchblade. By moving its body and tail in quick jerky movements, it hits an enemy, inflicting deep cuts. When not in use, the spike returns to its normal position in a deep recess within the body and is surrounded by a protective sheath.

Angler fish: Different fish use different types of lures to catch their prey. One type of angler-fish has a flexible "fishing rod" sticking out of its back with a luminescent "bulb" at the end of it. Other varieties have been found without this lighting display. Some are small and live in deep water, (about 1,500-1,600 feet) while other, larger varieties live in shallow water near shore. Most are broad, soft-bodied, with a huge mouth, and can grow up to four feet in length.

In each instance, the ingenious fishing rod device, equipped with a "light bulb" is certainly not assignable to the astuteness of the predecessors of this fish. Neither can it be implied that millions of years of patient, haphazard mutations, combined to generate such an intelligent display. Again, let us remember that the slightest aspect of this device can only grow if — and only if — it is properly encoded within the enormously complex DNA system. No stretch of evolutionary imagination can describe for us the logical step-by-step occurrences that took place so as to end up with such a whimsical appurtenance.

Shallow Angler: A modification of the above lure is found in the shallow angler, a small tropical fish. It has the same "fishing rod" growth, but instead of luminescence it displays a worm-like piece of flesh at the end of the rod which is actually the anterior spine of its dorsal fin. Other types of anglerfish grow different forms of bait, resembling shrimp, worms, or even small fish. An interesting aspect is that a variety of motions are performed by these anglers, depending upon the type of bait they sport. For example, and anglerfish with a shrimplike appendage will move it in a quick, backward-darting motion, simulating the movement of a real shrimp. An anglerfish with

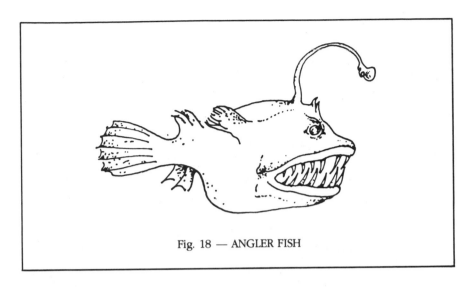

Fig. 18 — ANGLER FISH

a fishlike bait, imparts a kind of rippling effect so as to imitate the lateral undulation of a swimming fish. (Fig. 18).

By moving its lure at will, it attracts the attention of prospective prey which then ends up as a tasty repast for the angler. Interestingly enough, occasionally the "bait" is nipped off. Somehow "nature" must have anticipated such an event for it endowed this fish with the unusual ability to rapidly grow new "bait." The new appendage starts growing within a few days and is fully replaced within two weeks.

There must be enormously complex morphological mechanisms incorporated within the body of such fish which create precise actions. The forefathers of this particular anglerfish, before deciding to grow a shrimplike "bait," must have been astute observers of nature. Generations upon generations of baitless fish must have been engrossed in animal behavioral studies during an extended period of time, so as to determine the exact physical movements generated by a live shrimp. Having pinpointed that a sudden backward-darting movement is the normal motion displayed by a shrimp, it then became a matter of translating this into an anatomical change for its species and actually order the growth of such an appendage. The only way to achieve it would naturally have been to order its DNA to enlarge its program, incorporating a few million additional nucleotides, so as to generate:

135

a) a specific growth (as per some type of mental blueprint),

b) a special muscular coordination of that specific spinebone, to move the "bait" via a given type of motion,

c) and, lastly but not leastly, to create the internal mechanism that would grow a new appendage if the old one is lost.

No stretch of a fertile imagination can accept such a scenario, nor do we know of any capacity for a species to "order" its DNA to change so as to incorporate esoteric and bizarre physical appendages.

Deep-Sea angler: A number of years ago, a fish was discovered whose lure is within its mouth. Shall we assume that its forebears were probably too lazy to grow a "fishing rod" appendage? Instead, the deep-sea angler has a "light bulb" hanging from the roof of the palate. It swims around with open mouth, and dangles the lure from side to side. Small fish, attracted by this display, swim directly into the mouth of the predator to their death.

Shall we assign this display to random mutations or to "natural selection?" What are the probabilities of hundreds of millions of nucleotides (or even 10,000,000) to place themselves in the one specific alignment that would result in such an intelligent mechanism?

Lion-fish: The body of the lion-fish is covered with spikes, just like a porcupine. Each spine contains a potent poison which affects any living thing touching it. Humans experience severe pain and a leg so affected may swell to twice normal size, with the pain continuing for days. Any person wounded by a few of these spines, may die an agonizing death. No antidote to this venom had been found up to a number of years ago.

In this instance, we observe both a defense weapon, in the form of a spike, as well as chemical warfare capacities. This implies a veritable chemical production facility within the small body of the fish, so as to generate a very potent poison. Obviously, the morphology of this fish "knew" that the chemical to be created had to have venomous properties to affect predators. It could not be any haphazard chemical (and there are hundreds of them!) — it had to be a very poisonous one. How did this fish, or "evolution," know the difference between poisonous and non-poisonous chemicals? It implies purposefulness (i.e. intelligence) and a capacity to perform trial-and-error experiments so as to end up with the type of chemical that is venomous. Shall we consider that the antecedants of this fish hit upon, by accident, on the most poisonous concoction on the very first try and then decided not to try any other chemical combinations? Evolution cannot give us any possible explanation that makes sense. We are facing a very specific design, incorporated into a very specific DNA program, to perform a very specific result, all of which are obvious displays of intelligence.

Moses sole: Similar resort to chemical defense is displayed by the Moses sole, a fish found in the Red Sea. It appears to be harmless but can excrete a milky poison so potent as to paralyze large fish and kill small ones. About 240 poison glands are located along the dorsal and anal fin rays, each with an opening through a tiny pore. Through experimentation it was found that this fish would release small doses of this lethally toxic substance, which were sufficient to achieve the desired effect: small fish would die in a matter of minutes when placed in a tank containing 1 part poison to 5,000 parts of water. A charging barracuda, stopped cold in its attack, and withdrew hastily. Sharks that tried to bite the Moses sole, seemed to have temporarily paralyzed jaws that would not close; they too hurriedly swam away, with open jaws.

Such a weapon is certainly amazing in view of the "knowledge" that must have been incorporated within the morphology of the fish to create such a potency of lethal toxicity. Not only did the DNA have to control special glands to create specific chemical mixtures, but the anatomy of the fish had to be rearranged in such a manner as to include an entire piping system with 240 faucets, activated upon by the reflexive reactions of the fish. None of this can exist unless and until it is purposefully included within the DNA program. Chapter 2 indicates that the mathematical probabilities for such a program to occur haphazardly is zero.

Alligator: The alligator lays eggs in a mound-type nest which it builds. These eggs have moderately hard shells. Inside the egg, the baby alligator grows to a length of about 8 inches. When the time is ready to hatch out of the egg, the baby alligator pierces the shell of the egg with a special tooth on top of its nose. After breaking the shell with this "tool" it is able to step out of the egg into the outside world. In due time, the tooth falls off.

If we apply the thought process of the theory of evolution, we must consider that many millions of years ago, baby alligators had no egg-teeth. At a certain point in time, the necessity was felt, or a physical predisposition was present, or random mutations occurred to create such a "tool." Again evolution does not describe the step-by-step changes that took place so as to introduce the proper hundreds of thousands of nucleotides into the general DNA program — probably as an afterthought to the main, established sequence delineating the basic morphology of the alligator.

The alligator's egg-tooth may be compared with the human thymus gland, found in human beings — another type of tool used by the original genetic engineer to perform a specific job during the early months of new-born babies. In the case of the alligator baby, the tooth is present to perform a function during the early days of its existence. After that, it falls off — it will no longer be required during the balance of the alligator's life. Similarly with the human thymus gland; after it performs its function during the early months of a babies' life, it shrinks out of existence — it is no longer required during the balance of that person's life, (see pages 195, 196).

In both cases, we have the growth of an organ as a solution, elegantly executed, to perform a temporary requirement. Naturally certain sections of the DNA contain the type of sequences that will order the growth and demise of the "tool" in question. Such predetermination is a reflection of intelligence.

Egg-eating snake: A similar display of purposefulness, is seen in snakes who feed exclusively on eggs. These snakes grow to about 2-1/2 feet in length, have a narrow head and slender body. They have no sharp teeth, are not venomous and are harmless to humans.

The peculiarity of these snakes resides in the fact that they can swallow eggs that are wider than their mouths or bodies. Their throat can expand to fit the size of the food, while their jaws are especially hinged so as to engulf their prey. It seems to seek out eggs by smell. Upon locating a given egg, the snake coils itself around the future meal. It opens up its mouth a few times as if to exercise its jaw muscles and proceeds to engulf the egg by pushing forward the entire head, jaw, and throat so as to slide the egg into its body — an exercise that takes from 10 to 20 minutes of constant effort.

As the egg enters the throat, a remarkable sequence of events takes place. Along the top part of the throat, the snake has a row of about 30 teeth projecting downwards into the throat. The first 17 of these are knife-like and long, while the next few are broad and flat, and the rest have the form of solid spear stumps. The snake holds the egg tightly through exertion of its throat muscles. By moving its head backwards and forwards, it achieves a sawing effect of the teeth onto the egg. The broken egg exudes its contents that finds its way into the stomach. In front of the stomach is a valve which allows entry of the egg liquid but bars access to the shells. After the soft parts of the egg have been extracted, the snake performs a few additional contortions in order to spit out the broken shells. Interestingly this type of snake feeds only during one or two months of the year (the egg-laying season of other animals.)

Several observations are in order: The physical construction of this snake is amazing, in that it can swallow objects much larger than its throat. It would be equivalent to a human swallowing a basketball. In order to perform the job, it unhinges its jaw, and stretches its skin far enough to let the egg enter as a unit. Instead of having teeth in the mouth (as most other animals display) or fangs like other snakes, there is a unique construction: a single row of teeth starting at the end of the mouth and continuing into the body. These are, in fact, not true teeth but rather inward extensions of the snake's backbone. This serrated edge at the top of the mouth serves the meaningful purpose of sawing through the hard shell of the egg.

Every part of the morphology of this species is designed to perform specialized functions. If any one of these complex actions did not properly take place, the entire system would come to a dead stop. This means that every single component part had to be in functioning order from the very first day this snake was performing. It makes no sense to consider that the forebears of this snake used to feed on regular meals, until some members of the species decided to

139

go after eggs. It certainly would have taken "millions of years" of incremental evolution to grow all this paraphernalia for proper feeding. What did the snake do during those millenia? On the one side it proceeded to feed normally, and on the other side, it must have continuously pushed for the formation and growth of an entirely new system. When the tooth-sawing system was finally ready, did it then discontinue use of the old feeding system? To perform all these gyrations, did the DNA strands not have to contain all the millions of nucleotides necessary for regular feeding and at the same time, add constantly additional nucleotides for egg consumption? How was this achieved? At the point when this new feeding system was properly encoded within the DNA how did the same DNA arrange to discard the entire old program?

Obviously, imperceptible incremental evolution is not the answer. To implicate punctuated equilibria for an explanation (i.e., sudden jump into a completely new system) is equivalent to acknowledging creation of a given species as one fully perfected package. No matter how we evaluate these concepts, we must agree that we are witnessing the results of a pronounced predetermining intelligence.

Bombardier Beetle: Another amazing display of purposefulness is found in the bombardier beetle. This insect uses chemistry as a defense mechanism, but instead of having a single ready-made substance to squirt as needed (as some other species have) it stores two different chemicals in separate glands of its body, situated at the end of its abdomen. Two compartments within the beetle's body serve as reservoir and reaction chamber. When threatened, this beetle is capable to direct a hot stream of chemicals, in the form of an explosive spurt, onto the body of its enemies. The details of the ensuing actions are described by Milne and Milne[1]:

> "A cluster of gland cells transfers secretions through a duct into the first large chamber of a two-compartmented organ. The solution there consists of 25 percent hydrogen peroxide and 10 percent hydroquinones, which are the active ingredients. When the insect is alarmed, muscles surrounding the reservoir squeeze

[1] *Insect Worlds*, (Charles Scribner's Sons, New York 1980).

some of the solution into the second chamber, a sort of vestibule that leads toward the nozzle. The vestibule walls secrete enzymes that facilitate an instantaneous explosion: peroxidase causes the hydrogen peroxide to decompose into water and free oxygen, while catalase helps the hydroquinones change into toxic quinones and hydrogen. At the instant of the explosion, the hydrogen and oxygen combine to form water and release energy. The temperature of the discharge rises to the boiling point of water, with enough heat left over to vaporize almost a fifth of the discharge. Out goes an extremely hot jet of steam and minute droplets of quinone solution.

". . .the insect's gun is emptied by four or five little explosions in quick succession, although one beetle, examined by Thomas Eisner of Cornell University, responded to continuous stimulation with twenty-nine shots before giving up. Far fewer are needed to convince anyone that the gas feels warm on a fingertip, and that the skin turns brown as though it had been swabbed with a strong iodine solution. Large bombardiers are credited with burning a human hand so severely that only a few specimens can be captured with thumb and forefinger on any single day of collecting. All bombardiers earn high scores for markmanship, making direct hits in almost any direction by turning the flexible nozzle of the defensive organ."

How did the beetle know that hydroquinone and hydrogen peroxide, when properly mixed, would result in a powerful explosion? Once discovered that such a mixture is effective, how did it manage to manufacture these very same two chemicals? Did this occur on the first try or did the predecessors of this beetle have to try a great many other combinations that did not give them the expected effect? Did evolution "know" what it was after, and what type of a result it wanted to achieve? How did the beetle manufacture all the other trial chemicals that did not work out? Each time an unsatisfactory result was obtained, how did "evolution" arrange to dismantle the corresponding DNA sequence that translated into the manufacture of those ineffective chemicals?

What are the mathematical probabilities that a dumb beetle will hit upon the proper interacting combination of hydrogen peroxide and hydroquinone to generate an explosive effect? What are the probabilities for mutations to have haphazardly arranged themselves

141

in such a specific sequence so as to build two separate chambers within the body and fill them with two specific chemicals along with an inhibitor chemical?

If the readers get lost in the maze of these impossibilities suggested by the theory of evolution, then an obvious answer imposes itself: only predetermining superintelligence can generate specific DNA programs to create those desired effects. Genetic engineers can "create" programs as one complete functioning package, based on knowledge and intelligence.

Kangaroo: This animal is the best known of the marsupials indigenous to Australia. There are a great many other species built along the same principle of carrying their young in a pouch. Other marsupials are the wombat, bandicoot, opossum, koala, Tasmanian wolf, and banded anteaters.

The kangaroo has an interesting construction inside its pouch, where its lactic nipples are located. This animal weans her youngsters for a prolonged period of time, even after the offspring is able to jump out of the pouch and roam around. Nevertheless, the young continually return to the mother's pouch for comfort, relaxation, and nutrition. Because of a very short gestation period, a mother kangaroo is usually feeding two offsprings at different stages of development. It has been noted that she has different nipples for her two baby kangaroos. The amazing observation made is the fact that the milk consistency of each nipple is different. In other words, the mother kangaroo lactates different qualities of milk, adjusted to the nutritional requirements of the stages of growth of the offsprings. This also entails separate piping systems with a manufacturing system capable of producing, simultaneously, different milk, directed to the proper nipple.

Shall we consider that "evolution" decided unilaterally to create different qualities of milk *because* "it" realized that different stages of development needed separate types of nourishment? Even if we assign such a far-fatched purposefulness to the hazy concept of "evolution", how did it manage to rearrange millions of nucleotides according to a predetermined plan for such a very specific purpose? "Evolution" must be the most sophisticated genetic engineer we could ever imagine.

Australian frog: We have long marvelled that many of the animals indigenous to Australia have unusually different anatomical features. We understand but still wonder at the inner workings of the special morphological "system" of outside pouches where the young are weaned and carried. Yet even more wonderful is a small Australian frog which stands out because of its almost incredible and unique method of giving birth. Lacking both marsupial outside pouch and placental womb, this animal has a completely different internal arrangement that provides for its stomach to double as both digestive organ and womb.

When this frog becomes pregnant, the stomach stops performing its digestive processes and ceases to excrete enzymes. It rearranges its functions to become an incubator — a womb, where dozens of baby frogs are hatched and grow. At the end of the gestation period, the young frogs crawl up into the mother's mouth and are spit into the outside world. For all the time these baby frogs occupy the stomach, the mother frog eats no food. When the last offspring has been discharged through the mouth, the "womb" reverts to its original function of a normal stomach!

It certainly took creative imagination and expertise to design such a system and intricately encode all these activities into the frog's DNA spiral. Shall we again infer that "natural selection" and "mutation" were at work, over a period of millions of years, to create such a whimsically unique, yet enormously complex digestive and reproductive system incorporated into one organ?

Arctic Fish: The temperature of the waters in the Arctic regions is below the freezing point of fresh water. Why do fish swimming in that region not freeze? Amazing as it might sound, it was discovered that these fish have different blood constituents than other fish living in more temperate waters. Although many factors combine to provide protection against the cold, it was observed that the most important element was the presence of a special anti-freeze within the blood. It was discovered that the anti-freeze in question was a type of glycoprotein having three specific molecular weights, 21,500, 17,000, and 10,500 and consisting completely of repeating units of amino acids alanin and threonine. Tests have shown this type of anti-freeze to be far more effective than were an equal weight of sodium chloride

143

dissolved in the blood.

How did these fish arrange to introduce anti-freeze into their blood stream so as to survive the rigors of their ecology? How did evolution realize that a protein made of alanin and threonine would be the most effective compound to use so as to achieve the desired result? Probably through a period of trial-and-error? No matter how we look upon it, it represents a purposefulness of objective — which means, intelligence.

This indicates the DNA program includes a section that orders the creation of a chain of these two amino acids by being coded GCU (or GCC or GCA or GCG) alternating with ACU (or ACC or ACA or ACG) as displayed in the genetic code shown on page 56. For as long as the DNA master program was not properly encoded, the fish in question could not create the proper mixture of anti-freeze in its blood cells. Since the DNA was unknown 125 years ago, Darwin did not advise us how "evolution" would arrange such a situation.

Hawks: It is well known that animals in general have hollow bones to obtain the most efficient coefficient between bone strength and body weight. The degree of the ratio between these two factors depends upon the animal; large, heavy, terrestrial animals are built with more solid bony columns. We always seem to encounter the application of sound engineering principles in the ratio of strength to weight.

This concept applies particularly in the case of birds, where minimum weight is critical and yet high strength is essential so as to support the bird in flight and withstand changes in atmospheric pressure.

One of the more efficient and graceful of birds is the hawk, which can soar on thermal updrafts with wings held motionless. Even though hollow bones suffice for most birds, hawks and a few others are endowed with bones of still more efficacious construction. They have an internal bracing system which provides additional strength (Fig. 19). In effect their bones have inner diagonal struts (which connect the load-bearing bony beams) giving them maximum strength with the least possible bone structure. Engineering-wise, we observe an immensely advanced "know-how" performed in the smartest and most elegant fashion.

In engineering this construction is known as the "Warren truss." Ironically, it cost modern mankind millions of dollars expenditures and untold manhours to test and discover the structure in question! Much research time, money and sweat could have been saved if we had only appreciated the engineering implications of the anatomy of animals. Obviously "nature" was immensely more intelligent than our best engineering talents. Hawks were using the Warren truss construction millions of years ago — mankind "discovered" and applied it only recently.

How shall we explain the production of hollow bone systems and "Warren truss" structures through the application of random mutations expounded by evolutionists? The realization of meaningful ratios of strength versus weight, and the capacity to translate that into a physical mechanism, (in all the various species) cannot be random developments which *"happened"* to be programmed into the DNA. It displays much too much intelligence, forethought, and know-how to be glossed over by a meaningless generality such as "after millions of years land animals evolved wings and became birds." Such statements

Fig. 19 — "WARREN TRUSS" BONE STRUCTURE OF CERTAIN BIRDS.

are inane and express nothing. Sequences of nucleotides that have to be in a specific order, do not know structural engineering principles, so as to order the specific type of construction that will result in the most efficient ratio. Chemical molecules do not have research and development capacities to try out different combinations before deciding on the most efficient structure.

Again and again, basically the same question has to be asked: what are the probabilities for a few million nucleotides to line up haphazardly so as to generate most advanced aeronautical engineering principles?

In summary: the usual scenario depicted by evolutionists is to consider a species, labeled primitive, pronounce the magic words "after millions of years of mutation and natural selection," and derive a seemingly plausible conclusion for the existence of a different species defined as advanced. Such mental calisthenics conveniently blot out innumerable isolated events that must have taken place during those famous "millions of years." Instead, we would be better served if we try to understand events that could have taken place after twenty minutes, or after twentyfour hours, or after one month. Whenever one of those "millions of years" has been broken down into smaller meaningfully manageable time spans, the sequence of events has been seen not to follow the logical sequence evolutionists predicted. On top of it, if we translate all these events into our newly discovered DNA/RNA language, we conclude that the physiological and morphological changes necessary could not have been effected through chance mutations even if natural selection were there to sift through the debris.

What then is the message of all these examples from zoology? First, that there are extreme complexities and niceties in their physiology. There are intricacies in presumably simple primitive animals that match or exceed our best technology. Second, we find a lack of reason or means on the part of the animals concerned to have pressed, on their own initiative, from a presumed lower, more primitive existence to an, again presumed, advanced, higher level of life. Third, we note nearly complete inability to find, postulate, or even imagine the intermediate levels of development that would have led to the features common today. Fourth, there is the realization that no matter how insignificant the superficial changes may appear to be, each implies enormous changes in the makeup of the governing DNA/RNA systems that, if obtainable only by chance arrangements, are statistically impossible of attainment.

All these lead to inference of a fifth, that lacking better evidence than we now have, we must entertain the possibility, likelihood, even certainty that life as we know it on Earth cannot be ascribed to the oversimplifications of Darwinism. We observe morphological purposefulness in all phases of life forms — a display that can only be ascribed to "predetermining intelligence."

13
Botany

Intense fossil search in the animal world led to one conclusion: for all practical purposes, there are no preceding forms nor any connecting links leading from one species to the next. Each time, we observe species emerging as a whole packaged life-machine at a given point in time. From then on it continues in the very same form and complexity of systems till modern times (or until it becomes extinct).

In the plant kingdom we encounter very much the same thing — with even more pronounced abrupt appearances. The fossil record of plants similarly does not accord well with the predictions of evolutionists. Logical incremental, step-by-step histories generally are lacking. Again, we observe spectacular entrances upon this planet at quite specific moments in time of plants in essentially the same shape as observed today.

Usually, the plant world is only relegated as a small appendix to the discussion of evolution of the animal world. We lump them together under the same principles as applied to animal evolution, although there are fewer arguments, textbooks, and like literature which illustrate the step by step evolutionary processes that must have taken place during the "millions of years" we so conveniently formulate.

The reason is obvious: It is inconceivable for reasonable people to believe that a cauliflower became a tomato (or did a tomato evolve to become a cauliflower?, or did they have a common ancestor?). It is impossible to imagine that a potato, through a process of "natural selection" or "mutation" became a watermelon or a sequoia tree.

148

They are of such diversity that a direct evolutionary path cannot be considered in a serious vein. An artist, with a fecund brain, can always give us a picture depicting a sequential evolutionary progression, such as:

pea—olive—walnut—brussel sprout—tomato—watermelon

Apart from their round shape (as common denominator) these six life-forms have nothing else in common — except cells functioning along the same blueprint.

The difficulties we have in applying the principles of evolution in the animal world are compounded for the plant world. At least, in the animal world we have motion. An ant will move many yards, from one place to the other, in locating its food. A bird will fly across a great valley to court its mate and raise a new brood in a different spot. The wolf will run through miles to catch its prey and claim territorial rights of some different area. Yet constant motion is not available to plants. It is true that seeds, spores, and whole fruits will be carried by wind, water, and animals, but the basic concept of the plant in one of immobility. When we have a plant with roots almost tied to a given spot, it is difficult to postulate the evolutionary steps necessary to relate all plants from the original beginnings of cells to the trees, food plants, and flowers, sprouting all over the world, thousands of miles away from each other.

Nevertheless, evolutionists tell us that plants, too, are the result of "millions of years" of evolution starting with an insignificant cell and developing into the most complex flower. For how this development took place, there are few explanations. Yet it is insisted that this is the certain path that was taken. This is not reasonable logic; it is simply a statement of convenience with no evidence to show how the DNA helix of a weed did or could have changed into the DNA structure of an oak tree. Naturally, a great many questions are asked on this subject and, as usual, no logical answers are obtained.

For example, why would a single cell that, somehow or other, started the life process one or two billion years ago, develop into an animal with locomotion instead of developing into a plant without locomotion? On what premise did these single cells decide to create two different worlds of life-machines? Which did occur first?

We are given to understand that land plants occurred first. In the scope of things, animals seem to have taken to land at a later date. If that is so, how will we explain the pollination of a great variety of flowers which depend upon the action of insects, such as bees?

If the bees came millions of years later, than theoretically, there was no means to pollinate the flowers. If the flowers were not pollinated, then that species should have died out with the first generation since it would have had no means to reproduce. But then, we should not have had the "first" generation of that flower to start with! Yet, these flowers seem to have procreated continuously. Obviously, this means that the bees (or other pollinating agents) were present at the same time the plants evolved to bear flowers. If one keeps in mind that evolution has taken millions of years in one case, as well as in the other, one finds it difficult to understand how these flowers were able to come into existence through such a process, and how they coordinated their rate of evolution so as to end up as perfectly integrated mechanisms at the *same* time. And what happened during the intervening "millions of years?" How did each manage to survive?

The same argument can be made about a number of other insects and a number of other flowers and fruit trees. Obviously, there is a gap in logic in these instances. We cannot have these two living organisms follow their own evolutionary path over millions of years since they are so closely interdependent. Such dependency dictates that both appear at the same time, in full development of their own structure.

Just as in the case of animals, plant growth depends on the sequence of nucleotides that has been programmed into the DNA helix. Each cell of each flower, bush, or tree has its own unique DNA spiral with its own unique program that commands the growth of that particular species. Therefore, a change from one type into another type, no matter how superficially slight, means a tremendous reorganization within the links of the DNA. This cannot be performed with millions of years of patient wait, hoping that something will happen. The complexities and the precision in the DNA demands the introduction of outside intelligence.

150

We observe that various types of vegetation exist in various regions of the world, depending upon climate and soil, among other factors. How did all these plants happen to be the exact type required for that particular surrounding? According to the theory of "survival of the fittest", we are told that we now have only the survivors of plants that were able to make the grade under those climatic conditions, while the rest died out. However, under such circumstances, it would mean that, all areas had to have seeds of *all* existing plants, to start with. With years, the tender violet could no longer take the harsh winter of the Arctic Circle and died out. It doesn't make sense to expect that every single spot on earth started with all the possible samples of vegetation and then ended up with the flora that would survive the specific climate conditions of that particular ecology.

Another hypothesis would have it differently: originally, once just the right conditions prevailed, life started simultaneously in many different places in the world. In other words, we might have had 100,000 "warm little ponds" and in each instance the same extraordinary evolutionary sequences were repeated. In the final analysis, in each locality there developed the specific vegetation that would survive that particular ecology. If we have difficulty in following the sequence of events that created life out of one "warm little pond," imagine what it would mean to expect 100,000 little ponds, essentially duplicating the same evolutionary sequence over and over again — and ending up with a multitude of the same forms of life. Does that make sense?

The interdependence between some insects and plants is so complete that we cannot separate them from each other. They almost form one mechanism of life-form, built from two complementary parts. The life cycle of each is so minutely intertwined with that of its partner that we cannot conceive of one existing separate from the other.

There are numerous examples in nature that underline this relationship over and over again. For example: the fig tree depends on the pollination activities of a particular species of wasp. There are a number of different types of fig trees, and each has its own type of wasp. The intertwining life style of the two partners is a convincing display of complementary purposefulness.

151

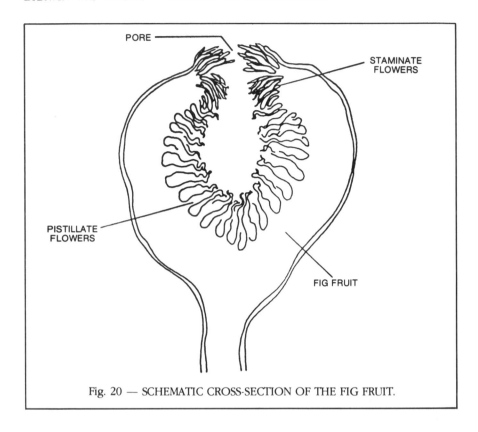

PORE

STAMINATE
FLOWERS

PISTILLATE
FLOWERS

FIG FRUIT

Fig. 20 — SCHEMATIC CROSS-SECTION OF THE FIG FRUIT.

The fig fruit itself is in effect a receptacle performing two functions. For the tree it represents the mechanism for reproduction, where staminate and pistillate flowers occur. These may be found in separate or in the same receptacle.

For the wasp, the fruit is the incubator for its larvae. The wasp enters through a pore at the end of the fig, pushes its way through a row of staminate flowers, and comes to rest on a bed of pistillate flowers found in the center of the fig (Fig. 20). The female wasp deposits eggs which hatch into larvae and which, in due time become a new generation of wasps. These mate with each other inside the fig. The males usually remain and die while the females escape through the pore; during this exit they become dusted with pollen from the staminate flowers of the fig. The wasps fly away and search for another fig tree of the *same* type to repeat the whole procedure. It is an eery sight to see millions of little wasps swarm away from the exit pores of thousands of figs.

These wasps performed their one function in life; within the scheme of things they are — so to say — the mobile extension of the fig tree, which is fixed in place and cannot on its own transfer pollen between male and female flowers. These particular wasps will always reside with the same species of fig tree — they are part and parcel of the tree. Why does every type of fig tree have its very specific type of wasp? Why do these wasps not pollinate any of the other types of fig trees? Because if they did, there would probably be cross-pollination and after thousands of years, we would have ended up with only one type of fig tree. Yet, after millions of years of existence, we still have different species of fig trees. How does each type of wasp know which species of fig tree to pollinate? We do not know as yet the mechanism that induces the wasp to search out its type of tree — possibly some sort of behavioral DNA. Without this interconnection, neither the fig tree nor the wasp could exist.

An interesting event is recounted by d'Entreves and Zunino in their book *The Secret life of Insects* (Chartwell Books, page 124):

"This phenomenon explains the misfortune which overtook California planters at the end of the last century. Having introduced the Turkish fig into California, they were disagreeably surprised when it did not bear fruit. The trees were covered with flower-buds which dropped off without ripening. The explanation was the lack of the capri fig, chosen host of the fig insect. After American entomologists had visited Smyrna in Turkey and realized the nature of the problem, it was fairly simple to import the wild fig with its attendant gall-forming insect *Blastophaga psenes*. This is a classic example of the importance of pollinating insects to the human economy."

A fig-tree is not a fig-tree unless it is serviced by its own type of wasp. They are part and parcel of the same unit.

Again we observe an enormous display of purposefulness and ingenious architecture to perform a job elegantly. This implies that incremental evolution over "the millions of years" was not the route of development of these two partners. There is a delicate system of coexistence here which has to be in perfect working order, for each one of the partners to survive. If any aspect in the biological structure of the tree and the wasp is not in order and properly functioning, neither species can survive. It follows, that both had to be fully developed and functioning from the beginning of both species.

Today we can apply a more precise type of evaluation and inquire into the mathematical probability for each of the two DNA systems in question. Is there a chance for each one of millions of nucleotides to have found their proper positions within the program, so as to create a meaningfully performing end product? What are the chances for this program to have developed at random, but in such a way that it would coordinate its activities with the DNA program of another species, so that the combined survival of both would then be assured? The answer given by probability concept is: no chance.

Many examples of this delicate interweaving of functions can be observed in nature between flowers, trees, fruits, on the one hand and insects and birds on the other hand.

A particularly unusual display is found in the carnivorous — more precisely, insectivorous plants (Fig. 21). We are accustomed to see insects feed on plants. The tables are turned this time — the insect is the prey and the plant is the predator. There is an extraordinary variety of architecture and intelligence displayed in this section of botany — stationary plants that derive nutrients from the insects they catch. The type of supersophisticated systems and amazing engineering executions that went into creating so many different catching mechanisms is sobering.

These carnivorous plants are equipped to capture insects from which they extract nutrients by secreting digestive enzymes. The best known of these plants is the Venus flytrap in which the snaring mechanism is a leaf blade, the two halves of which can swing together as though hinged. Along the outer edge of the leaf are tough bristles, while within the space between the halves are very fine, sensitive hair like filaments. When an insect touches these filaments, it triggers a mechanism that causes the two halves to close quickly to a form much like that of a Mexican taco. Enzymes are soon secreted from special glands in the leaf, which in turn digest the trapped insect.

Another type of trap is known as the sundew plant. It possesses a

154

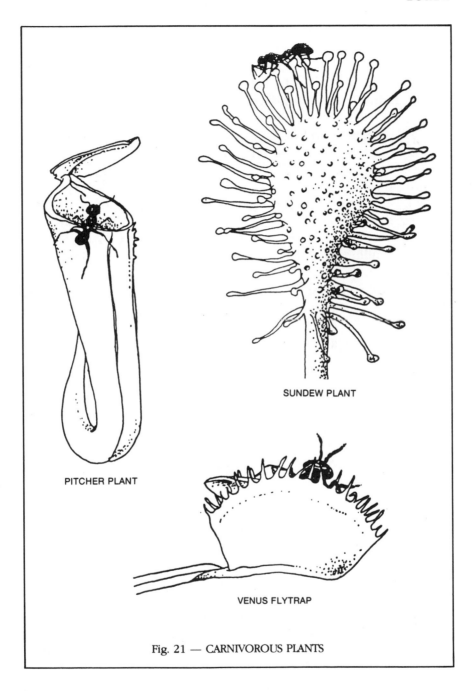

PITCHER PLANT

SUNDEW PLANT

VENUS FLYTRAP

Fig. 21 — CARNIVOROUS PLANTS

quantity of filaments that stick out. At the tip of each filament is a globule of a sticky substance that holds any insect touching the plant. Adjoining filaments even bend towards the prey so as to assure its entrapment. Like the Venus flytrap, certain glands excrete enzymes, which, in turn, digest the insect and feed the plant.

Pitcher plants are built along a different principle. They display the form of an elongated pitcher with numerous fine filaments on the inside — all of which point downwards. At the bottom of the pitcher, the plant maintains a pool of water and digestive enzymes. The insect can enter the pitcher but is prevented from leaving by the downward-pointing filaments. The more the insect tries to escape, the more surely it is trapped; it moves inexorably further into the pitcher eventually falling into the stagnant liquid where it is digested.

There are great many additional varieties all of which display enormously sophisticated mechanisms created so as to act as efficient traps.

It is as though a class of engineering students were assigned homework: to design life-machine mechanisms that will catch insects. Each student, using the basic building blocks known to him, put together a working system dictated by his imagination. If there were a hundred engineering students in the class, a hundred different designs were generated (and probably some of them quite faulty and unable to survive). One cannot escape the realization of the enormous intelligence reflected in the physical design of the various carnivorous plants.

If based on evolution we must conclude that these carnivorous plants evolved after all the insects were fully formed and roaming the earth, otherwise the plants could not have survived without their main food. Obviously, it must have taken evolution many more millions of years to "evolve" such incredible plants *after* the insects were fully formed. If we have to apply Darwin's brain-child of "natural selection" leading to "survival of the fittest," we should assume that the forebear of these plants could not extract enough sustenance through their roots (as all other plants were doing) and — by sheer desperation — were forced to generate such intelligent systems to catch and digest insects! Of course, we don't know how these plants survived during "the millions years" it took them to develop this immense engineered trap mechanisms (evolutionists usually don't address themselves to those intervening millenia.) And why so many different systems for catching insects, each one superbly displaying amazing intelligence — almost with a touch of whimsical irony? Why did evolution not create one carnivorous plant system? After all, it is much easier and logical to evolve one system rather than create so many different supersophisticated mechanisms. This amazement was also expressed by Niles Eldredge when he stated:

> "But we are left to explain the most striking fact about these fossils — their diversity. What does all this variety suggest? How and why did ancestral trilobites evolve into so many kinds of descendants, so anatomically varied?[1]

Evolution is the most farfetched and improbable answer to the multifarious constructions we encounter in the plant world. There is too much purposeful engineering in each one of the millions of plants. If we stop to think through the step by step situations involved, we must conclude that evolution could not have been the method by which the world of plants with its myriad systems and colored architectural marvels, came into being.

Each plant, each flower, each shrub can only be the result of a precise engineering program created as an individual, specific life-machine, and based upon a very unique alignment of nucleotides within their particular DNA.

---

[1]*An Extravagance of Species* (Natural History, Vol. 89, No. 7, 1980, Page 50).

14
Behavioral DNA

A queen bee, the lone layer of eggs within a beehive, places a fertilized egg in each hexagonal honeycomb cell. The worker bees follow her, deposit honey and seal the top with a layer of wax. When the egg hatches, the infant bee has all the nourishment it needs in its cubicle as it grows to a point where the cell can no longer hold her. At that stage, the baby bee pierces the wax roof and moves into the outside world.

The first action after puncturing the wax is to turn around and clean up the comb within which it grew. Once this is done, the new member joins the colony and shares the other chores to be performed.

How does a newly hatched baby bee know that its first duty is to clean up her pen and have it ready for the next generation? What propels that baby bee to perform such an act upon emerging from the honeycomb? At that point it had no physical contact with the grown-ups nor could it have been taught what to do and how to do it. Yet this infant knows exactly what to do and how to do it. Where did this knowledge come from?

Tsetse fly: We all know about flies; there are big ones, small ones, green ones, blue ones, and pesty ones. In general, basically all are built along similar architectural principles. However, one fly seems to be quite different — one where its various organs developed in a completely different direction. It is the tsetse fly found only along a certain belt in Central Africa. Although outwardly it looks like any other fly, inwardly it has a completely different set of organs. To start with, this fly lives only on blood. It attaches itself to a living creature and sucks blood through the skin. To a great extent, it acts like a mosquito although it looks like a fly. The most interesting aspect of the tsetse fly is that it does not lay eggs as other flies do but has a completely different system of reproduction. Even courting between male and female is different. The tsetse is not particularly interested in attracting the opposite sex and does not go out courting it. Somehow or other, by sheer chance the male meets female where both are sucking blood from a victim. It is only by this haphazard meeting that the two mate over a period lasting an hour or more. In relationship to its life span (1 to 5 months), this seems to be an unusually long period. We also observe that the tsetse fly mates only a few times in a lifetime, again an unusual aspect.

An extraordinary aspect is their method of birth. While all the other flies lay many eggs, the tsetse produces a cocoon within which the baby fly is ready-built and living. The birth of the cocoon-type hull is unusual insofar as it is about half as long and weighs half as much as the mother tsetse. Once this hull has come out of the womb it immediately tries to dig itself into the ground. There is an instantaneous motion performed as the top part of the head of the small tsetse sticks out and apparently propels the entire structure through the rotational movement of the eyes. The newborn wastes no time but tries desperately to dig itself into the ground where it stays for a certain period of time. As soon as the baby tsetse is mature enough and has absorbed all the food within that hull, it pries itself loose and starts digging upwards out of the ground. At that stage we have a completely ready tsetse fly, whose wings are in place but have to be pried loose. The baby tsetse starts flying promptly without coaxing or instruction from other adult flies.

Each new-born generation knows exactly what to do as soon as hatched. In this particular case, a feverish action takes place so as to dig into the ground as soon as possible. Since the tsetse mother never had the opportunity to teach the youngster or perform the digging itself, the question has to be asked: how is the new-born able to know what steps it has to take, upon coming out of the mother's womb? Without any lesson, without any directions, the youngster knows

159

exactly what to do and how to do it.

Kangaroo: Another example is the birth of a kangaroo. This large animal produces an offspring in the form of a blind small worm, about an inch long. As soon as it comes out of the mother's womb, it wriggles its way up on the outside of the mother's stomach to the pouch which it enters and then attaches itself to a lactic nipple within the pouch. It continues to live there until it grows to the point where it can move out into the outside world, even though it continually returns for comfort and milk.

Interestingly, the doe kangaroo does not help at all in this process. She simply waits for the infant to find its way into the pouch through its own capacities. If that newly born entity does not get into the pouch within a short time, it dies.

How does the new-born kangaroo know that its first urgent requirement after birth, is to move posthaste in the direction of the pouch and enter the pouch? Obviously, the mother kangaroo did not teach its offspring nor did it help put it into the pouch. This leads us to conclude that the newly formed kangaroo must have a built-in "knowledge," that propels it into a specific direction for a specific purpose. It does not have thinking capacities to have evaluated the risks involved and have decided that the safest haven would be to move upwards into the mother's pouch.

From the above three examples, we may deduce that there is some built-in mechanism that forces the offspring to perform in a specific manner. For lack of a better word, we could theorize that such a built-in mechanism might be a "behavioral DNA."

Since we established that the biological DNA is the order-giver, based on the program that it contains, one may logically infer that it also contains instructions commanding the behavioral activity of the newly born life.

There are hundreds of similar examples throughout the animal world, all of which are enormously interesting and most surprising. A great many research projects have been undertaken and fascinating books have been written on this subject by such zoologists, as V.K. Frisch, K. Lorenz, and N. Tinbergen.

Whether animals actually have a behavioral DNA or not has not been scientifically determined as yet. There are strong indications that it or something equivalent exists; but as yet, no section of any DNA structure has been shown to be the order-giver for behavioral activity.

Despite this, we discern certain overall patterns, as though there are connections between built-in behavioral patterns and self-generated actions. The first one seems to be genetically supplied as a ready-made program. The second one is produced through the brainy activities of the individual itself. This means, that we observe a display of intelligence either as a prepackaged product built into the species; or as the result of an independent brain that has decisions-making capacity applied from day to day. Insects are close to one end of the spectrum, and human beings on the other. In between, there seem to be all sorts of gradations, some who display part prepackaged intelligence, and part instantaneous evaluation capacities. The ratios among these two sources of "thought" capacities, varies from species to species.

Bees do not know geometry, yet they produce the one shape of cell (hexagonal) that is the strongest and most space-efficient type of construction given the raw materials they control. The wall thickness of each cell is exactly 0.073 mm with a plus or minus tolerance of 0.002 mm (as per Frisch). This is an extraordinary precision performed by an "uneducated bee." The strength of this thin construction can be appreciated when we consider that with only 1.4 ounces of wax, bees construct a comb capable of holding four pounds of honey.

How did the bee settle on the hexagonal shape as the most economical and sturdy? Millions of years ago, when the first bee appeared on this earth or finally evolved as a functioning life-machine, did it experiment with different shapes, and then pick the one logical, scientific principle of construction that makes sense? Hardly; even if it wanted to and tried, a bee cannot build honeycomb cells in any shape other than hexagonal. To a very great extent, the bee is nothing more than a robot, programmed to perform a task in a precise predetermined fashion. It cannot act in any different way than what its built-in "floppy disc" orders it to do. A bee seems to rely completely upon the "thinking" that preceded it and which incorporated the orders in the "behavioral DNA." It does not seem to

161

have an independently functioning brain, that will evaluate new situations, and through thought, change the orders as seen fit. A bee will perform only as another predetermining brain decided it should act and forced it to act through a program engraved in the DNA.

We have ants who create all sorts of homes. We have the Australian termites that have been described as the master architects and civil engineers of the insect world. These termites produce towers nearly 25 feet high. In relationship to their size, this would mean that they are creating a building comparable to humans erecting a one mile high tower. The same termites also make roofs with overhanging eaves so as to protect themselves against heavy rains. Some termites build homes in the shape of an ax-head with a broad side and a narrow side. They position their structures in such a way that the broad side is exposed to the sun's rays as it progresses from east to west. Termites of the African desert dig holes as deep as 130 feet in order to reach the water table. Again, in terms of human scale, this would be equivalent for us to dig a hole 5.2 miles into the earth.

In the same vein, we find that the Caddis fly that lives in water, builds protective cases out of materials which it finds in that particular brook. This is done by using saliva to form a silky thread-like substance which is then would around the pebbles or other raw materials located. One species uses small wooden branches, cut precisely to length, in building its protective case. It then spins a sticky thread to anchor itself to a rock and extends its legs to catch free-floating food.

Another type of Caddis fly, cements grains of sand together to build its structure. Yet another builds a case of plant debris in the fork of a twig; all mesh segments are exactly the same size.

There are jawfish that produce homes made out of stone; wasps build extremely strong gourd-like structures within which they make their homes.

One aspect stands out: all these species are only able to perform exactly in the same manner — they are robots following implanted orders. As we go into the larger, more complex animals we observe that this ingrained building capacity has faded out or is even non-existent. Chickens, dogs, ducks, cats, horses, apes, cows, and their likes, do not seem to have the "knowhow" to create structures of any form. They have certain different behavioral patterns that become obvious to us, but no architectural or engineering capacity. They have, rather, a greater ability to decide on actions to be taken — but less to follow built-in preprogrammed orders.

And finally, in man, we observe the fewest well-defined, imposed behavioral patterns; the brain seems to be the predominant factor regulating day-to-day activities.

The process of living requires performance of action. This, in turn, means constant decision-making ability for purposeful behaviors. Any decision depends upon intelligence (which is equivalent to a thought process.) Either a species can generate its own intelligence, or it comes supplied with a package of intelligence determined by somebody else. Depending upon the species, there are various percentage admixtures of these two sources of intelligence.

Behavioral DNA is certainly an enormously interesting field — one that evolution has not explained away as yet. Shall we consider that the first bees to populate this planet decided among themselves on a specific behavior which they taught forever-after to all the ensuing generations? How is it that since the original forebears of the bees decided on certain activities, newer generations were not "clever" enough to add new behavioral patterns to the list? So far as we know, a bee has always behaved in the same manner — which seems to be along the specific program encoded within its "behavioral DNA."

15
The Complexity
of Birth

A superficial description of the DNA/RNA mechanism was submitted in the previous chapters along with the principles of mathematical probability. Based on strictly mathematical terms, there is no probability that 11,000,000 or 1,000,000 or even 5,000 nucleotides could haphazardly arrange themselves in a meaningful sequence (meaningful as far as the ultimate result, or species, is concerned.) Consequently, evolution as described by the Darwinian school of thought, was not the road followed by unintelligent chemical molecules so as to generate 6,000,000 or more different species on this world.

There is another logical approach that can be developed to assess the probability as to whether evolution, as understood by Darwin, could have taken place through a slow incremental process, extended over millions of years. Let us evaluate the requirements necessary for birth.

The birth of a child is an extraordinarily complex, awe-inspiring event. Unfortunately, we take it for granted and fail to fully appreciate its significance. That the baby is able to come at all out of the mother's womb is in itself a near-miracle. There are dozens of intricate actions taking place within the body of the mother, either simultaneously or synchronized to follow in necessary progression. Of further significance is that all of these steps take place without conscious control by the mother. Except perhaps for a pressing action, a woman in labor need take no deliberate action — "nature" takes care of all necessary actions to deliver the baby. The internal organs "know" exactly what they will do, when they will be activated, for how long they will perform and when they will stop acting in cooperation with each other. Everything seems to be preprogrammed within the body of the woman. Under normal circumstances, with precise regularity and timing, the new life will begin automatically. The mother is incapable of directing or ordering her internal organs, muscles, nerves, or glands to act or not to act. Although our modern civilization provides the laboring mother with help and medical equipment, the female body was built and programmed to give birth with no outside help. Aborigines are living proof of this fact; they have no 20th century medical conveniences to help them give birth to their children. Animals don't even have any medical attention when giving birth, and yet millions of species continued to reproduce from time immemorial. From that point of view the laboring mother is but a semi-robot — performing exactly as programmed by a master program center (i.e. the DNA). Every move, every chemical action, every reaction is completely outside the mother's decision; she is only an interested bystander, waiting for "nature"to take its course and perform its synchronized activities.

Let us stop and think through, some of the simple and obvious necessities needed to make birth possible — which, in turn, means reproducing and perpetuating a particular species.

For this new life to have begun, it needed a womb, ovaries that created an egg at regular intervals, and male sperm. Naturally, such additional appurtenances as fallopian tubes, umbilical cord, cervix, and vagina are necessary to round out the mechanism necessary for a new life. This means, that each of these organs (in the broadest sense of the word) would have to be fully developed and functioning. Pregnancy is not possible if the ovaries are not functioning, or if the fallopian tubes did not exist, or the uterus had not been invented, or if the umbilical cord were not in place. If any of these were not fully developed and not properly tied to the others, inception and birth could not take place; that species could not reproduce but would die out. In fact it could not even have begun as a species — to start with! If we had to wait for "millions of years" for an ovary to "create itself" and finished being ready for action, we would still be faced with an impossible situation: no birth during those "millions of years." For example, an ovary without fully developed fallopian tubes or uterus or egg forming capacity, is worthless. It cannot create and sustain new life by itself. Thus all of these parts of the "birth-machine" had to develop in parallel, so as to reach perfection, at the same time.

If such a premise is not accepted, then it means that eons of years ago, when the whole system began, "nature" (or whatever other name we wish to employ) had a single-track mindedness to push towards the creation and growth of a series of organs and mechanisms, knowing that eventually, after "millions of years," it would reach perfection and perform the function of birth. At that stage — and only at that final stage — life could start to multiply — life as we know it today. But if the evolution of all these cooperatively acting organs continued its progress over a long period of time, then a plan, or a design, had to exist from the very moment "nature" decided to push towards ultimate creation of all these various organs and their appendages.

Naturally, when evolution was busy creating and developing the female reproductive organs, it was, again simultaneously, but independently, working hard at generating a different system in the male variety of the same species. Yet, the design had to be such, that it coordinated its functions and performances with those of the female variety.

There must have been a synchronized development between male and female reproductive organs so that they could function together. After all, what good is a fully developed ovary or uterus, if the male organs are not ready to function properly: That species would simply not reproduce.

How will we explain the fact that two different, yet interconnected beings were independently evolutionizing over "milllions of years?" How shall we rationalize that two different organs, coordinated with each other so as to complement each other's functions, were inexorably moving in unison toward perfection? In other words, besides developing in itself as a specific reproductive system (or better said: one half of a whole system), that particular species had to match the development taking place in the female counterpart and vice versa.

166

This means, that from the very beginning, a cooperative action must have taken place — one with a *design* in mind, working along two separate fronts to reach a combined goal, "million of years" hence.

Or are we expected to believe that the development of the male variety took place completely independently from the development of the female one? And eventually, by sheer luck, by the time they reached the point of functioning perfection, they simply fit with each other and lived happily forever after? How did they reproduce and survive up to the time of reaching functional perfection?

If such a separate development and eventual fit on a haphazard meeting of male and female is accepted, will we also accept the same scenario for approximately 6,000,000 or more species on this planet? Can we conceive the idea of 6,000,000 haphazard, independent evolutions of male and female of the same species? If the answer is negative, then we must conclude that male and female of every species must have developed in unison, synchronized with each other, on the basis of a specific plan for a specific goal.

The mammalian species rely completely on the mother's milk in order to feed the newborn infant. Would that not imply that the enormously complex system of milk production had to be ready and functioning the moment the first offspring was born? Can we conceive of a situation when our primate ancestors gave birth, but their lactic system was not ready to perform? If we go back hundreds of millions of years, we should — evolutionarily speaking — reach the day when the newborn life had no mother's milk on which to depend. Did these original specimens survive the first day eating plants or insects? If they did, then "nature" did not have to continue evolving a lactic system — since they were adapting to a different food intake rather than mother's milk. Or else, mother's milk was available as soon as the offspring was born. How were these organs and hormones perfected so as to be ready for the first birth? Shall we consider that the entire reproductive system evolved at exactly the same rate as the lactic system, so that the one was ready at the same time the other was functionally perfect?

Let us go one step further: For the female reproductive organs to function, every part of it has to be fed by blood. After all, it is blood that carries the nourishment to sustain the function of each part of the reproductive organs. Naturally blood has additional functions, but for the present let us follow through this part of its function.

Blood flows through a series of vessels, which end up in thousands upon thousands of capillaries — that means smaller tubes. They direct the circulation of the blood to every section of the reproductive organs. Blood has to be present, so that the reproductive organs can survive and perform. Without the circulation of blood, each and every organ would die and could not perform. Again it signifies coordinated action, as every organ or every part of an organ, has to be simultaneously supplied with blood. If the ovary reached the point of having obtained a proper tie-in with hundreds of capillaries, this in itself would be useless, unless all the other parts of the reproductive machine had simultaneously been tied in to additional thousands of separate capillaries. Each part of it has to be nourished so as to survive and perform. Thus, for life to exist, we can conceive only of a simultaneous connection of all the parts to thousands of capillaries.

These capillaries, in order to function, require certain minimum capacities:

1) They have to be constructed in such a way as to feed every part of the reproductive organs; they have to be of such material that will allow the flow of blood plasma and permit nutrients to permeate through its walls. For all the time that "evolution" had not yet created the proper raw material for the arteries, or capillaries, they could not perform as required.

2) These capillaries had to grow into a widespread network, encompassing every part of the reproductive organs, as well as every other part of that body. This network had to be properly tied in both to the blood vessels on one end, and to the organs, on the other end. A network that is ready to feed the reproductive organs but is as yet unattached to the stomach, or the lungs, or the liver, becomes useless. The entire system would fail. Any non-functioning or malfunctioning organ would interfere with the proper

activities of the entire body — the species would die.

3) For all these arteries, blood-vessels and capillaries to perform, they had to be supplied with blood. Evolution would have had to have created blood, that enormously complex fluid performing a great many activities within the body. Blood would have to be readily available at the moment the capillaries were formed and in place. After all, what good is blood if it does not have the necessary piping to move from place to place? Reversely, what good are all these capillaries if they are not filled with blood? Logically speaking, the two had to exist at the same moment.

4) Once blood was available and fully developed with its myriad components, it needed a pump to circulate this liquid. Without a pump, blood becomes useless. Thus the heart had to be functioning at the same time blood was available. It had to be properly tied in to the blood-vessel network, so as to circulate this important fluid to every part of the body.

Without the heart, the capillaries are useless, as they could not discharge their functions. This means that the entire reproductive system could not exist, if the heart and its distribution network of blood-vessels did not exist and perform properly. Furthermore, both systems — the reproductive and the circulatory — had to exist at the same time and function perfectly from the outset. Each system depends upon the other one. Reproduction cannot take place if the heart does not properly pump blood to support reproductive organs. A heart could not exist for long, if reproduction did not have the means to create a new heart for the ensuing generation of that species.

But a functioning heart is not enough to satisfactorily support the system. Bood that is continuously pumped has the additional function of removing waste and excess metabolic water.

To regulate the water content of the blood, we need a filter — the kidneys. A great many complicated functions take place in this organ. One aspect is certain — if there were no kidneys or if kidneys did not function properly, the blood circulation would suffer to the extent that life would stop. Consequently, all the reproductive organs, the heart, the blood distribution systems become useless, unless and until the kidneys are in functioning order.

The kidneys have to discharge unwanted waters. Luckily for the body, "evolution" seems to have foreseen this necessity long ago, and created ureters (urine tubes) which discharge into a storage tank: the bladder.

The blood carries blood cells, which have a remarkably short life span — up to about four months. These cells require a system which will destroy old blood corpuscles, create new ones, and store them on a continuous basis. Nature must have realized the need for such an organ, and astutely evolved — again "over milions of years" — the proper mechanism: the spleen. Without a well-functioning spleen, all other organs would stop performing.

Furthermore, blood has to carry fresh oxygen to all the organs named above. A special mechanism evolved (seemingly "all by itself") to inhale atmospheric air, pass it through millions of finely ground sponge-like particles, and then exhale it. A precise and wonderful instrument was created — the lungs. Once again, without a precisely functioning lung, the reproductive organs would not get their required oxygen through the bloodstream and as a result they could not continue to live and exist.

On the other hand, for all of these organs to survive, they certainly require nourishment in the form of myriad chemicals to be extracted from food. To perform such a delicate job still another mechanism was necessary — the stomach. However, such a machine tool requires intake pipes and discharge pipes. "Nature" seemingly understood the necessity of the problem and created a whole digestive system with a mouth, lined with teeth so as to chop down the food, and with yards-long intestinal tracts to discharge the refuse through the rectum.

Although we will skip over a plethora of actions taking place simultaneously in this digestive system, we may remind ourselves, that this part of the human machine could not perform properly were it not for the help of at least three more organs — the liver, the pancreas, and the bile. These are important for secretions furnished to the intestines and for metabolic functions of food already digested.

Naturally if any part of the digestive system stops functioning or is not performing as it should, it triggers a chain reaction of malfunctions, which in turn brings the whole human machine to a stop. Thus, during those "millions of years" of evolution, the digestive system had to evolve in parallel with all the other systems, within a coordinating plan to support and tie into the other systems.

As though all these complexities were not enough, we must realize that a new life cannot be born, if proper muscles were not in place and functioning at perfection. After all, it is the muscles that expel the new life out of the mother's womb. A number of these muscles are tied to and act upon the womb as well as on the other organs. The vast majority of them perform without scient knowledge of the adult being. They are automatically activated by nerves or nerve cells tied in to the various organs, and carrying the messages to and from the central computer room — the brain. For the nerve strings to reach the head, "nature" cleverly created (over a span of millions of years, no doubt), a cavity within the spinal bones, so as to stash away the spinal cords. We must recall, that without a properly functioning nervous system and its command post located in the brain, no actions could have taken place in any of the organs discussed up to now. As a result childbirth could not have taken place.

As for the brain — this most complex and semi-understood organ — can we imagine a functioning body without the head and the brain, without eyes, or ears, or nose? This means that these had to evolve at the same time as all the other organs, so as to complement and support their existence.

Although a great number of additional details are omitted, it is worthwhile to note that all these organs could not function if they were not supported in place by a rigid framework — the bony skeleton. Nor would they have been active, if not protected by layers of flesh and skin.

One does not have to be a paleontologist or a physician to realize the obvious: Every organ, and the thousands of subparticles that form them, are but only a part of a whole unit. They work in conjunction with each other, support each other, complement each other and could not possibly exist without the proper functioning of the others. It is not enough that all these organs and subsections be on hand — but each and every one of them must work *properly* and must be functionally tied in to all the others.

If that is so, then no single organ could have developed by itself within one or ten or fifty million years. As an independent unit, that organ would have been useless. It was only in conjunction with all the other parts, as part and parcel of an overall predetermined plan or program that an organ can function. This means that all the other organs had to develop simultaneously and be ready at the same moment so that the particular species could function and reproduce. We are faced with the need for an alternative to traditional evolutionary theory to derive the entire package.

Every species of the animal or vegetation world raises similar questions. Each displays enormously complex interconnected parts — parts that function only if all the other parts are perfect and working flawlessly.

Evolutionists have a tendency to counter the above arguments by pointing out that many organs were performing in other species millions of years ago. For example, they state, a lung was actually performing in "lungfishes" of the Devonian period. Likewise, muscles must have been in place in trilobites, some 600 million years ago.

These arguments are not proper evidence. They simply push the problem back in time, without solving it.

How did the lungfish generate a lung? Was it not necessary for its lung to be active at the very second its stomach, or heart, or digestive system was functioning? How did the trilobite generate muscles? Did they not have to be available the moment the heart or nerve system were functioning?

The example of the laboring women has been used since it is so close to our own experiences. However, the very same arguments could be advanced for any of the species on this world, no matter what position they hold within the so-called evolutionary tree of life. Each one of these species perform the basic functions: They need some sort of breathing apparatus, they feed themselves, they digest and extract sustenance from their food, discharge the refuse, and reproduce themselves. The same logic could be applied to the smallest insect or to the biggest whale. Even the single cell bacteria perform along the same blueprint of the cycle of life.

No matter how simple a construction a species displays, the conclusion is the same: no organ could survive and reproduce itself without all the rest of the system being functional at the very same moment. Each one of the few million species on earth could only survive and reproduce if — and only if — it was a complete and

172

perfectly efficient life-machine on the very first day of its existence, with both male and female, fully formed and performing their coordinated functions.

An old-age facetious statement poses a philosophical question: which came first, the chicken or the egg? This question is not as stupid as it appears at first sight. Scientifically speaking, it is thought-provoking and contains the core of the dilemma of evolution: are we going to consider that evolution, acting over "millions of years," was pushing for the creation and perfection of the chicken's egg? Or was it attempting to first perfect the whole chicken? If evolution was perfecting the egg first, then we had no chickens on this world during "millions of years," to lay additional eggs. If evolution was acting on the chicken first, and since it took just as many "millions of years, " (anyhow who counted them?) to reach the viable final product, does it mean that there were no eggs on this world during those eons of millenia? But if we had no eggs developed, how did succeeding generations of chickens follow each other? We reach a circular impasse in our incremental evolutionary thought process. For any species to exist and constantly reproduce, it must be an efficiently performing unit on day No. 1 — both the female *and* its male counterpart! This is the only objective, logical conclusion we can reach with the facts on hand.

The chicken together with its eggs, represent a single perfected mechanism, with thousands of sub-mechanisms, all performing at the same time. The rooster is the complementary mechanism, integrated within that particular system to form one complete entirety of a life machine. Each section is part and parcel of the same complex system. They can exist and procreate only if *all* aspects of the complete system are in perfect working order — and working at the same moment.

It is a matter of *all* or *nothing*.

16

Genetic Engineering

It is ironic that scientists are practicing the very same act which they stubbornly deny could possibly exist. They are presently *creating* forms of life in their laboratories and are confidently predicting the creation of further, more complex forms of life within a few decades. Nevertheless, they insist that *creation* may not be entertained as possible means of accounting for abrupt stops and starts in the fossil record.

Genetic engineering is another phrase for creative control of life. Whether we call it by one or the other phrase, is irrelevant. The process will be, and was, an act of creation. As time goes on, as our knowledge of the DNA/RNA complex increases, and as our laboratory techniques improve, we will literally *create* more and more types of life-machines — species. Admittedly there are still formidable technical hurdles to overcome and much additional knowledge will be needed before *we* become full-fledged *creators.* Yet, we can be almost certain that the day will come when scientists will be able to establish a completely new species, one that survives and reproduces. The key to such success will depend on our depth of understanding of the workings of the DNA/RNA system and our degree of sophistication in putting molecules to work for us. This, in itself, is a scary prospect as we will have the power to create all sorts of life-forms, including monsters or robots. Such a technical capacity can be put to work for honest and elevating purposes — or for the opposite. In the hands of unscrupulous politicians, this could spell the end of life on this planet — just as nuclear weapons now threaten our collective future.

At that stage of our progress, the procedures might be as follows:

1) The genetic engineer will decide on the end product he desires to create. He has to predetermine such physical characteristics as height, number of limbs, systems of organs, and performance capabilities. He will have to know ahead of time, the behavioral pattern desired. On the basis of these specifications, he can draw the first blueprints (just as in machine drawings.)

2) Once the wanted characteristics are established, he will determine which proteins, how many of them, and at what intervals, are necessary to generate the growth of such a species.

3) When the sequence of the protein production is determined, it becomes a matter of translating them into amino-acid components.

4) At that point, the genetic engineer can apply the proper genetic code and translate back these amino acids (in the sequence required) into codons, which in turn would be broken down into their component C-G-A-T chemical molecules.

5) By going backwards several additional steps, he will be able to determine the composition of the various RNA strands, their numbers, and their operative sequences. He can then determine and design all the other functions required within the cell.

6) Eventually he will be able to backtrack and determine the sequence of nucleotides needed within the DNA structure to have the desired effects.

7) The next step might be determination of the magnitude of energy each component cell must supply. Accordingly, the genetic engineer will calculate how many mitochondria belong in each cell, so as to generate the proper energy amounts required.

175

8) As in other engineering activity, a prototype will have to be "created" to be sure that it will grow and perform as designed. Observed flaws would be corrected by introducing necessary improvements in the DNA program and retesting them.

9) After an extended period of all types of tests, the genetic engineer will launch his newest model of species, to live and procreate forever, unless destroyed by either accident or design.

This hypothetical procedure may seem a Buck Rogers fantasy. It is not. It is much too real, and within the grasp of human technology in the not too distant future. There can hardly be doubt about it: new species will be *created* by future generations of humans.

A scrutiny of the DNA/RNA details indicates a precise relationship between program and end product — the given species. It means that specific sections of the DNA are coded in such a way as to translate into specific subparts of that species. Thus the growth of a straight nose might need, say, 3,000,000 specific nucleotides,[1] all in a very particular sequence, so as to order production of a given quantity of proteins for a given length of time at specified intervals of time. These, in turn, will perform the job of growing a straight nose. The growth of a hooked nose, however, might need 3,300,000 nucleotides. The growth of a pug nose might need 3,360,000 nucleotides, a portion of which might be in the same sequence as the previous example. The growth of a flat nose could need 2,800,000 nucleotides, or the growth of a gorilla type nose might need 4,500,000 nucleotides.

---

[1]It should be noted that the numbers cited in this chapter are completely theoretical and are not based on statistical facts. They have been chosen at random so as to give a general feeling of the type of magnitude of figures we are facing. Science does not know yet how many million nucleotides, nor which exact ones, translate into the production of a nose. For the argument being presented here, it is immaterial whether future research proves that a nose is equivalent to 3,000,000 or 10,000,000 or any other large number of nucleotides.

176

Product	Numbers of Nucleotides	Sequence of Codons		Notes
Straight nose	3,000,000	AACTAG … ATA		Option 1 for species #37459
Straight nose	3,105,340	AACGAC … GGA		Option 1 for species #38440
Straight nose	3,099,811	AACTTT … CTA		Option 2 for species #38441
Hooked nose	3,300,000	AACCAC … ATA		Option 9 for species #37459
Hooked nose	3,404,000	AACGAC … AAA		Option 9 for species #38440
Thin lower lip	2,215,633	GAGTTA … TGA		Option 14 for species #37459
Thick lower lip	2,441,777	GAGGAA … ATA		Option 15 for species #37459
Thick lower lip	2,454,449	GAGCAG … CTA		Option 15 for species #38440
Two eyes	8,775,400	TTTACT … AGA		Option 20 for species #37459
Three eyes	8,994,700	TTTACC … AGA		Option 21 for species #37459
Four eyes	9,347,750	TTTACC … TGA		Option 22 for species #37459
Infrared sight	1,440,000	TTTATA … TGA		Option 36 for species #38440
U.V. sight	1,230,550	TTTGAT … CGA		Option 37 for species #38440
Six legs	7,330,000	GGACTT … TAA		Option 1 for species #38945

Table 22: HYPOTHETICAL DNA REQUIREMENTS
FOR CREATION OF SPECIES.

(The reader is again reminded that all the information contained in this table is hypothetical and does not refer to any experimental data. These figures are used only as examples of possible situations.)

In due time, scientists will be able to break down the exact meaning of the position of each nucleotide and relate its performance to the overall program in which they are found. This job has already begun on very small bacteria. In short RNA sequences, microbiologists know exactly the orders extended for example, by nucleotides between numbers 1008 and 1200, between 1201 and 1444, between 1445 and 1667. As research capabilities improve and as our analysis of the complicated programs advances, genetic engineers will be able to set up an equivalence catalogue for future reference purposes. Such a bank of information will give them precise details for each desired effect they wish to achieve. They might end up with specifications not unlike the hypothetical entries in table 22.

Such a catalogue of specification would tell the genetic engineer, at a glance, which sequence to use so as to obtain newer varieties of men, or gorillas, or horses or "baboozes" — a completely new species.

It would be similar to what today's automotive engineers do in specifying the requirements of different car models. They give us a number of options when ordering a new car. We have the option to include a 4-speed transmission or a 3-speed one, with stick shift, or columnar shift, with or without air conditioning, or with a four cylinder or six cylinder engine. However, there are other components that exist but would not fit into the general design of that particular car. For example, a 10-speed transmission would not work properly with a four cylinder engine of a sub-compact car.

Genetic engineering will probably follow the same general procedures, except that their problems would be immensely magnified, involving complex molecular biology and interactions that have to be taken into consideration when building a new species.

Or else, instead of building up a program from scratch, they could start with existing programs. They could cut a specific section from the DNA of a serpent and splice it to a section from the DNA of a leopard; they would obtain a new species: a serpent-headed leopard. The ancient Egyptians depicted for us such a serpent-headed leopard, which was referred to as the God SETCHA. The Egyptians (and other ancient civilizations) had a whole collection of these types of "gods": half-human, half-animal. Some of them were combinations of different animals. These mythical species were shown clearly on paintings in

178

various graves and temples. The orthodox explanation of our archaeologists was: the ancient Egyptians were symbolically uniting the attributes of one type of animal with those of another. Perhaps so — and perhaps not! Would such a combination survive on a continuous basis? This question cannot be answered as yet — it would depend on a great many factors — factors that are, at the present time, beyond our capacities to evaluate and determine.

This idea of combining known forms of present animals should not be considered outrageous science-fiction dreams. It is being applied in England, where they have, for example, succeeded in creating a peculiar-looking new species: a goat-sheep combination, called the *chimera*. It has the head of a goat, the horns of a sheep, the lower part of the body is covered with sheep's wool, while its back and sides grow goat's hair. The animal is alive and performing as a viable species — a new form of life — a new program.

A great many additional techniques are being developed in our laboratories. Thoughts that were laughable 20 years ago, are now appearing on the draftboard of genetic engineers. It all boils down to simple principles: science has discovered the mechanical key to life, the DNA/RNA. We are learning about the meaning of each nucleotide and its translation within the overall program in which it is present. When we reach the point of mastering the exact translation of every sequence of nucleotides, we will be able to "create" whatever life forms our imagination prescribes.

Can we still continue to deny that life on Earth may have been the result of intelligent creation?

If we, with our limited scientific knowledge are able to and will be able to "create" life forms, why is it impossible to consider that a superior intellect or civilization did, in fact, follow the same procedures billions of years ago and *created* life on Earth?

On the basis of the factual scientific evidence we have today, and on the basis of mathematical probability concepts, we can conclude that:

1) The evolutionary process, as described by the Darwinian evolutionists, could not have been the path leading to the

179

6,000,000 or more species now believed to live on this planet.

2) Species are "created" forms of life, achieved by a superintelligence through a process of purposefully producing and arranging the awe-inspiring DNA/RNA system.

3) Genetic engineering means the ability to *create* life-forms.

17
Evolution

Thousands of books have been written in support of evolution. In many the author tries to prove evolution graphically. The average book explaining evolution submits beautifully drawn pictures showing comparative features. We are shown all sorts of serial drawings, such as the

— skulls of various hominids
— forelimbs of different vertebrates
— various horse types through the ages
— shapes of hand in vertebrates
— different mandibles
— various beaks in birds

All of these studies imply that from the similarities shown among the samples, we should infer a straight line descent (as ascent) from one stage to the next. That there are similarities between the specimens illustrated in the lineup is obvious. But to conclude, as a logical deduction, that each of the stages rearranged itself to become the next stage, is unwarranted. We have no factual basis to conclude that just because two things look alike that one descended from the other. In terms of strict scientific evaluations, we have no right to jump to conclusions of this sort, simply because they suit our imaginary concepts. There is a wide chasm between observable fact and conclusions drawn from our imagination. The skulls of various hominids will illustrate the point (Fig. 23).

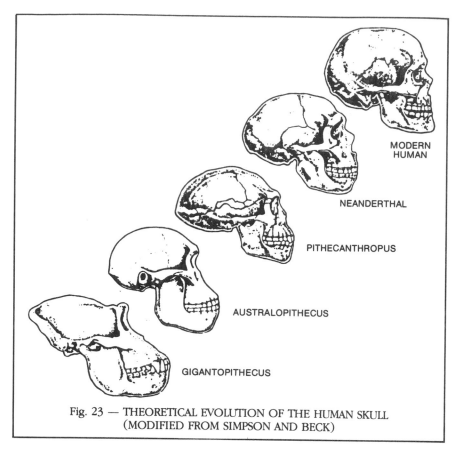

Fig. 23 — THEORETICAL EVOLUTION OF THE HUMAN SKULL
(MODIFIED FROM SIMPSON AND BECK)

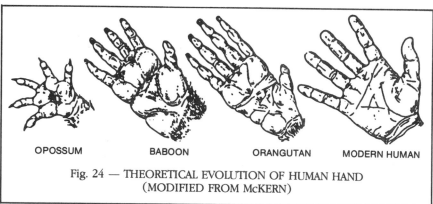

Fig. 24 — THEORETICAL EVOLUTION OF HUMAN HAND
(MODIFIED FROM McKERN)

We start with the skull of a species called gigantopithecus of a few million years ago, and proceed through various fossil finds, until we end up with modern *Homo sapiens.* We certainly observe a resemblance: jaws, teeth, eye sockets, nose sockets, and cranial covers.

What real evidence do we have that more developed species (at least in our evaluation) are the descendants of previous less developed species? None. How many millions of nucleotides must be added or rearranged to jump from one stage of development to the next? Millions! What is the probability factor that these millions of molecules realigned themselves haphazardly? Zero.

The fact that apes and humans have certain resembling features is obvious. Translated into the DNA/RNA language, it means that a certain portion of their DNA sequence is similar, or even the same. Yet the balance is different. If we recall that a mammal has about 3 billion nucleotides, a mere 20 percent difference would result in 600,000,000 different bases — quite enough to guarantee a zero probability factor! Even if there is only 1 percent difference between the DNA nucleotides of an ape and a human, it would still translate into 30,000,000 bases — which will mean zero probability of random occurrence.

In Fig. 23 we observe a uniform usage of similar mechanisms to create the same effect. The shapes, the sizes, etc. are quite different. If we transpose these into the DNA/RNA language of nucleotides, we realize that there is a world of difference between these skulls, as each one would have to be described by a completely different sequence in their respective DNA. We understood that the slightest change in morphology meant a tremendous alteration of the master program. We also concluded that every alteration of as few as 84 nucleotides has no probability of occurring on a haphazard basis through independent mutations. Consequently the cranial depictions shown in Fig. 23 could not be results of random mutations.

The best alternative explanation would be a specific creation of each one of these samples of hominid-type heads by a superintelligence. It is more plausible to consider that a genetic engineer who knew how to handle DNA could create separate programs for separate designs than to expect 50 million molecules to line up haphazardly in a meaningful program.

183

In another sequence (Fig. 24), we are shown illustrations of hands. Again, we are offered the explanation that the human hand is generated through the process of evolution when starting with a baboon or an orangutan (or an unknown common ancestor whose presence we were never able to locate.) Again the same question can be asked: What real evidence is there that the one hand reflects direct descent from the previous shape? None.

We can only establish the fact that there is a resemblance between these hands: they all have five fingers and a palm. They all seem to be the most efficient arrangement to fit the requirements of the particular species. It is just as logical to infer that they were specific designs for specific applications. In fact, we are on far more solid ground because now we realize that these models of hands are separated from each other by hundreds of thousands of nucleotides (if not millions.) Let us remember, again, that any sequence above 84 nucleotides has no probability whatever to be created via random mutations and still end up into a meaningful program. They have to be specific creations with predetermined DNA programs.

In a sense, evolution did exist, but it is a different concept than the one imagined by Darwin. It is the evolution of thought of a design engineer. With each new blueprint, he matures to the extent of evolving new thoughts which translate into more complex forms of life-machines. He introduces new systems of substructures, new linkages, to fit new requirements and new performances — still using the same general building blocks. We agree that there is a resemblance between a monkey and a human; for that matter, there is also resemblance between Ford and Buick cars. In each case we have entities that are constructed from similar components, but their rearrangements are different. This does not allow us to jump to the conclusion that a Buick is a directly evolved product from a Ford car. They can be (and certainly are) started from scratch and built up with the same general mechanisms known to both the Ford and Buick engineers. By the same token a monkey and a human can reflect two separate blueprints. The distinctions we observe are not necessarily differences generated by self-evolving forces of a given life-machine. They are differences that start as an idea in the designer's mind, as a new species, before he puts them down on paper as blueprint for a new DNA program

From that point of view, evolution exists — in the mind of the genetic engineer.

18
The Origin of Life

This subject has long preoccupied scientists, who felt challenged to pinpoint the exact method that must have been applied 3 or 4 billion years ago when the first "life" was formed. These researchers usually start with the premise that a rocky world came into being some 4.5 billion years ago. (The method by which the world was created is uncertain but it is irrelevant to the present argument). It is conceded that no oxygen was present, nor did Earth have an ozone layer to protect it from the sun's ultraviolet light. After all, ozone is a form of oxygen. A number of chemicals seemed to have been present, including hydrogen, nitrogen and carbon.

Based on this assumption, Darwin expressed himself as follows in a letter he wrote: *"But if we could conceive in some warm little pond, with all sorts of ammonia and phosphoric salts, light, heat, electricity, etc., present that a protein compound was chemically formed ready to undergo still more complex changes. . ."* This general thought then captured the imagination of evolutionists who spent time, effort, and talent to duplicate the primordial conditions that must have prevailed when "life" was presumed to have begun.

Since we know that life requires protein, and since proteins are made from amino acids, scientists experimented with the view of generating amino acids. Some placed ammonia, methane, water and hydrogen in a container and passed an electric charge through the mixture for a number of days. Others used ultraviolet radiation, or heat, or electric discharges. In many cases amino acids were thus actually synthesized, and some experimenters were able to create certain sugars (i.e. ribose), using similar procedures.

At that point, many scientists were very happy and proud that they had finally discovered the process to recreate the essential building blocks of life — which, in turn, implied that they had strengthened the theory of instantaneous beginnings of "life" on Earth — at least so they said. Darwin's theory was thus supposed to be reinforced!

What did these experiments prove? They simply proved that if one combines hydrogen, nitrogen, oxygen, and carbon under proper conditions, one will obtain certain organic chemicals that contain these elements. After all, we all know that a great many different organic compounds are merely rearrangements of these four chemical atoms.

Consequently these results simply indicated that amino acids can be synthesized under certain conditions. That is wonderful — but how does that relate to the existence of "life?" There is a world of difference between a building block and a finished building. Building blocks do not rearrange themselves — all by themselves — to form a 50-floor building. *Somebody* has to put them there, and *somebody* has to follow purposeful blueprints so as to generate a specific building. A heap of blocks will remain a heap of blocks; they have no intelligence, no logic, no ambition, no fervor, no sophistication, no organizational capacities to carry out a predetermined purpose.

Likewise, amino acids have no purposefulness of their own. They cannot decide by themselves the type of DNA intricacies that should be created, which, combined with RNA, together with the half-understood actions of ribosomes, all of which, being based on a standard language code, will finally result in additional protein chains. At that moment they would wait for further instructions from RNA strands so as to line up additional protein chains! Are we not expecting too much from a deaf, dumb, and blind molecule of amino acid?

Further, amino acids are one of the *end products* of a chain of awe-inspiring events controlled by DNA and its helpers. The prime mover, the order giver, is the DNA structure — that is where the entire purposeful action starts. Consequently, the beginning of "life" has to be determined by the moment in time when the entire DNA/RNA system became functional. Only then, when this complex system performs, can we consider that "life" started.

The evolutionist model leads to a vicious circle. How did the DNA system, with all its complexities, come to be, in the first place? For so long as the component parts were not cooperating with one another within a larger plan, there was no "life." Shall we accept the premise that lonely atoms got together to dream up, design, and execute such an incredible scheme as the DNA/RNA? Or shall we seriously consider that separate molecular "evolution" took place, nucleotide by nucleotide?

When and how did the cell create and incorporate ribosomes, endoplasmic reticula and the Golgi apparatus? Were these also the end result of creeping evolution, where the necessity was felt to induce the molecules in the cell to create some sort of an organelle that would perform the functions required? Can a cell exist and function — and thus be alive — without a ribosome? Obviously a cell can function as a cell, only if it has all the necessary component parts in place, ready to cooperate with each other towards the goal of maintaining the system. Chemical molecules, left to their own devices, cannot invent complex mechanisms and then go out, create and apply them within a localized area — which in turn would produce a functioning cell. Repetitive though it might sound, each one of the organelles within the cell are masterpieces of inventions necessary for the execution of very specific and essential functions within the cell. Such purposefulness can only be the mark of intelligence — it simply cannot be the result of haphazard events.

According to Darwin, with enough time (i.e., millions of years) one species will lead to another species through chance mutations and natural selection. This would be equivalent to generations of monkeys pounding on a typewriter, pressing down the letters of the keyboard. What are the chances that they would type — sequentially and by sheer luck — all the proper letters which, when read from left to right, represent the entire play of Hamlet? No matter how many millions of years this exercise continues, the probabilities for the proper sequence of words to appear on the monkey's paper is zero. Darwin's concept that given enough time, random events will eventually end up one day as something meaningful, simply does not stand. Mathematical probability concepts give us a big NO for an answer.

No matter how we evaluate this problem, we reach the same logical conclusion:

a) "Life" as we know it on Earth, started only when the DNA/RNA system was fully operative in the cell.

b) The enormous complexity built into that system indicates directed purposefulness, which in turn, is an expression of superior intelligence. Consequently "Intelligence" came first — DNA/RNA came after.

Naturally these conclusions do not answer all our questions — for we can continue to ask: where did the superior intellect or civilization come from? We don't know — possibly from outer space. How did it originate in outer space? We don't know.

Let us solve one problem at a time. Let us agree at least to the above conclusions, before we direct our search to outer space. For the present we can only conclude that "life" is not an organism that sprouted haphazardly on this earth three to four billion years ago. It required superintelligence to precede it.

19
Intellectual Schizophrenia

The dilemma of the modern evolution scientist has become schizophrenic. On the one side he is caught up in the herd-like onrush of his discipline that channels his thinking into a rut. On the other side (and provided he is an inquisitive scientist) he is shaken by his thoughts that generate heretical questions — questions whose likely answers frighten him, since they undermine the well-rehearsed and oft-repeated teachings of his discipline.

On the one hand, he has the cozy feeling of "safety in numbers" — and on the other hand, the loneliness, though dangerous, of individuality. Which shall it be?

The most fruitful progress is often initiated by the loner who cherishes intellectual individuality and is willing to disagree with his peers and take an unpopular stand dictated by his research — even if the scientific community has reached an opposite consensus on what constitutes "truth."

Science can judge "truth" only on the basis of its knowledge. But since we know that our knowledge is limited, then obviously our "truths" are limited too. We know of many top scientists who, at the zenith of their reputation, were certain of their "truths" and ridiculed any suggestion that they be reconsidered. And yet, the inexorable advance of science proved them wrong. This, in itself, is to the everlasting credit of science — which is not afraid, in the long run, to change completely its outlook and position. Good science provides for a continuing search for new ground and review of old.

In his book, *The Immense Journey,* Dr. Loren Eiseley exhibits thoughts and feelings on this subject that warrant review.

Eiseley (1907-1977) is acknowledged to have been one of the more learned anthropologists of the past 50 years. He was head of the Department of Sociology and Anthropology at Oberlin College in Ohio, became the head of the Department of Anthropology at the University of Pennsylvania in 1947, and lectured in various universities such as Harvard and Columbia. He then became curator of Early Man at the University Museum, University of Pennsylvania. Dr. Eiseley wrote a number of books, including *The Immense Journey, The Unexpected Universe, Darwin's Century.* Although he was basically a Darwinian evolutionist, his inquisitiveness and logical thinking led him to ask pertinent questions which he could not answer by means of evolutionist theories. This does not mean that he rejected evolution during his lifetime, but it is significant that he started to realize that there was no satisfactory answer that could be obtained by following the path of evolution. His intellectual independence was not yet so pronounced as to reject Darwinian theory as being an impractical rationalization, at best. However, he was moving in the right direction by asking very discomforting questions. His general approach was that of an anthropologist faced with skeletal remnants found in various archaeological digs trying to make sense of the different human skulls in front of him. Yet the interrelationship did not make sense.

A surprising aspect (at least to the evolutionists), is the fact that modern humans have a much larger brain than their various "forebears." There is a big jump between the previous plateau and that of the human skull. In-between steps seem to nave been completely skipped as we jump from one stage to the other — for no explainable reason. Eiseley had the following to say in his book *The Immense Journey:*[1]

"... As we have already indicated, most of our collection of human fossils is derived from the last half of the Pleistocene, even by the old chronology. In this new arrangement the bulk of

[1] From *The Immense Journey,* by Loren Eiseley, Copyright ©1957 by Loren Eiseley. Reprinted by permission of Random House Inc.

191

this material is found to be less than two hundred thousand years old. Man, in Dr. Emiliani's own words, had "the apparent ability to evolve rapidly." This is almost an understatement. The new chronology would appear to suggest a spectacular, even more explosive development than I have previously suggested.

"... an essentially modern brain at so early a date can only suggest, in the light of Emiliani's new datings, that the rise of man from a brain level represented in earliest preglacial times by the South African man-apes took place with extreme rapidity.

"If man approximating ourselves is truly much older than we imagine, it is conceivable that his physical remains might for long escape us. It seems unlikely, however, that a large-brained form, if widely diffused, would have left so little evidence of his activities. It would appear, then, that within the very brief period between about five hundred thousand to one hundred fifty thousand years ago, man acquired the essential features of a modern brain. Admittedly the outlines of this process are dim, but all the evidence at our command points to this process as being surprisingly rapid.

"Such rapidity suggests other modes of selection and evolution than those implied in the nineteenth-century literature with its emphasis on intergroup "struggle" which, in turn, would have demanded large populations. We must make plain here, however, that to reject the older Darwinian arguments is not necessarily to reject the principle of natural selection. We may be simply dealing with a situation in which both Darwin and Wallace failed, in different ways, to see what selective forces might be at work in man.

"How did this brain first come? How fast did it come? Probing among rocks and battered skulls, scientists find that the answers are few. There are many living members of the primate order — that order which includes man — who live in groups, but show no signs of becoming men. Their brains bear a family resemblance to our own, but they are not the brains of men.

"If one attempts to read the complexities of the story, one is not surprised that man is alone on the planet. Rather, one is amazed and humbled that man was achieved at all. For four things had to happen, and if they had not happened simultaneously, or at least kept pace with each other, the bones of man would lie abortive and forgotten in the sandstones of the past:

1) His brain had almost to treble in size.

2) This had to be effected, not in the womb, but rapidly, after birth.

3) Childhood had to be lengthened to allow this brain, divested of most of its precise instinctive responses, to receive, store, and learn to utilize what it received from others.

4) The family bonds had to survive seasonal mating and become permanent, if this odd new creature was to be prepared for his adult role.

"Each one of these major points demanded a multitude of minor biological adjustments, yet all of this — change of growth rate, lengthened age, increased blood supply to the head, moved apparently with rapidity. It is a dizzying spectacle with which we have nothing to compare. The event is complex, it is many-sided, and what touched it off is hidden under the leaf mold of forgotten centuries.

"Somewhere in the glacial mists that shroud the past, Nature found a way of speeding the proliferation of brain cells and did it by the ruthless elimination of everything not needed to that end. We lost our hairy covering, our jaws and teeth were reduced in size, our sex life was postponed, our infancy became among the most helpless of any of the animals because everything had to wait upon the development of that fast-growing mushroom which had sprung up in our heads."

These questions, without answers, coming from a Darwinian anthropologist, are significant and touch the core of the problem. The fact that they were asked at all, is gratifying as it shows that in the recesses of his intellect, the impossibility of evolution was starting to creep up.

Over the past century we dutifully repeated that man is the next stage after apes. The proof was lacking. Then we changed the approach and said that both man and the ape had a common ancestor, shrouded in the darkness of the forgotten past. Who and where was that common ancestor? We did not know. Again, there was little fossil evidence beyond what our imagination supposed was the theoretical possibility of a common ancestor. Why? Because it was so simple an explanation for an extraordinarily difficult problem, and fitted beautifully with the generalities invented by the theory of evolution. It satisfied our communal ego of apparent "knowledge" — when, in fact, it was ignorance.

The fact remains, as Eiseley pointed out, that our brain size all of a sudden jumped threefold. How that happened, we simply do not know. Where were the stages through which it moved in order to get there? What major biological adjustments had to take place in order to move into this new dimension? After each change, how was the DNA rearranged in order to transmit the new form or organ to the next generation? That too is unknown. The only thing we know for sure is, that there are certain resemblances between an ape and ourselves. Yet, that cannot be considered as sufficient, solid scientific proof — not even partial — that we are descendant from the ape or from a common ancestor. We are only aware that, all of a sudden man was on this planet with a ready-built, developed brain.

The interesting aspect about our brain is the fact that we know so very little about it despite all the advances in biological research during the past hundred years. We still do not understand why we possess such a large brain, especially as the functions of much of it are a mystery.

Our brain apparently functions much like a computer. It receives input, has a storage capacity, and has a recall mechanism. But it also displays intelligence — that means, a reasoning and decision-making capacity. Somewhere within that cranial grey matter, there seems to exist a deductive capacity to interconnect bits of input information, and display the result — a process we call "thought." It is a most complex process and one is not certain that the various medical sciences understand the step-by-step processes that lead to "thought." We may logically — albeit only theoretically — conclude that our human computer must have a much larger potential, a larger built-in capacity, than the one presently used.

194

Our various experiences in the study of nature indicate a fundamental fact — one of least wastefulness. In nature every organ seems to be found in its most efficient state. We do not seem to have superfluous organs that perform unneeded functions. Everything is accounted for and in the most efficient state. Yet when it comes to the brain of man, we seem to have a wastage: an additional part of an organ for which there seems no usage — at least, as determined by our present stage of knowledge. This is contrary to the universal law we have encountered in all our studies of the various life forms. It is most surprising that we should meet in nature so contradictory a situation.

Whenever specific situations do not fit the rule, the chances are that we did not quite understand the occurrence and, thus, our logical deduction is probably at fault. We are faced with subjective error, not objective. In the case of the brain, we should bow to nature's inexorable perfection in its end products, and consider that this "excess" is not a matter of chance. Instead, it is pre-determined, just as all our other organs proved to be efficiently intergrated into the human body.

Unfortunately, evolutionists were quick to jump at misunderstood information and used them to bolster their Darwinian theories. An outstanding example is the thymus gland, located close to the point where the chest and throat meet. This gland seemed peculiar since it was always found in a shriveled state, inactive, or at best almost non-functioning.

Evolutionists had a field day; they pointed out that this gland constituted the best proof for the existence and functioning of evolution. According to them the thymus was a stunted leftover from very old times, when it might have had some sort of ill-defined function. As our ancestors of millions of years ago "evolved," this appendage lost its meaning and had no value for the more modern body. This was supposed to be evolution in action, with the proof in front of our very noses. How wrong they were!

The truth of the matter was that we had no knowledge about the functions of the thymus gland. It was true that it hardly functioned in grownups, that it was stunted, and seemingly a useless appendage in an otherwise perfectly efficient machine.

However, medical research ultimately realized that the thymus gland has a function — an extemely important one. It was not the left-over from some hazy evolutionary process that took place over "millions of years ago." Newborn babies have a large thymus gland, in perfect functioning order. As the child grows, the gland degenerates, becoming almost non-existent in the fully grown adult. But this gland plays an important role in the growth of the human body.

The thymus gland produces large doses of antibodies for the protection of the newly born baby, so as to protect it against the various germs present in its new surroundings. We must realize that the child who spent nine months in the mother's womb was protected by her immune system. All of a sudden the baby leaves that sterile ambiance and is thrust into a new world. teeming with germs and bacteria. It needs a constant, reliable flow of antibodies to defend itself and survive. The thymus gland constitutes that defense mechanism until the body can adjust and the other organs and glands can develop and take over the job of biochemical protection. When the other body mechanisms grow enough to shoulder the responsibility of protecting the body against germs, the thymus gland starts to shrink and phases itself out of existence. This is a long way from the reasons submitted by evolutionists! It did not prove the theory of evolution — it simply underscored our ignorance of our state of ignorance.

For so many years we did not know what the thymus gland was and how it performed. Rather than acknowledge that we had an unsolved problem on our hands and keep searching, evolutionists jumped to conclusions — they invented standard answers picked up from a hazy past, based on non-existing "facts." They insisted that a specific function did exist millions of years before, (which ones, they did not know), a fact that could no longer be ascertained since all the in-between evolutionary stages had died out — soft tissues did not leave any fossilized remnants! Yet, the same argument did not make sense even when applied to bony appendages. For example, we are told that humans, at a certain point of the evolutionary process, have lost their tails — since our ancestors (the simians or a non-existent common ancestor) used to have a tail. How did we lose our tail? In one complete step or as a gradual shrinking appendage? The theory of evolution cannot give us a clear-cut answer, except to imply that the coccyx, at the end of our spine, is our vestigial tail. We never found a human skeleton that had a one-half or a one-quarter tail. It was a clean-cut jump from a full-tail to a no-tail stage. Such a jump infers an incredibly huge change within the morphological system of that animal.

Whenever we ask about the existence of intermediate steps in evolutionary forms, we are told that they are not available because the old species had died out in the meantime. We are given as evidence the words "survival of the fittest," or "natural selection" to account for what was going on in the meantime. Actually, this is not evidence but a self-serving statement. That a stronger animal will survive is obvious and quite natural — but that still does not change the anatomical or physiological structure of those that are left. There could be certain slight hereditary tendencies that might or might not be accentuated. However, it is a huge leap in logical thinking to consider that this "survival of the fittest" idea can explain the lack of intermediate stages. It only helps to paint a screen and lose it in the depth of the haziness of "millions of years."

This reminds one of an old magazine cartoon. An ultra modern art gallery had a showing of modern paintings. On one wall they displayed a beautiful frame with a completely white canvas, conspicuously lit, bearing the title "THE GRAZING HORSE." It carried a price tag of $10,000. A potential patron is seen viewing the white canvas with a puzzled and thoughtful look. The floor manager approaches and dutifully asks whether he could help the customer out. The baffled patron explains that he does not understand the title and could not connect it to the utterly white canvas. The floor manager, in an authoritative and condescending manner explains that the white canvas represented a grazing horse.

"But where is the horse?" naively asks the patron.

"The horse has left since it has finished feeding on the grass."

"But, then, where is the grass?" asks the patron.

"Well," replies the manager, "the horse ate all the grass and that is why there is no grass left on the picture."

We, too, are left with such a baffled quandary when trying to

197

understand the in-between steps of the evolutionary ladder that do not seem to exist at all, because they all died out — as we are told.

Darwin's theory is incapable of showing in-between stages or any missing links. We are asked to simply accept such an existence on "faith."

Scientists rejected statements of the Old Testament precisely because of this matter of "faith." Yet, in the same breath, they substituted their own tenets — also to be accepted on "faith." In other words, we were asked to have "faith" in the statements made by a person 125 years ago, but not in those made by someone about 3,250 years ago. *If* we have to accept the evolutionary theory on "faith," why is it any different from accepting the statements of the Old Testament on "faith?" Reliance on "faith" is neither better nor worse in either case.

A further quotation from Eiseley's book, *The Immense Journey*, will typify the approach and intellectual schizophrenia of a modern scientist who is almost completely convinced about Darwin's theory of evolution. It shows a faithfulness to the principles and yet, at times, serious questions are raised in his mind which should have shaken the foundations of his faith in that theory. Still, Eiseley did not seem to have had the mental capacity to breakthrough out of the rut and discard the theory of evolution.

> "It was only with the rise of modern biology and the discovery that the trail of life led backward toward infinitesimal beginnings in primordial sloughs, that men began the serious dissection and analysis of the cell. Darwin, in one of his less guarded moments, had spoken hopefully of the possibility that life had emerged from inorganic matter in some "warm little pond." From that day to this biologists have poured, analyzed, minced, and shredded recalcitrant protoplasm in a fruitless attempt to create life from nonliving matter. It seemed inevitable, if we could trace life down through simpler stages, that we must finally arrive at the point where, under the proper chemical conditions, the mysterious borderline that bounds the inanimate must be crossed. It seemed clear that life was a material manifestation. Somewhere, somehow, sometime, in the mysterious chemistry of carbon, the long march toward the

talking animal had begun.

A hundred years ago men spoke optimistically about solving the secret, or at the very least they thought the next generation would be in a position to do so. Periodically there were claims that the emergence of life from matter had been observed, but in every case the observer proved to be self-deluded. It became obvious that the secret of life was not to be had by a little casual experimentation, and that life in today's terms appeared to arise only through the medium of pre-existing life. Yet, if science was not to be embarrassed by some kind of mind-matter dualism and a complete and irrational break between life and the world of inorganic matter, the emergence of life had, in some way, to be accounted for.

Nevertheless, as the years passed, the secret remained locked in its living jelly, in spite of larger microscopes and more formidable means of dissection. As a matter of fact the mystery was heightened because all this intensified effort revealed that even the supposedly simple amoeba was a complex, self-operating chemical factory. The notion that it was a simple blob, the discovery of whose chemical composition would enable us instantly to set the life process in operation, turned out to be, at best, a monstrous caricature of the truth.

With the failure of these many efforts science was left in the somewhat embarrassing position of having to postulate theories of living origins which it could not demonstrate. After having chided the theologian for his reliance on myth and miracle, science found itself in the unenviable position of having to create a mythology of its own: namely, the assumption that what after long effort, could not be proved to take place today had, in truth, taken place in the primeval past.

My use of the term *mythology* is perhaps a little harsh. One does occasionally observe, however, a tendency for the beginning zoological textbook to take the unwary reader by a hop, skip, and jump from the little steaming pond or the beneficent chemical crucible of the sea, into the lower world of life with such sureness and rapidity that it is easy to assume that there is no mystery about this matter at all, or, if there is, that it is a very little one.

This attitude has indeed been sharply criticized by the distinguished British biologist Woodger, who remarked some years ago: "Unstable organic compounds and cholorophyll corpuscles do not persist or come into existence in nature on their own account at the present day, and consequently it is necessary to postulate that conditions were once such that this did happen although and in spite of the fact that our knowledge of nature does not give us any warrant for making such a supposition... It is simple dogmatism — asserting that what you want to believe did in fact happen."

Yet, unless we are to turn to supernatural explanations or reinvoke a dualism which is scientifically dubious, we are forced inevitably toward only two possible explanations of life upon earth. One of these, although not entirely disproved, is most certainly out of fashion and surrounded with greater obstacles to its acceptance than at the time it was formulated. I refer, of course, to the suggestion of Lord Kelvin and Svante Arrhenius that life did not arise on this planet, but was wafted here through the depths of space. Microscopic spores, it was contended, have great resistance to extremes of cold and might have come into our atmosphere with meteoric dust, or have been driven across the earth's orbit by light pressure. In this view, once the seed was "planted" in soil congenial to its development, it then proceeded to elaborate, evolve, and adjust until the higher organisms had emerged.

This theory had a certain attraction as a way out of an embarrassing dilemma, but it suffers from the defect of explaining nothing, even if it should prove true. It does not elucidate the nature of life. It simply removes the inconvenient problem of origins to far-off spaces or worlds into which we will never penetrate. Since life makes use of the chemical compounds of this earth, it would seem better to proceed, until incontrovertible evidence to the contrary is obtained, on the assumption that life has actually arisen upon this planet. The now widely accepted view that the entire universe in its present state is limited in time, and the apparently lethal nature of unscreened solar radiation are both obstacles which greatly lessen the likelihood that life has come to us across the infinite wastes of space. Once more, therefore, we are forced to examine our remaining notion that life is not coterminous with matter, but has

200

arisen from it.

If the single-celled protozoans that riot in roadside pools are not the simplest forms of life, if, as we know today, these creatures are already highly adapted and really complex, though minute beings, then where are we to turn in the search for something simple enough to suggest the greatest missing link of all — the link between living and dead matter? It is this problem that keeps me wandering fruitlessly in pastures and weed thickets even though I know this is an old-fashioned naturalist's approach, and the busy men in laboratories have little patience with my scufflings of autumn leaves, or attempts to question beetles in decaying bark. Besides, many of these men are now fascinated by the crystalline viruses and have turned that remarkable instrument, the electron microscope, upon strange molecular "beings" never previously seen by man. Some are satisfied with this glimpse below the cell and find the virus a halfway station on the road to life. Perhaps it is, but as I wander about in the thin mist that is beginning to filter among these decaying stems and ruined spider webs, a kind of disconsolate uncertainty has taken hold of me.

I have come to suspect that this long descent down the ladder of life, beautiful and instructive though it may be, will not lead us to the final secret. In fact I have ceased to believe in the final brew or the ultimate chemical. There is, I know, a kind of heresy, a shocking negation of our confidence in blue-steel microtomes and men in white in making such a statement. I would not be understood to speak ill of scientific effort, for in simple truth I would not be alive today except for the microscopes and the blue steel. It is only that somewhere among these seeds and beetle shells and abandoned grasshopper legs I find something that is not accounted for very clearly in the dissections to the ultimate virus or crystal or protein particle. Even if the secret is contained in these things, in other words, I do not think it will yield to the kind of analysis our science is capable of making."

The above illustrates very clearly the dilemma of a thinking scientist who wants to remain faithful to the principle of evolution and yet starts realizing the flaws in the logic behind it.

When Darwin referred to the possibility that life "has emerged from inorganic matter in some warm little pond", this was again a conclusion with no basis in fact. After 125 years, no scientist, no laboratory, no research, has been able to provide convincing evidence that inorganic matter can be turned into life-bearing organisms. The only thing we had to go by were statements such as "it *seemed inevitable. . .* that we *must* finally arrive at the point where, under the proper chemical conditions, the mysterious borderline that bounds the inanimate must be crossed." The logic simply escapes us as to why it is *"inevitable"* that we *must* reach the point of being able to create "life" out of inanimate objects. Yet this was the certitude expressed by the scientific community for the past 125 years. It is gratifying to see Eiseley admit that all these statements and expectations were self-deluding and that the secret of life continued to remain a secret. Still Eiseley did not seem to have the mental fortitude to unshackle himself from the yoke imposed upon us by decades of theoretical pronouncements — concepts which humankind propounded during the infancy of our nascent scientific era.

It is important to observe Eiseley acknowledge that *"even the supposedly simple amoeba was a complex self-operating chemical factory."* We finally realized the complexity of the most simple life-bearing cell. During Darwin's time and later on, these supposedly insignificant little cells were taken for granted and were not properly analyzed. In fact, 125 years ago there was not enough knowledge to analyze and realize the complexities built into the simple cell. That means they were looking at something, seeing the outer surface, but not penetrating the intricate inner mechanism that made this cell perform. On the basis of our semi-ignorance, we generated momentous theories and believed in them wholeheartedly for 125 years. Even if we did have the courage to sort of question the validity of certain aspects, as Eiseley did, we still did not have the mental courage to follow these new questions to their inexorable conclusions, and discover the world to which they would have led us. To simply ask a question is not sufficient. It is a step forward, but it requires additional mental discipline to research it further without being tied down by old conceptual habits. We must then draw the logical objective conclusions — no matter where these might lead us.

As Eiseley so very aptly pointed out, the evolutionists were *"left in the somewhat embarrassing position of having to postulate theories of living origins which it could not demonstrate."* He conceded that he had come to finally realize that *"This long descent down the ladder of life, beautiful and instructive though it may be, will not lead us to the final secret. In fact, I have ceased to believe in the final brew or the ultimate chemical."* Let us hope that other scientists will spend a good many lonely hours with themselves to rethink the impossibility of the theory of evolution. Certainly, sooner or later, they will come to the same realization which led Eiseley to state that he has ceased to believe in this castle built on thin air in order to explain a phenomenon for which neither our mental capacity nor our scientific knowledge, was advanced enough to face and explain. We have to admit that for the past 125 years, we were too incompetent and too ignorant to understand the process of life and the steps that might or might not have led from one form of animal or vegetation to the next. An oft-repeated illusion does not automatically become an established "fact."

The constant repetition of a speculation did, unfortunately extend it an aura of unwarranted credibility, which, in turn, imbedded itself into our collective minds as established facts. Factually, the theory of evolution, stripped of its repetitive glamour, still remained but a theory — and a very dubious one at that.

Even the evolutionist Gould displayed doubts in Darwinism. Just as in the case of Eiseley, he has raised pointed questions — remarks that prove the deep search for more logical answers that continuously churn in his mind. Among other statements, we read:

> ". . .I am led to wonder why the old, discredited orthodoxy of gradual origin ever gained such strong and general assent. Why did it seem so reasonable? Certainly not because any direct evidence supported it."[1]

It is gratifying to see Gould seriously and publicly acknowledge that gradualism is discredited — and yet commands the blind allegiance, *a priori,* of the general scientific community. One hopes that this objective evaluation by Gould will be further pursued by

[1]Stephen Jay Gould, *The Panda's Thumb,* page 225 (published by W.W. Norton & Company, 1980).

other inquisitive scientists — those who are not afraid to face sequential conclusions which ensue from scientific, logical thinking, even if the results contradict the general opinion prevailing at that moment. Science is not a popularity contest; nor should it be a vehicle for intellectual schizophrenia.

Now that we have learned a few of the secrets of the cell, we should come to realize that some of the big theories expounded during our ignorant stages, can no longer be maintained during our more mature search for scientific "truths."

20

Summary

A summation of the foregoing argument is advisable. so as to have a combined overview of the subject. Since the same basic argument of the DNA complex applies to, and has to be compared to, the different concepts of evolution, the summary that follows perforce repeats a number of premises.

Based on the probability factors depicted in Chapter 2 any viable DNA strand having over 84 nucleotides cannot be the result of haphazard mutations. At that stage, the probabilities are 1 in 4.80 x 10^{50}. Such a number, if written out, would read

480,000,000,000,000,000,000,000,000,000,000,000,000,000,000,000,000

Mathematicians agree that any requisite number beyond 10^{50} has, statistically, a zero probability of occurrence (and even that gives it the benefit of the doubt!) Any species known to us, including the smallest single-cell bacteria, have enormously larger numbers of nucleotides than 100 or 1000. In fact, single cell bacteria display about 3,000,000 nucleotides, aligned in a very specific sequence. This means, that there is no mathematical probability whatever for any known species to have been the product of a random occurrence — random mutations (to use evolutionist's favorite expression.)

The theory of evolution was based on certain basic premises.

These have to be translated into and evaluated against a background of the DNA/RNA realities and their probabilities of occurrence. Using these measuring sticks, do the basic Darwinian concepts accord with modern paleontologic and microbiologic realities? Let us analyze it:

A) *Various forms of life started suddenly from inert inorganic matter.* This concept was essentially abandoned long ago — and for good reason. No neo-Darwinian evolutionists could stretch their imagination that far. Today we know why: inorganic matter does not have a functioning DNA. For life to exist (at least as we know it) requires cells whose activities are controlled by the incredibly complex DNA/RNA system. We cannot imagine a situation that will create functioning DNA systems out of previous "nothingness." The border between inert inorganic material and living organic cells is not a line but an immense chasm that cannot be crossed without the instantaneous appearance of the DNA helix (and all its other controls.) Mathematically speaking that is impossible, given the millions of nucleotides, all aligned in a specific meaningful sequence.

B) *The first forms of unicellular life were formed through the interactions of pressures, temperatures, chemicals, water, air, and related physical conditions.* No experiment has yet created unicellular life by mixing these ingredients. The reason is obvious: we may mix chemicals to our heart's content, for as long as we desire, but we would only achieve, at best, the synthesis of some other chemicals — we will not achieve "life." Again, let us remember that "life" means the proper functioning of the immensely sophisticated DNA/RNA system (and all its subsystems) within the cell. For as long as this system is not functioning at hundred percent efficiency, there is no "life." Chemicals, mixed in any manner or ratio, do not create DNA spirals. A simple single cell bacteria has about 3,000,000 nucleotides, all aligned in a very specific and purposeful sequence. Chemical molecules are dumb — they have no brains — they cannot design supersophisticated systems by their own volition, they cannot decide to become actors within an immensely complicated drama and actually play in it. Because of their robotic existence they cannot get together and agree among themselves to generate a sequence of 3,000,000 nucleotides, in a *very specific order.* Such meaningful action would be an expression of intelligence — which chemical molecules do not possess.

This means that no amount of chemical mixing, with or without heat, with or without pressures, would ever result in a 3,000,000 nucleotide sequence. For as long as this does not occur, we have no living species. Consequently, the evolutionist's concept of the origin of life is untenable: the first living cell on Earth could not have been the result of haphazard interaction of chemical molecules. Mathematical probability theories deny us completely any possibility for 3,000,000 units (or even 5,000 units) to align themselves haphazardly, and end up into a most purposeful sequence.

Furthermore, the evolutionist's concept that such chance meeting created the "simple" cell is also inaccurate. What Darwin considered as a "simple" cell is anything but simple — it is the most complex, and sophisticated chemical factory humankind has ever tried to analyze. In fact the complexity is so advanced and so deeply intertwined that modern science has not yet deciphered all the interactions taking place within Darwin's so-called "simple" cell!

C) *The simple cell split, multiplied and formed newer forms of life — new species.* This proposition also has not been demonstrated scientifically, and the DNA/RNA existence emphatically denies the possibility. Multiplications or splits of a specific cell, do not and cannot create new species. A new form of life can be only generated by rearranging and adding millions of nucleotides to a DNA helix — all in a *very specifically meaningful sequence.* Nothing else creates new life-bearing species. If a single cell splits, we now know that it will generate two separate cells, of the *very same* species. The reason is obvious: its DNA will split and reconstitute itself into two identical cells with the very same DNA structure. This is not creation of new species.

A cell has no capacity to decide by its own wit, to change its own DNA sequence and create a different alignment of 50,000,000 other nucleotides. Then, and only then, would we have obtained a new species; and even then, if the sequence was not purposefully constructed, no viable species would ensue.

Darwin's theoretical concepts were not based on awareness of DNA/RNA structures. We cannot expect him to have guessed the intricacies microbiology would have discovered one hundred years later. Predictions pronounced during the kindergarten stages of our scientific growth cannot be expected to stand up during our

207

sophomore years, when additional scientific knowledge has been acquired.

D) *With the passing of millions of years, species added to their physiological and anatomical structures and thus evolved into other structured species; for example fish with gills became land-animals with lungs.* This concept is similar to the previous one, although it deals with the evolution of more complex species (macroevolution). Again, it is untenable for the same reasons given above. Any DNA with millions of bases cannot change by "itself" into a DNA with other millions of bases, all arranged in a meaningful order. The mathematical probabilities for such events to occur is zero.

E) *Acquired characteristics were genetically transferred from generation to generation and thus created new or altered species.* This refers, for example, to the classical theoretical example submitted: a short giraffe that stretches its neck will become a taller one, a few generations hence. Science has proven that acquired physical characteristics cannot be transferred genetically. The reason is clear: any physical growth is the result of a very specific sequence of hundreds of thousands of nucleotides in its own DNA. The order giving sequence starts at the DNA and seeps down to the growth mechanisms. It never acts in the reverse direction. Growth cannot instruct the DNA to rearrange itself. A giraffe that stretches its neck has no capacity to order its DNA to change so that the next generation automatically acquires the amount of the stretch achieved by the previous generation.

F) *Evolution proceeds through sustained incremental changes.* This concept too is not supported by paleontology nor by the DNA/RNA mechanism. An increment of any size (no matter how small) means an addition to, or a rearrangement of, the DNA chain. There is no system within the complex cell that will provide such an action. In fact the addition of a *single* nucleotide would upset almost completely the reading of the ensuing three-letter codon sequences (refer to Chapter 8). The theoretical addition of large quantities of nucleotides (if it could be achieved at all — and it cannot), could result in a viable living species only *if* these molecules were in a purposeful sequence — a sequence that coordinates its meaning with the rest of the billions of nucleotides in the existing DNA. This, again, is an impossibility based on random molecular realignment probabilities. The suggestion submitted by Gould/Eldredge in their hypothesis of "punctuated equilibria" (as a correction to earlier Darwinian theory) is unrealistic and untenable. Because of clear-cut evidence displayed by the fossil record, these two scientists concluded that the rates of incremental change proceed much faster than originally thought by Darwin — in fact paleontology tells us that most changes are sudden.

Whether the change occurs one nucleotide at a time, or whether it occurs 300,000,000 nucleotides at a time, is immaterial. Nucleotides cannot be added at will; even if they did, they could not align themselves in a meaningful sequence.

G) *"Survival of the fittest" and "natural selection."* No matter what phraseology one generates, the basic fact remains the same: any physical change of any size, shape, or form, is strictly the result of purposeful alignment of billions of nucleotides. Nature or species do not have the capacity of rearranging them nor to add to them. Consequently no leap (saltation) can occur from one species to another. The only way we know for a DNA to be altered is through a meaningful intervention from an outside source of intelligence — one who knows what it is doing, such as our genetic engineers are now performing in their laboratories.

It follows that every single concept advanced by the theory of evolution (and amended thereafter) is imaginary as it is not supported by the scientifically established facts of microbiology, fossils, and mathematical probability concepts.

Darwin was wrong.

209

21
In Retrospect

The theory of evolution may be the worst mistake made in science. The fact that an erroneous hypothesis was submitted is not in itself reprehensible. In fact, it is the normal procedure in science to evaluate and seriously consider any theory that seems to have value in solving problems. Concentrated study based on factual data then determines the probable validity of the proposed theory.

The error does not, therefore, lie with submission of this theory 125 years ago. The real problem arises much later on, when the scientific world should have realized from convincing evidence (i.e. fossils and DNA) that previously assumed base for evolution had been effectively negated. Especially when the DNA/RNA complex was understood, scientists should have questioned anew Darwin's conclusions, Why did they not?

The answer to that question is probably best left to psychologists specializing in mass attitudes. Nevertheless, one can speculate that it goes back to our earlier educational background. We were taught:

a) Science considers and accepts only factual data; there is no room for the metaphysical or unseen.

b) The Bible seems to submit a metaphysical answer to the problem.

c) Ergo: Science cannot consider and accept the biblical solution as a matter of principle. Thus the concept of

Creation is automatically dismissed as not warranting scientific consideration. It is not an option even to be considered.

This dogmatic teaching becomes subconsciously part of our thinking process. Mentally we are preprogrammed to have our logic rebel at the moment when "creation" becomes a probable solution; such an option is taboo. Scientists reflexively *invent* any other plausible solution that might have some relevance — even if it is outrageously farfetched, so long as it skirts *"creation."*

Does that mean that there is something wrong with science and scientific methodology? Certainly not.

Is there anything wrong with scientists? Nothing whatsoever — except when they stray away from solid scientific sequential thought processes and shy away from reaching conclusions which, subjectively, they do not like.

The majority of scientists became too deeply identified with the theory of evolution and thus, considered that they were personally committed, as a matter of professional honor, to defend this theory to the bitter illogical end. This approach generated its own momentum which fed on itself and ballooned into an orthodoxy from which there was no turning back. Any criticism of the theory was perceived as a personal insult, since their self-esteem apparently was at stake. It was no longer a matter of searching for the objective truth; instead it degenerated (knowingly or unknowingly) into the spirit of an unassailable rampart, static in position, and eager to repulse any approaching newcomer — any new ideas. In fact it relied on known "myths" and grasped for or invented plausible-sounding reasons to vindicate the theory. This is certainly not the path that science should travel.

The present book is not the first attempt to apply mathematical principles when evaluating evolutionary concepts. One of the past confrontations between evolutionists and mathematicians took place in 1966, during a symposium held at the Wistar Institute of Anatomy and Biology in Philadelphia, Pa. Professor Eden of MIT submitted sound observations about the improbability of randomness that constitutes the basic structure of evolution. The logic the mathematicians developed during that conference was to critically evaluate the haphazard occurrence of protein chains. By applying mathematical concepts, it was deduced that there would be 10^{325} possible protein combinations created through the genetic code, based on the assumption that each protein chain contained 250 amino acids. It was further argued that the number of different proteins that ever existed was, at best, 10^{52} — which means a very small fraction of the available pool of protein possibilities. Consequently, the mathematicians pointed out that instead of searching out haphazardly the proper combinations of protein chains that would create life-machines (as known to us today), there must have been a mechanism in "nature" that was able to focus rapidly on the infinitesimally small portion of all conceivable protein chains that could exist. The theory of evolution does not tell us what this mechanism was nor how it functioned to perform a statistically improbable job. Other examples of the improbability of the theory of evolution were submitted at that conference.

Although the mathematics displayed is correct and the ensuing conclusion accords with the results submitted in this book, it was a more complicated way to prove the point. In my humble opinion, the present approach is simpler and more direct. Protein chains are complex structures that represent the end result of the actions in the cells. Rather than being concerned with the final product, my approach goes back to basics — the DNA — and evaluates its probabilities. Fewer assumptions are required and more precise results can be obtained. However, no matter which approach is used, the final answer is the same: there is no mathematical probability whatever for evolution to have been the mechanism that created 6,000,000 species on this world.

That conference was attended to by such well known evolutionists, as Mayr, Lewontin, Wright, Eiseley, and Bossert. Eighteen years have elapsed since then, and for all practical purposes the impact of mathematical logic on the evolutionist school of thought has been almost nil. The beauty of mathematics is its precision and its universality of application — attributes that are not open to questions. Mathematical concepts and ensuing results are provable and reproducible. Evolutionary theories are verbiages that derive from and rely on one's imagination. We have two completely different worlds; no wonder that they cannot understand each other. A mathematician, with his precise and objectively structured logic, cannot be at home and concur with the world of the evolutionist who deals with imaginary concepts — concepts that are neither provable nor reproducible. On the other hand, the evolutionist accustomed to his utter freedom of flight of fancy can hardly squeeze himself into a structured discipline imposed by the strict logic of mathematics. In fact, he prefers not to face mathematical logic and reality as that would destroy the foundation of his theories.

Is there any wonder that mathematics and probability theories have not been allowed to influence the artificial world of the evolutionists? Is it a wonder that, for all practical purposes, the solid arguments presented by mathematicians at the Wistar conference have been discarded and forgotten?

However, if we broaden our horizons and accept to evaluate the "unthinkable," if we open our minds to consider outside infusion of knowledge and intelligence, then we may discover a completely different picture — a picture that makes sense. It would introduce a new factor — a new option that was *forbidden* to be evaluated up to now by the evolutionist community. They restricted their options, and thus reduced the scope of their sights. True scientific research should be free and unhampered to wander into *any* nook and cranny of our inquisitiveness and our experimental world. As soon as we place eye patches on a scientist, so as to channel his sights into one direction only, we get lame results. His field of action and his views *must* extend around an arc of 360°. Anything less is restrictive, oppressive, and *must* lead to faulty final results.

There are certainly a good number of scientists who now reject the concepts of evolution — not on religious grounds, but on strictly scientific grounds. Most of them are keeping their own council.

Outwardly they support evolution (so as to be in step with their peers) but inwardly they have second thoughts on the subject. It is not too easy to take a stand against the beliefs of the majority, and expose oneself to ridicule, especially when one's job and academic and professional prospects are on the line. It is only the very brave and those highly placed scientists whose standings are universally acknowledged (and thus, secure) that can afford to contradict the general trend. In fact, a few of these scientific superstars have publicly raised pointed questions. Some, for example, have advanced the thought that amino acids might not be the end result of chemical evolutionary interactions that took place on Earth during the Precambrian era. Instead they have suggested that amino acids were probably available in outer space, and have been "imported" to this planet. This type of thinking is a step in the right direction. It does not go far enough, but it does acknowledge that there is something wrong with our accepted concept of organic chemicals getting manufactured all of a sudden in a "warm little pond." The fact that some amino acids arrived here from outerspace does not, in itself, solve the question of how 6,000,000 or more species became established on this planet. Amino acids are not life-machines, nor can they order the DNA to generate a meaningful program, so that they — the amino acids — play their proper role within specific protein chains. They are only the tail of the dog, not the dog itself.

Nevertheless, the fact that topnotch scientists are at least starting to think in those terms, and have the courage to publicly make such heretical statements (heretical from the point of view of the orthodox majority of evolutionists) is very gratifying. As time goes on, one unanswered question will lead to the next, and eventually, they will have to seriously consider as probable the existence and assistance of outside superintelligence.

After all, it is not the duty of science to defend the theory of evolution, and stick by it to the bitter end — no matter what illogical and unsupported conclusions it offers. On the contrary, it is expected that scientists recognize the patently obvious impossibility of Darwin's pronouncements and predictions. If in the process of impartial scientific logic, they find that creation by outside superintelligence is the solution to our quandary, then let's cut the umbilical cord that tied us down to Darwin for such a long time. It is choking us and holding us back.

An incredible amount of time, effort, talent, and money was spent during the past 125 years to argue and defend this theory. Modern microbiology has proven how the DNA works, mathematics has proven that no meaningful alignment of millions of molecules could possibly take place haphazardly, and fossils have constantly supported the ensuing conclusions. These are solid scientific facts that cannot be denied — in favor of creation by a superintelligence. Any further denial would simply be blindfolded bigotry — it would no longer be science.

At times the rigidity of some evolutionists is perplexing, even for their own standards. For example, Lewontin, one of the foremost modern evolutionists, expressed himself as follows:

> "It is time for students of the evolutionary process, especially those who have been misquoted and used by the creationists, to state clearly that evolution is fact, not theory. . . Birds arose from nonbirds and humans from nonhumans."

Such dogmatic finality is most surprising when uttered by a scientist who should know that, to start with, he is navigating on very insecure grounds, since the foundation of the theory of evolution has not been scientifically proven as yet.

For this academician, however, the matter is closed; for him any logical argument submitted will only prove the ignorance of the utterer. Probably Gould, the Neo-Darwinian evolutionist, had this in mind when he stated in *Ever Since Darwin* (published by W.W. Norton & Co., 1977, pages 40 and 44):

> "I am a strong advocate of the general argument that "truth" as preached by scientists often turns out to be no more than prejudice inspired by prevailing social and political beliefs.

> ". . .I also deplore the unwillingness of scientists to explore seriously the logical structure of arguments."

Likewise, even Mayr warned against "myths" in science:

215

"Yet all of us must keep a careful watch for manifestations of both pitfalls, (i.e. chauvinism and whiggishness) so that we can correct misleading statements before still other inaccuracies are added to the all too rich repertory of myths in science." (*The Evolutionary Synthesis,* Harvard Univ. Press, 1980, page 2).

Loren Eiseley very eloquently warned the scientific community against the static condescendent approach of those who are so certain about the evolutionary process. During the symposium held at the Wistar Institute of Anatomy and Biology in 1966 in Philadelphia, Pa. he stated, in part:[1]

"...we should give serious thought to the question of whether we have reached a certain point of hesitation in our seemingly clear explanation of the way evolution comes about. Have we really answered all the questions; or is there something peculiarly attractive, almost like a Kipling "Just So" story, about natural selection? The range of ideas and the possibilities which they cover are so extensive that it is in a sense a bit deceptive. Perhaps, after all, there is still a veil of mist hanging over this seemingly sharp, clearly defined landscape. I think one of the things we will have to be wary of today ... in our attempt to analyze the pros and cons of whether a neo-Darwinian position satisfactorily accounts for all aspects of evolution or not, is to avoid getting this tangled up with a theological debate, vitalism versus mechanism. The point, it seems to me, no longer lies here so much as it does over in another domain of the organismic approach, the problem of whether there are some aspects of life, and of chemistry under the control of life, which are not as yet totally accountable for with the means at our command. To say this is not to run off into mysticism. It is to be examining an unknown, just as Darwin in his time was examining an unknown. If we keep this is mind I think that we are less apt to be emotional over some lingering and archaic fear that we will be precipitating ourselves into outmoded nineteenth century controversies.

Not long ago I received for comment a book praising the achievements of science. The author said, in essence, "It is the duty of the historian to hold up all scientific men of achievement

---

[1] *Mathematical Challenges to the Neo-Darwinian Interpretation of Evolution* (pages 3 and 4), monograph number 5; Reprinted by permission of Wistar Institute of Anatomy and Biology, Philadelphia, Pa.

as saints for the benefit of oncoming students of science."

What an ironic reversal, in a sense, of our whole conception of what science ought to be, compared with its struggles in the nineteenth century! Now we hold the platform; but let us not engage, either as historians or scientists, in either regarding ourselves as saints or failing to recognize that over the apparently hard, empirical landscape across which we gaze there may still lie some morning haze, some shadows, which we may hopefully illuminate."

Challenges to old established concepts must not be brushed aside in an emotional and dogmatic manner. Mathematics is not a lightweight science. It is probably the most objective and "scientific" of all sciences. It is the duty of every scientist to sit up and evaluate very carefully what mathematics is telling us. We all have (or should have) a deep respect for the constant precision and clarity of logic expressed by mathematical theorems and concepts.

It is true that science is a conservative discipline, but, in the long run, it always corrects its mistakes. It is only to be hoped that, in the case of evolution, this correction occurs sooner rather than later. There is too much work to be done than to continue shuffling around sterile debates based on impossible dreams.

If we insist on maintaining and supporting the theory of evolution, we are then forced to eliminate and disavow mathematical probability concepts. If we are convinced that mathematics is correct, then we have to discard the present concepts of evolution. The two teachings do not seem to be compatible with each other.

As objective scientists, which shall we support?

Remember the story of the Emperor's New Clothes?. Not a single vasal dared point out the obvious fact that the Emperor was naked; instead they competed with each other to vociferously praise the wonderful tailoring of the new suit. They even described in detail the fine and exquisite stitching to be found in the lower left corner of the imaginary coat. They were all gratified — to their own satisfaction — to hear themselves describe the virtue and beauty of the coat.

It was left to the simplistic mind of a naive child to exclaim: "but that is not so — the Emperor is naked!"

Does this sound familiar?

History has a way of repeating itself.

Bibliography

There are thousands of books on the subjects mentioned in this volume. The vast majority of them defend the evolutionist point of view. Very few books submit true scientific arguments against the concept of evolution. The books mentioned hereunder, represent but a small fraction of the available literature which could be of interest to readers as a guide for further study of these subjects.

Ackerman, E. — *BIOPHYSICAL SCIENCE* (Prentice Hall Inc., Englewood Cliffs, N.J., 1962)

Allaby, M. — *ANIMAL ARTISANS* (Alfred A. Knopf, New York, 1982)

Altman, J. — *ORGANIC FOUNDATIONS OF ANIMAL BEHAVIOR* (Holt, Rinehart and Winston, Inc., New York, 1967)

Arms, K. and Camp. P.S. — *BIOLOGY* (Holt, Rinehart and Winston, Inc., New York, 1969)

Barnes, R.D. — *INVERTEBRATE ZOOLOGY* (Holt, Rinehart and Winston, Inc., New York, 1980)

Bates, M. — *ANIMAL WORLDS* (Random House, New York, 1975)

Bethell, T. — *DARWIN'S MISTAKE* (Harpers, Feb. 1976)

Boyer, P.D. — *THE ENZYMES, 3rd ED.* (Academic Press, New York, 1970)

Bylinsky, G. — *LIFE IN DARWIN'S UNIVERSE* (Doubleday and Co. Inc., Garden City, N.Y., 1981)

Campbell, B.G. — *HUMAN EVOLUTION* (Aldine Publ. Co., Chicago, 1973)

Chedd, G. — *THE NEW BIOLOGY* (Basic Books Inc., New York, 1972)

Christie, W.W. — *LIPID ANALYSIS* (Pergamon Press, Oxford, England, 1973)

Cohen, G.N. — *CELL REGULATION* (Holt, Rinehart and Winston Inc., New York, 1969)

Conn, E.E. and Stumpf, P.K. — *OUTLINES OF BIOCHEMISTRY* (John Wiley and Son, Inc., New York, 1976)

Crick, F. — *LIFE ITSELF — ITS ORIGIN AND NATURE* (Simon and Schuster, New York, 1981

D'Entreves, P.P. and Zunino, M. — *THE SECRET LIFE OF INSECTS* (Chartwell Books, London, England, 1976)

Davidson, J.N. — *THE BIOCHEMISTRY OF THE NUCLEIC ACIDS* (Academic Press, New York, 1972)

Diamond, S. — *THE WORLD OF PROBABILITY* (Basic Books, Inc., New York, 1964)

Dickerson, R.E. and Geis, J. — *THE STRUCTURE AND ACTION OF PROTEINS* (Harper and Row, New York, 1969)

Dobzhansky, T. — *GENETICS OF THE EVOLUTIONARY PROCESS* (Columbia Univ. Press, New York, 1970)

Dobzhansky, T. — *GENETICS AND THE ORIGIN OF SPECIES* (Columbia Univ. Press, New York, 1937)

Eiseley, L. — *THE FIRMAMENT OF TIME* (Atheneum, New York, 1960)
Eiseley, L. — *THE IMMENSE JOURNEY* (Random House, Inc., New York, 1957)
Eiseley, L. — *THE UNEXPECTED UNIVERSE* (Harcourt, Brace and World, New York, 1969)

Eldredge, N. — *THE MONKEY BUSINESS* (Pocket Books, New York, 1982)
Eldredge, N. — *AN EXTRAVAGANCE OF SPECIES* (Natural History, Vol 89, No. 7, American Museum of National History, New York, 1980)

Fabre, J.H. — *THE LIFE OF THE SPIDER* (Horizon Press, New York, 1971)

Fingerman, M. — *ANIMAL DIVERSITY* (Holt, Rinehart and Winston, Inc., New York, 1969)

Frankel, E. — *DNA: THE LADDER OF LIFE* (McGraw Hill Book Company, New York, 1979)

Freese, A.S. — *THE MIRACLE OF VISION* (Harper and Row, New York, 1977)

Frisch, V.K. — *BIOLOGY* (Harper and Row, New York, 1964)

Fuller, H.J. — *THE PLANT WORLD* (Henry Holt and Co., New York, 1957)

Futuyma, D.J. — *SCIENCE ON TRIAL: THE CASE FOR EVOLUTION*(Pantheon Books, New York, 1983)

Ghiselin, M.T. — *THE ECONOMY OF NATURE AND THE EVOLUTION OF SEX* (Univ. of California Press, Berkeley, Calif., 1974)

Gish, D.T. — *EVOLUTION — THE FOSSILS SAY NO!* (Creation Life Publishers, San Diego, Calif., 1981)

Goldberg, S. — *PROBABILITY — AN INTRODUCTION* (Prentice-Hall Inc., Englewood Cliffs, N.J., 1960)

Goldschmidt, R. — *THE MATERIAL BASIS OF EVOLUTION* (Pageant Books, Inc., N.J., 1960)

Gordon, B.L. — *THE SECRET LIVES OF FISHES* (Grosset and Dunlap, New York, 1977)

Gould, S.J. — *EVER SINCE DARWIN* (W.W. Norton and Co., New York, 1977)

Gould, S.J. — *THE PANDA'S THUMB* (W.W. Norton and Co., New York, 1980)

Gould, S.J. — *THE MISMEASURE OF MAN* (W.W. Norton and Co., New York, 1981)

Gould, S.J. — *HEN'S TEETH AND HORSE'S TOES* (W.W. Norton and Co., New York, 1983)

Gould, S.J. — *BATHYBIUS MEETS EOZOON* (Natural History, Vol 87, No. 4, 1978)

Gould, S.J. and Eldredge, N. — *PUNCTUATED EQUILIBRIA: THE TEMPO AND MODE OF EVOLUTION RECONSIDERED* (Paleobiology 3: 115-51)

Grasse, P.P. — *L'EVOLUTION DU VIVANT* (Albin Michel, Paris, 1973)

Greene, J.C. — *DARWIN AND THE MODERN WORLD VIEW* (Louisiana State Univ. Press, Baton Rouge, La., 1973)

Gribbin, J. and Cherfas, J. — *THE MONKEY PUZZLE* (McGraw-Hill Book Co., New York, 1983)

Griffin, D.R. — *THE QUESTION OF ANIMAL AWARENESS* (Rockefeller Univ. Press, New York, 1976)

Halstead, B.W. — *DANGEROUS MARINE ANIMALS* (Cornell Maritime Press, Cambridge, Md., 1959)

Harker, J.E. — *FACTORS CONTROLLING THE DIURNAL RHYTHM OF ACTIVITY OF PERIPLANETA AMERICANA* (Journal of

Experimental Biology, 33, 224-34)

Hickman, Hickman, Hickman, and Roberts — *INTEGRATED PRINCIPLES OF ZOOLOGY* (C.V. Mosby Co., St. Louis, Mo., 1979)

Hitching, F. — *THE NECK OF THE GIRAFFE* (Mentor Books, New York, 1982)

Hodges, J.L. and Lenmann, E.L. — *ELEMENTS OF FINITE PROBABILITY* (Holden-Day, Inc., San Francisco, Calif., 1964)

Hooton, E.A. — *UP FROM THE APE* (Macmillan Publ. Co., N.Y., 1946)

Hoyle, F. and Wickramasinghe, N.C. — *LIFECLOUD* (Harper and Row, New York, 1978)

Jacob, F. — *THE POSSIBLE AND THE ACTUAL* (Univ. of Washington Press Seattle, Wash., 1982)

Jacob, F. — *THE LOGIC OF LIFE* (Pantheon Books, New York, 1973)

Jordan, D.S. and Kellogg, V.L. — *ANIMAL LIFE* (D. Appleton and Co., New York, 1903)

Judson, H.F. — *THE EIGHTH DAY OF CREATION* (Simon and Schuster, New York, 1979)

Keeton, W.T. — *BIOLOGICAL SCIENCE* (W.W. Norton and Co., Inc., 1967)

Kent, G.C. — *COMPARATIVE ANATOMY OF THE VERTEBRATES* (C.V. Mosby Co., St. Louis, Mo., 1978)

Kornberg, A. — *DNA SYNTHESIS* (W.H. Freeman, San Fransico, Calif., 1974)

Land, M.F. — *ANIMAL EYES WITH MIRROR OPTICS* (Scientific American, Dec., 1978)

Lear, J. — *RECOMBINANT DNA — THE UNTOLD STORY* (Crown Publishers Inc., New York, 1978)

LeGros Clark, W.E. — *HISTORY OF THE PRIMATES* (Univ. of Chicago Press, Chicago, Ill., 1971)

Lessing, L. — *DNA AT THE CORE OF LIFE ITSELF* (Macmillan Publishing Co., New York, 1967)

Levi-Setti, R. — *TRILOBITES* (Univ. of Chicago Press, Chicago, 1975)

Lewontin, R. — *HUMAN DIVERSITY* (Scientific American Books, New York, 1984)

Levy, J. and Cambell, J. and Blackburn, T.H. — *INTRODUCTION TO MICROBIOLOGY* (John Wiley and Sons, Inc., New York, 1973)

Lloyd, F.E. — *THE CARNIVOROUS PLANTS* (Dover Publication, Inc., New York, 1976)

Loewy, A. G. and Siekevitz, P. — *CELL STRUCTURE AND FUNCTION* (Holt, Rinehart and Winston, Inc., New York, 1969)

Lorenz, K. — *KING SOLOMON'S RING* (Signet Books, New York, 1972)

Luria, S. E. — *LIFE — THE UNFINISHED EXPERIMENT* (Charles Scribner's Sons, New York, 1973)

Macbeth, N. — *DARWIN RETRIED — AN APPEAL TO REASON* (Gambit Inc., Boston, 1971)

Mayr, E. — *THE GROWTH OF BIOLOGICAL THOUGHT* (Harvard Univ. Press, Cambridge, Mass., 1982)

Mayr, E. and Rovine, W.B. (eds.) — *THE EVOLUTIONARY SYNTHESIS* (Harvard Univ. Press, Cambridge, Mass., 1980)

Meister, A. — *BIOCHEMISTRY OF THE AMINO ACIDS, VOLS I AND II* (Academic Press, New York, 1965)

Milne, L. and M. — *LIVING PLANTS OF THE WORLD* (Random House, New York, 1975)

Milne, L. and M. — *INSECT WORLDS* (Charles Scribner's Sons, New York, 1980)

Moorhead, P.S. and Kaplan, M.M. (eds.) — *MATHEMATICAL CHALLENGES TO THE NEO—DARWINIAN INTERPRETATION OF EVOLUTION* (The Wistar Institute Press, Philadelphia, 1967)

Mosimann, J.E. — *ELEMENTARY PROBABILITY FOR THE BIOLOGICAL SCIENCES* (Appleton-Century-Crofts, New York, 1968)

O'Neill, T. — *THE FOUR-EYED FISH SEES ALL* (National Geographic, March 1978)

Pellegrino, C.R. and Stoff, J.A. — *DARWIN'S UNIVERSE* (Van Nostrand Reinhold Co., New York, 1983)

Perry, R. — *THE UNKNOWN OCEAN* (Taplinger Publ. Co., New York, 1972)

Pinna, G. — *THE DAWN OF LIFE* (World Publishing, New York, 1972)

Ponnamperuma, C. — *THE ORIGINS OF LIFE* (E. P. Dutton and Co., Inc., New York, 1972)

Ransom, J.E. — *FOSSILS IN AMERICA* (Harper and Row, New York 1964)

Schmalhausen, I.I. — *FACTORS OF EVOLUTION* (Blakiston Co., Phila., 1949)

Schmidt-Nielson, K. — *HOW ANIMALS WORK* (Cambridge University Press, Cambridge, England, 1972)

Schnell, D.E. — *CARNIVOROUS PLANTS* (John F. Blair, Winston Salem, 1983)

Segal, I.H. — *ENZYME KINETICS* (John Wiley and Sons, Inc., New York, 1975)

Simpson, G.G. and Beck, W.S. — *LIFE — AN INTRODUCTION TO BIOLOGY* (Harcourt, Brace and World Inc., New York, 1965)

Slack, A. — *CARNIVOROUS PLANTS* (MIT Press, Cambridge, Mass., 1980)

Smith, J.M. (Ed.) — *EVOLUTION NOW: A CENTURY AFTER DARWIN* (W.H. Freeman and Company, San Francisco, 1982)

Stanley, S.M. — *THE NEW EVOLUTIONARY TIMETABLE* (Basic Books, New York, 1982)

Stansfield, W.D. — *THE SCIENCE OF EVOLUTION* (Macmillan Publ. Co., New York, 1977)

Stebbins, G.L. — *DARWIN TO DNA, MOLECULES TO HUMANITY* (W.H. Freeman, San Francisco, Calif., 1982)
Stebbins, G.L. — *VARIATION AND EVOLUTION IN PLANTS* (Columbia Univ. Press, New York, 1950)

Stent, G.S. — *MOLECULAR GENETICS* (W.H. Freeman and Co., San Francisco, 1971)

Street, P. — *ANIMAL WEAPONS* (Taplinger Publ. Co., New York, 1971)
Street, P. — *ANIMAL PARTNERS AND PARASITES* (Taplinger Publ. Co., New York, 1975)

Strickberger, M.W. — *GENETICS* (Macmillan Publ., New York, 1968)

Sturtevant, A.H. — *A HISTORY OF GENETICS* (Harper and Row, New York, 1965)

Tinbergen, N. — *CURIOUS NATURALISTS* (Anchor Books, Garden City, New York, 1968)
Tinbergen, N. — *THE ANIMAL IN ITS WORLD* (Harvard University Press, Cambridge, Mass., 1975)

Villee, C.A., Walker, W.F. and Barnes, R.D. — *GENERAL ZOOLOGY 5th EDIT.* (W.B. Saunders Company, Philadelphia, 1978)

Watson, J.D. — *MOLECULAR BIOLOGY OF THE GENE* (W.A. Benjamin Inc., New York, 1965)
Watson, J.D. — *THE DOUBLE HELIX* (Mentor Books, New York, 1969)
Watson, J.D. and Tooze, J. — *THE DNA STORY* (W.H. Freeman and Co.,

San Francisco, 1981)

Weier, T.E., Stocking, C.R. and Barbour, M.G. — *BOTANY* (John Wiley and Sons, Inc., New York, 1970)

Wells, H.G., Huxley, J.S. and Wells, G.P. — *THE SCIENCE OF LIFE* (Literary Guild, New York, 1929)

White, M.J.D. — *ANIMAL CYTOLOGY AND EVOLUTION* (Cambridge Univ. Press, Cambridge, England, 1945)

White, M.J.D. — *MODES OF SPECIATION* (W.H. Freeman and Co., San Francisco, Calif., 1978)

Whyte, L.L. — *INTERNAL FACTORS IN EVOLUTION* (George Braziller, Inc., New York, 1965)

Williams, B.J. — *EVOLUTION AND HUMAN ORIGINS* (Harper and Row, New York, 1973)

Winchester, A.M. — *GENETICS* (Houghton Mifflin Co., Boston, 1977)

Young, J.Z. — *THE LIFE OF VERTEBRATES* (Clarendon Press, Oxford, England, 1981)

For the past 125 years, we were taught that Darwin's theory of evolution, based on imperceptibly gradual incremental changes, was the mechanism that created the 6,000,000 (or more) species believed to exist on this planet.

In the 1950s a momentous event occurred — the discovery of the DNA and RNA systems within the cell. We finally had a specific understanding of the blueprint of life. It allowed us to explain biology in terms of mathematical probabilities and the principles of mechanical engineering. For the first time we were given a measuring device of great precision — a precision once possible only within the physical sciences and mathematics.

The author evaluates the highlights of past concepts of evolution and translates them into the new mechanistical meaning of the DNA/RNA. He then applies mathematical probability concepts and concludes that the millions of nucleotides within a DNA spiral, aligned in very specific sequences, could not be the result of random mutations; thus, species could not be the result of evolution.

In his factual style, Cohen leads us through most interesting details on subjects such as the cell, gemmules, trilobites, the birth of a kangaroo, the fig tree, and the timing of the horseshoe-crab's mating activities.

Submitted with the least amount of formulae and statistical tables, the author addresses his arguments to the Darwinian scientist as well as to the average educated reader — the one who wants to understand the argument without getting lost in high-level scientific jargon.